Nation-Building in Central Europe

German Historical Perspectives Series
General Editors:
Gerhard A. Ritter, Werner Pöls, Anthony J. Nicholls

Volume I
Population, Labour and Migration in 19th- and 20th-Century Germany
Edited by Klaus J. Bade

Volume II
Wealth and Taxation in Central Europe:
The History and Sociology of Public Finance
Edited by Peter-Christian Witt

German Historical Perspectives / III

Nation-Building in Central Europe

Edited by
HAGEN SCHULZE

BERG

Leamington Spa / Hamburg / New York

Distributed exclusively in the US and Canada by
St. Martin's Press, New York

First published in 1987 by
Berg Publishers Limited
24 Binswood Avenue, Leamington Spa, CV32 5SJ, UK
Schenefelder Landstr. 14K, 2000 Hamburg 55, W.-Germany
175 Fifth Avenue/Room 400, New York, NY 10010, USA

The editors wish to thank the Stifterverbund für die Deutsche
Wissenschaft for their generous grant towards the production costs
of this volume.

British Library Cataloguing in Publication Data

Nation-building in Central Europe.—
    (German historical perspectives; 3)
    1. Germany—History—1815–1866
    2. Germany—History—1866–1871
    I. Schulze, Hagen   II. Series
    943'.07   DD204

    ISBN 0–85496–529–7

Library of Congress Cataloging-in-Publication Data

Nation-building in Central Europe.

    (German historical perspectives; 3)
    Bibliography: p.
    Includes index.
    Contents: The revolution of the European order and
the rise of German Nationalism / Hagen Schulze —
German Catholics and the quest for national unity /
Adolf M. Birke — German liberalism and the national
question in the 19th century / Alexander Schwan — [etc.]
    1. Germany—History—1789–1900.   2. Nationalism—
Germany—History—19th century.   3. Nationalism—Central
Europe—History—19th century.   I. Schulze, Hagen.
II. Series.
    DD204.N38   1987   943   86–33463

    ISBN 0–85496–529–7

Printed in Great Britain by Billings of Worcester

Contents

Editorial Preface

The purpose of this series of books is to present the results of research by German historians and social scientists to readers in English-speaking countries. Each of the volumes has a particular theme which will be handled from different points of view by specialists. The series is not limited to the problems of Germany but will also involve publications dealing with the history of other countries, with the general problems of political, economic, social and intellectual history as well as international relations and studies in comparative history.

The aim of the series is to help overcome the language barrier which experience has shown obstructs the rapid appreciation of German research in English-speaking countries.

The publication of the series is closely associated with the German Visiting Fellowship at St Antony's College, Oxford, which has existed since 1965, having been originally funded by the Stiftung Volkswagenwerk, later by the British Leverhulme Foundation and, since 1982, by the Ministry of Education and Science in the Federal Republic of Germany. Each volume will be based on a series of seminars held in Oxford, which will have been conceived and directed by the Visiting Fellow and organised in collaboration with St Antony's College.

The editors wish to thank the Stifterverband für die Deutsche Wissenschaft for meeting the expenses of the original lecture series and for generous assistance with the publication. They hope that this enterprise will help to overcome national introspection and to further international academic discourse and cooperation.

Gerhard A. Ritter   **Werner Pöls**   **Anthony J. Nicholls**

HAGEN SCHULZE

Foreword

There are stereotypes and axioms which survive world wars, revolutions, economic catastrophes and social upheavals and which, even after a hundred years of use, are still fresh. The German *Sonderweg*, the concept that the Germans and their history have deviated from the general course of European or West European history, at least since the eighteenth century, is one of these stereotyped notions. Originally this idea had a positive connotation; it had to do with the assertion of the Prussian mission in Germany and the German mission in the world, an assertion which presupposed the metaphysical elevation of the Prussian–German State and its special moral quality in polemical contradiction to the Western nations. This approach can be traced back to Hegel and the historical tradition of German historicism; it found its most famous expression in the prophecies of Heinrich von Treitschke and determined the picture Germans had of themselves during the German Empire, the Weimar Republic and the Third Reich, only to disappear without trace after the collapse of 1945.

This idea was then replaced by its mirror image. On the level of social psychology one claimed that the Germans had a peculiar tendency toward authoritarianism. As a result they had the misfortune in their history not to have experienced a bourgeois revolution, and therefore moved ever further from the 'normal' West European progress towards freedom and equality, thus plunging Europe into wars, until finally the Germans were bound to become National Socialists. There is a lot of the English Whig historiographical tradition in this train of thought, a tradition which considers British constitutional history synonymous with the history of liberty. As a matter of fact, it was primarily Oxford historians who developed this interpretation of

1

German history during the First World War. The experience of the Third Reich followed, and so the ground was prepared for a scathing criticism of the apparently misguided history of the German national state; the *raison d'être* of the Federal Republic of Germany appeared in this light as a linking up with Western traditions which had no parallels in German history. German historical research focused on presenting the German past as a continuity of anti-liberal, authoritarian and repressive traditions, whose ultimate truth was Adolf Hitler.

For several years opposition to this theory of the German *Sonderweg* has been growing. Anglo-Saxon historians in particular seem to be dissatisfied with the all too simple interpretation of German history; 'Reinterpreting the German past' is Geoff Eley's programme,[1] and David Calleo criticises German historians as follows:

> First of all, Germany is too often treated as an isolated case, a country with broad characteristics presumed not to exist elsewhere. Many German writers appear to take a certain perverse relish in claiming for their society a unique wickedness among humankind. Obviously, every national society is in many senses unique. And although no one should wish to rob the Germans of their hard-earned reputation, theirs is not the only European society with . . . authoritarian traditions. Nor is Germany the only nation that has hoped to play a great role in bringing the world to order or taken pride in military prowess . . .[2]

In my opinion such complacent accusations are reason enough to submit to review our knowledge of the causal relationships of German national history and to present it to a critical public. It is of course impossible to give an overview of historical research on a thousand years of German history in a single volume, but that is not necessary. Our main concern is the phase of the formation of the German national-state from the end of the eighteenth century, when the idea of German nationality found broad interest in connection with the decline of the Holy Roman Empire and the French Revolution, until the year 1871, when the Prussian King William I was declared German Kaiser in the Hall of Mirrors in Versailles. In the span of two generations what we call the 'German Question' emerged. The German national state, which could never be identical to the German cultural nation, and its peculiarities as well as its pure existence were to become the cause of European anxiety.

1. Geoff Eley, *From Unification to Nazism, Reinterpreting the German Past*, Boston, 1986.
2. David Calleo, *The German Problem Reconsidered. Germany and the World Order, 1870 to the Present*, Cambridge, 1978, pp. 2f.

I used the occasion of my presence as a Visiting Fellow at St Antony's College in Oxford during 1985/6 to invite, together with Anthony Nicholls, a number of German experts to a seminar during the course of which we discussed the rise of the German national state in Central Europe during the nineteenth century and the problems which arose from it. The lectures held during this seminar are presented in this volume.

Certainly no simple answers to our questions were found; the methods, points of view and temperaments of the lecturers are too varied for that. In addition, we had to confine ourselves to handling a number of important aspects and perspectives, without trying to furnish a total picture; this volume is not a substitute for a historical reference work. But it is precisely the variety of perspectives which permits the reader to look at the difficult and ambiguous process of nation-building in the centre of Europe with different eyes. Dieter Düding analyses the liberal and democratic associations as the main acting force 'from below' against the Central European order of 1815. While Alexander Schwan confirms the classical view of the failure of German liberalism to bring about the nation-state as an act of popular liberal emancipation, Adolf M. Birke does away with the widely-held view that the Catholic minority in Germany was merely the victim of a hunger for power on the part of Prussia and the Liberals. Quite unconventional also are Hubert Kiesewetter's findings in a carefully researched study on economic history: the economic unification of Germany, the Deutsche Zollverein of 1834, did not lead inevitably to the Empire of Bismarck, as is often maintained — the effects of the Industrial Revolution on the national question remain ambivalent.

Harm-Hinrich Brandt uses the Revolution of 1848 as an example to illustrate how closely the question of German unification was related to the national ambitions of the other peoples in the Russian and Austro-Hungarian Empires: the national mixture in East-Central Europe was so complex that any attempt at nation-building had to be at the expense of the neighbouring peoples. Klaus Zernack's lecture shows how intricate these interconnections were — Poland and Germany are virtually Siamese twins, who remain inescapably connected despite profound antagonisms. And Michael Stürmer points to the basic problem of the viability of a German national-state within the European balance of power: the French–German dualism was the logical consequence of the conditions which enabled the creation of the French and German national-states, but at the same time it posed the fundamental danger to the European Concert, which guaranteed the existence of the states of Europe. The case study by Günther Heydemann about British policy towards the German national parliament during the Revolution of 1848 also shows the concern with which Palmerston's Ministry followed the events in the heart of Europe and how difficult it was from the British point of view to relate the German unification process to the politics of the classical balance of power.

Summarising from these various perspectives one can say that the German question was always inseparably connected with European politics, it influenced European politics and was affected by it. Whoever speaks of Germany must speak of Europe.

I sincerely thank all co-authors of this volume for their cooperation and the editors of the series *German Historical Perspectives* for their support. I am very indebted to the Stifterverband für die Deutsche Wissenschaft, which furnished the financial means for the guest lecturers to Oxford, and Marion Berghahn, who took the risk of publishing a book with a rather exotic theme. Above all, I would like to thank Anthony Nicholls, who with great patience not only tolerated my continental concepts regarding the organisation of a seminar, but who took upon himself the task of transforming our more less Teutonic Anglo-Saxon into legible English.

HAGEN SCHULZE

The Revolution of the European Order and the Rise of German Nationalism

In 1766 the Imperial Reichshofrat Friedrich Carl von Moser asked 'What are the Germans?' He gave his own answer: 'For centuries we have been a puzzle with respect to our political constitution, a source of booty to our neighbours, an object of ridicule, disunited and weak'.[1] The reasons for Moser's lament were obvious: the Holy Roman Empire was split up into 314 larger and smaller states and free cities, was marked by deep confessional discord, was economically far behind Western Europe, and was the theatre of war of the Continent. Whereas on Europe's periphery modern nation-states were coming into being, Central Europe remained without a political, economic and cultural focus, without a central power, without a real identity. The population was loyal to its respective ruler, one considered oneself a subject of Prussia, Bavaria, Austria, Saxony–Coburg–Gotha or Schwarzburg–Sondershausen; the Emperor and the Empire were very distant, more of a myth than a reality. In 1806, when, under pressure from Napoleon, Emperor Franz II abdicated from the Roman–German throne, thus terminating the thousand year history of the old Empire, the Germans hardly took any notice. Goethe commented that the quarrels of his coachman interested him more than this piece of news.[2]

Two generations later, with the founding of Bismarck's Empire in

---

1. F. C. von Moser, *Von dem Deutschen Nationalgeist*, Leipzig, 1766, p. 5.
2. J. W. Goethe, 'Diary', 7 August 1806, in *Artemis-Gedenkausgabe, Tagebücher*, Zurich, 1964, p. 267.

1871, a national concentration of power came into being in Central Europe the likes of which this area had not experienced before. Benjamin Disraeli declared before Parliament on 9 February 1871, that the creation of the German nation-state meant 'the German revolution, a greater political event than the French revolution of last century'.[3] Between Moser's lament and Disraeli's apprehensions lay a century of the fastest and most profound change yet experienced by Europe. When we ask in the following what led to the rise of nationalism and the nation-state, we should not speak only of Germany. The 'German Question' was always a question posed to history and to the political constitution of Europe.

First of all there was the demographic problem. Since the middle of the eighteenth century, after centuries of demographic equilibrium which had been brutally achieved through wars, epidemics and famine, Europe's population began to increase by leaps and bounds. In 1750 the continent had a population of approximately 130 million people; around 1800 it was already 185 million and in 1900 it had jumped to 410 million. Central Europe was no exception in this regard: in 1750 about 17 million people would have been living within the borders of the empire to be founded later by Bismarck; by about 1800 the figure already reached 23 million, and in 1900 it was up to 57 million people. Thus, not only did the population figures increase steadily, the growth rate also went up, although already at that time (around 1800) Western and Central Europe was already the most densely populated part of the world.[4]

Several factors were responsible for this population explosion: one cause was the sharp increase in agricultural productivity thanks to new methods of cultivation. The previous large fluctuations between the annual harvests became more seldom, famines were a thing of the past. The people, who were better nourished, were also more resistant to illnesses. New methods of combating diseases, such as the vaccination, but also improved hygiene contributed to the containment of epidemics and helped increase the average life expectancy. In particular, the mortality rate of infants and of women in childbirth went down.

3. W. F. Monypenny, G. E. Buckle, *The Life of Benjamin Disraeli, Earl of Beaconsfield*, vol. 2, London, 1929, p. 473.
4. W. Köllmann, 'Bevölkerungsgeschichte 1800–1970', in H. Aubin and W. Zorn (eds.), *Handbuch der deutschen Wirtschafts- und Sozialgeschichte*, vol. 2, Stuttgart, 1976, B. R. Mitchell, *European Historical Statistics 1750–1970*, Cambridge, 1975; W. Köllmann, *Bevölkerung in der industriellen Revolution*, Göttingen, 1974.

This was an accomplishment not only of medicine, but also of a new attitude towards children and the family. In many parts of Europe the social or legal barriers to marriage disappeared; more couples married both at an earlier age and for longer periods. In this way numerous factors, many of which have not yet been adequately studied, combined to produce an unprecedented population rise.

People began to migrate *en masse*. The rural society of old Europe was gradually disintegrating; one of the symptoms being that the increase in food production could not keep pace with the increase in population. During the nineteenth century people migrated to countries which were relatively underpopulated, such as America, Australia and Canada, or they crowded into the rapidly expanding cities giving rise to social, hygienic and moral grievances that can hardly be described today. The novels of Charles Dickens or Eugène Suë offer only a pallid, romanticised notion of the harsh and miserable reality.

This development could have culminated in a terrible catastrophe; the Scottish clergyman Thomas Malthus had already made the sombre prediction that the sustained population growth on the basis of the given economic resources would result in the collapse of mankind. That his prophecy did not come true was due to the simultaneous economic transformation which we generally refer to as the 'Industrial Revolution'. It is not possible to describe here the countless preconditions which set off this unique process in world history, a subject which even today is a rewarding topic for learned discussion. At any rate this process would have been unthinkable without the background of the scientific, philosophical, cultural, religious and institutional history of Old Europe since antiquity. I certainly don't need to point out that England was a pioneer in these developments, among other reasons: because of the good location of its iron and coal mines; because of a good transportation network, which was not impeded as in the rest of Europe by customs barriers; because of the strong motivation on the part of capitalists to invest and to take a risk; and, furthermore, because of the existence of a highly developed banking and credit system and of liberal economic policies. All this and more led within a few decades to an unusual rise in productivity and to sustained economic growth, although interrupted by crises — a process that also took place in other European countries with similar political, economic, social and especially ideological preconditions.[5]

5. D. S. Landes, *The Unbound Prometheus*, Cambridge, 1969; C. M. Cipolla (ed.), *The Fontana Economic History of Europe*, vols. 3 and 4, London, 1973; R. M. Hartwell, *The Industrial Revolution and Economic Growth*, London, 1971; C. Fohlen, *Que'est-ce que la*

The rise in population and production was accompanied by a third secular transformation: the revolution in communications. In the old days the speed of a coach and team of horses defined time and space. Now, with the development of steamship lines and the railroad, masses of men and goods were transported greater distances much more quickly and at lower cost. Large markets, essential for the interaction of national and European economic spheres, were now possible. The news of a military victory or of a politically or economically important decision used to take a week to cross Europe — with the invention of the telegraph all such distances became meaningless. The number of schools and universities — and thereby the literacy rate — increased rapidly. Messages, news, books and magazines were no longer restricted to a small educated elite, but were available to masses of people; a change which was facilitated by inexpensive printing owing to mechanised printing processes and the introduction of the linotype technique.[6]

These revolutions in demographic growth, industrial production and communications were all interconnected, conditioning one another mutually. It was inevitable that the European political system would react to this. All the constitutions of Old Europe were based on the rule of small, closed aristocratic elites which derived their legitimacy, as interpreted by the churches, from God. No doubt a tendency to centralise and monopolise political power had already existed for a long time. This could be achieved by rendering the administration of the State more efficient by introducing a rational bureaucracy, by standardising legal conditions, and by legitimising the exercise of power by a single ruler, thus taking it away from the estates. But the absolutist State of the eighteenth century, which in its various forms characterised Europe during this age, could no longer fulfil its task on the three decisive levels of political power: the levels of legitimacy, of participation and of performance for the socio-political system.[7]

---

révolution industrielle?, Paris, 1971.

6. A general history of the revolution in communications is not yet published. Some provisional titles: P. S. Bagwell, *The Transport Revolution from 1770*, London, 1974; W. Schivelbusch, *The Railway Journey*, Leamington Spa and Berkeley, Calif., 1986; R. Wittmann, *Buchmarkt und Lektüre im 18. und 19. Jahrhundert*, Tübingen, 1982; J. W. Carter, P. H. Muir, *Printing and the Mind of Men*, London, 1967; C. M. Cipolla, *Literacy and Development in the West*, London, 1969.

7. L. Binder et al., *Crises and Sequences in Political Development*, Princeton, 1971; S. N. Eisenstadt, S. Rokkan (eds.), *Building States and Nations. Models and Data Resources*, 2 vols.,

We are interested here primarily in the problem of legitimacy. The politically effective myths of the *ancien régime* lost appeal; the divine right of kings and the 'good old law' became obsolete. The crisis in Europe was above all a crisis of values, and it is noteworthy that this crisis of values set in *before* the population explosion and industrialisation began to have their disintegrating effect on the social system of the estates. The de-Christianisation of large parts of Europe had already begun at the end of the seventeenth century and had already made itself felt not only as an elitist philosophy of the Enlightenment, but also as a change in collective mental attitudes. This is apparent when one studies, for instance, the changing concept of death or the popularisation of birth control measures during the eighteenth century.[8]

New forms of legitimacy replaced old ones. Initially, the idea of the right of each individual to freedom and happiness came to the fore; the American Revolution and, for a while, the French Revolution found in this idea their main justification. But already toward the end of the eighteenth century, there was a change in tone: the idea of the general quality of citizenship, in which all should participate, joined with Rousseau's idea that only the sum of individuals, their unity as a people, was politically viable. The unity of a people was not maintained merely by the rational idea of a common citizenship, but rather by the all encompassing consciousness of the common nation. The nation was the incarnation of the common will, and all rule owed its legitimacy to this common will.

This modern concept of nation was first developed during the French Revolution. It was a rational idea evolving from the French Enlightenment, and its goal was the unity of the French people in the form of the 'third estate' with the French state and the French language within the boundaries of the hexagon, between the Mediterranean and the Maas, the Rhine and the Pyrenees, the Alps and the Atlantic. But the 'nation une et indivisible' was by no means an abstract principle. In the enthusiasm of the *jeu de paume* oath, in the common attack on the Bastille, in the spontaneous outbursts of violence of the revolutionary masses the concept of nation was experienced physically as a supra-individual, ecstatic unity in which the doubts and fears of each individual disappeared in the emotional confirmation of the national com-

Beverly Hills, 1973; C. Tilly (ed.), *The Formation of National States in Western Europe*, Princeton, 1975.

8. M. Vovelle, *Piété baroque et déchristianisation en Provence au XVIIIᵉ siècle*, Paris, 1973; J. Dupaquier/M. Lachiver, 'Les débuts de la contraception en France ou les deux malthusianismes', in *Annales* E.S.C., 1969, pp. 1391–406.

munity. This mass experience created stimuli which later facilitated the appeals to the feeling of national community. Pseudo-religious rituals and symbols were developed, which reassured the 'believers' of their membership in the community. And a language came into being which combined the key words of national devotion and exaltation with a peculiar literary–religious kind of pathos. In this way the extraordinary mass experience could be applied to everyday life. The liturgy of revolutionary celebrations brought the symbols of the common people into a mythological context and the experience of the nation could be artificially renewed. The language of journalism ensured that every citizen was informed daily of his new emotional tie to the nation for which he could be mobilised.[9]

The French model, however, did not function on the other side of the Rhine. There were two hindrances: the social and the territorial conditions. In Germany, too, there was a bourgeoisie, but its structure was totally different from that of the French. In France we see a self-confident commercial bourgeoisie beside a broad stratum of state employees, then the lawyers of the *parlements* and the counsel — all of whom were kept away by the upper class of nobles from the higher, financially and politically interesting state positions and who were thus discontented. Then we have the artisans who were dependent on the King and the nobility's demand for luxury goods and who were cast into misery by the severe financial crisis of the French state. This factor had revolutionary potential especially in the capital.[10] In Germany, on the other hand, an educated elite of aristocratic bureaucratic academicians came into being in the course of the eighteenth century, which was without corporate status. This elite consisted of higher civil servants, professors, high-school teachers, Protestant clergymen and lawyers, whose opportunity to climb the social ladder by being promoted in the state's service was much better than that of their French colleagues. They were, to be sure, the public of the German Enlightenment, but at the same time they shared the opinion of Baron Knigge who said: 'I claim that we in Germany need neither wish nor fear a

9. M. Vovelle, *Die Französische Revolution — Soziale Bewegung und Umbruch der Mentalitäten*, Munich and Vienna, 1982.

10. A. Cobban, *The Social Interpretation of the French Revolution*, Cambridge, 1964; H. Schulze, 'War die Französische Revolution eine bürgerlich-kapitalistische Revolution?', in H. Boockmann et al. (eds.), *Geschichte und Gegenwart*, Neumünster, 1980, pp. 149–60.

revolution'.[11]

The new concept of nation was also discussed in these educated circles, but it remained abstract and without consequences for politics, which in reality were apparently bearable for the vast majority of the German people. Madame de Staël, the French writer, observed that 'the educated class of Germany quarrels with great liveliness about the realm of theory and does not tolerate any fetters in this respect. Rather happily, however, they leave the realities of life to the earthly rulers'.[12] In the concept of this educated class, the unity of Germany consisted in language, literature and culture, and nothing else. And for that reason, Goethe and Weimar were for the Germans what the King and London were to the English, what Napoleon and Paris were to the French: the centre and incarnation of the nation. The German nation existed, but not in the form of a nation with its own state, but rather as a cultural unity.

It required the shock of the collapse of the fragile giant Prussia on the battlefields of Jena and Auerstedt in October 1806 and the occupation by Napoleonic troops to make the concept of nation a physical experience for the Germans. The Wars of Liberation of 1809 and 1813 replaced the revolutionary flame. No doubt, the national enthusiasm for the wars against the 'Corsican Monster' did not reach the same social depth as the Revolution in France. It is true that the sons of the educated bourgeoisie eagerly joined the voluntary battalions, while their daughters exchanged their jewellery for weapons; and the artisan class, which enjoyed special privileges as a result of the Prussian reforms, could also be mobilised; but notably the rural mass, which was, after all, almost 80 per cent of the total population, was hardly touched by the new national movement.[13]

Death on the battlefield, surrounded by a pathetic–aesthetic halo in the spirit of Neohellenism, replaced the revolutionary blood sacrifice. The units of volunteers felt themselves to be 'the nation in arms'. In the poet Theodor Körner, who died in battle, and in the woman Eleonore Prohaska, who, wearing a soldier's uniform, also fell on the battlefield, the movement had its martyrs. The French enemy was attacked with a hatred and fury that anticipated the horrors of the total wars of the twentieth century. The common hatred of the enemy made Germans out of the Prussians, the Bavarians, the Hanoverians, the Austrians — but what was 'Germany' in reality? The most famous song of the Wars

11. A. Frhr. von Knigge, *Joseph von Wurmbrand (1792)* (ed.) G. Steiner, Frankfurt, 1968, p. 11.
12. G. de Staël, *De l'Allemagne*, vol. 1, London, 1913, p. 68.
13. R. Ibbeken, *Preußen 1807–1813*, Cologne and Berlin, 1870.

of Liberation, composed by Ernst Moritz Arndt in 1813, begins with
the question: 'What is the fatherland of the Germans?' and ends with
the answer: 'As far as the German tongue rings'. After the Wars of
Liberation Germany was still only vaguely defined by language, culture, history, a utopian projection of the past. The German Confederation, which was created by the European powers in Vienna in 1815,
besides having the nebulous vision of a nation-state of all Germans,
never had the chance to win the hearts of the people. It remained a
multinational complex, in which there lived, apart from Germans, also
Poles, Italians, and Czechs, whereas German-speaking populations in
Denmark and France and even in East Prussia were not to belong to
Germany. Foreign princes, the kings of England, Denmark and the
Netherlands were members of the German Confederation, an indica-
tion that Central Europe was organised not as a German nation-state
but as a region where European interests were balanced out. The
federal institutions served the restorationist aims of the Holy Alliance,
of the Austrian and soon also of the Prussian courts: the suppression of
liberal and nationalist movements in the population. The German
Confederation never won the approval of the people, it remained a
despised and hated symbol of bondage and suppression.

During the decades after the Wars of Liberation, as the once strong
ties between the State and the citizen in Germany gave way, as
dangerous social tensions emerged and the mass poverty of the pre-
industrial lower classes anticipated a future social revolution, German
nationalism developed such an emotional attraction for the masses that
all competing ideologies appeared weak by comparison. German
nationalism was open to all kinds of ideas, could have liberal, religious,
democratic or egalitarian colouring, could accommodate demands for
any type of state or constitution — briefly, it was the ideal vehicle for
any kind of idea inimical to the existing political system: it was the
common denominator for any form of opposition.

The German Revolution of 1848 failed for this reason among others.
The Revolution stood for unity and freedom, freedom primarily in the
sense of liberal constitutional ideas, sometimes even in a republican
framework. But what was unity? In Frankfurt the elected representatives of the German people came together to constitute a national
assembly, a host of famous names of intellectual and libertarian Germany: three-quarters of the representatives were university-educated, a
quarter were professors — the educated class was still the backbone of

the national idea. With the motto from the Wars of Liberation: 'It must be all of Germany' the debate began, and as with every discussion among professors, it had no end. Heinrich von Gagern, the President of the National Assembly, proposed a motion to exclude Austria from the future German state: this was the 'lesser Germany' (*Kleindeutschland*) solution under Prussian leadership as it already existed on the economic level in the form of the German Customs Union (Zollverein). Here we have them — the stable borders, the reasonable solutions, for without Austria one was rid of the whole mess of involvements in East and South East European conflicts, the whole ballast of the non-German peoples with the exception of the Prussian Poles. But this solution appealed only to reason, not to emotions. Was Germany to be a greater Prussia? Opposition was quickly forthcoming, from all fractions of the Assembly. One invoked 'the bulwark of the Carpathian Mountains'; one invoked Bohemia — 'the body and head of Germany'; and one the Tyrol — the 'German fortress in Italy', and first and foremost the civilising mission of the Germans in the Balkans and in Eastern Europe. That other nations were also fighting there for their freedom and union did not matter. A 'greater Germany' (*Großdeutschland*) under a Habsburg emperor, the revived 'old empire' anointed with a drop of the oil of liberalism — that was the Germany the majority of the liberal notables dreamt of.[14]

The Revolution collapsed due to its own internal contradictions — the various revolutionary wings each had their own concepts of freedom and unity and when the radicals among the revolutionaries threatened with a second, social revolution, the moderate lovers of freedom were overcome with the archetypal fear of the guillotine, which had swept over all of nineteenth-century Europe, and quickly sought a compromise with the old ruling powers. The Revolution also failed because of the threat of intervention on the part of other European powers, who saw in the realisation of the German nation-state the end of the European Concert and who feared the revolutionising of the whole continent. At the last moment, just before the Frankfurt National Assembly was about to disperse in total despair, a last effort was made: — the unpopular 'lesser Germany' solution was proposed, but Frederick William IV of Prussia refused the 'pig's crown', as he called it, because 'the smell of revolutionary excrement' clung to it.

Thus the dream of encompassing all Germans in a nation-state on the basis of liberty faded away. But in some respects the Revolution

14. G. Wollstein, *Das "Großdeutschland" der Paulskirche*, Düsseldorf, 1977.

also brought forth clarity: for the first time the Germans had to realise that their national hope was one thing, the reality of European power-politics something entirely different. In East Central Europe — that was clear — it was impossible to find a just solution for the territorial ambitions of the Germans, Poles and Czechs. The German national movement had lost its innocence by ignoring the national wishes of its eastern neighbours. Since the supranational solutions of Old Europe had lost their legitimacy, the national question in East Central Europe could only be solved by renunciation of demands or by subjugation. And it had become evident that there was little leeway for the tolera-tion of German unity in a European framework. Every attempt to establish a German nation-state at the expense of the system of Euro-pean peace treaties of 1815 met with the decided opposition of the European community of nations.

And finally, in the course of the debates of the National Assembly in Frankfurt, the question of what was the German fatherland was clarified. The alternatives were either 'greater Germany' under Habs-burg leadership and including the German parts of the Habsburg monarchy or 'lesser Germany', without Austria, under Prussian rule.

The contradictions which had split the Frankfurt Parliament, were fought out and decided eighteen years later on the battlefield of Königgrätz in accordance with the programmatic statement of the Prussian Chancellor Otto von Bismarck: 'The great questions of time are not decided by speeches and votes of the majority — that was the great mistake of 1848 — but by iron and blood'.[15] This insight of the 'Iron Chancellor', which shocked the liberals of all factions, was only the logical consequence of the previous defeats. 'Blood and iron': that meant that the German Question had to be solved by resorting to the *ultima ratio* of politics, by taking to arms. Decisive here was not the old German longing for their own nation-state, such as the peoples of western and northern Europe had achieved long before, but the still older political rivalry between the two German powers, Austria and Prussia. The war of Prussia against Austria in 1866 was a classical war for hegemony. The result had little to do with the wishes of the German nationalists. Whereas Austria finally ceased to play a role as a power on the Central European scene and thereby in German history, north

15. O. v. Bismarck, *Die gesammelten Werke. Friedrichsruher Ausgabe*, vol. 10, Berlin, 1926, p. 139.

of the Main river the Northern German Confederation came into being, a union of all northern German states with overwhelming Prussian dominance. Prussia officially recognised the independence and sovereignty of the southern German states. It could not be foreseen in 1866 that only four years later, after the victorious war against France, the German Empire would be proclaimed in the Hall of Mirrors of the palace of Versailles. Two factors led to this: one was the aggressive policy of Napoleon III towards Germany. Napoleon feared the concentration of Prussian power on his border and wanted to maintain the classical French role as the guarantor of the status quo in Central Europe. The second factor was the temporary collapse of the European balance of power after the Crimean War, as England and Russia became deeply estranged and a Central European power such as Prussia enjoyed greater manoeuvrability. Thanks to a unique historical constellation, the German Empire was moulded on the battlefields of Sedan and Mars-la-Tour and, for that matter, as a union of German princes, not as a creation of the German people. The King of Bavaria discovered his German heart and joined the Empire only after having received a handsome bribe from a secret Prussian fund.

At first glance it seems that the stories of 1813, 1848 and 1871 have nothing to do with each other, and, as a rule, this is confirmed in historical writing: it is usually said that the national and liberal movement of the people failed in Germany. The Second German Empire was created not by a 'revolution from below', but by the forces of reaction and an authoritarian state, the 'revolution from above'.[16] This is an interpretation with carries considerable weight when trying to explain later German history. And at first glance much seems to support this point of view. We know that Bismarck's politics of hegemony until 1866 met with the irreconcilable opposition of the German national movement, the 'party of chatterers and swindlers', as Bismarck mockingly called the Liberals. And when one calls to mind the proclamation of the Empire in Versailles, the abundance of colourful uniforms and the shining helmets of the feudal society which cheered William I enthusiastically, and when one considers further the constitutional structure of Bismarck's Empire with an Imperial government independent of parliamentary control and the strong position of the

---

16. E. Engelberg, 'Über die Revolution von oben. Wirklichkeit und Begriff', in idem., *Theorie, Empirie und Methode in der Geschichtswissenschaft*, Berlin (East), 1980, pp. 339–84; B. Vogel, '"Revolution von oben" — Der "deutsche Weg" in die bürgerliche Gesellschaft?', in *Sozialwissenschaftliche Informationen für Unterricht und Studium 8*, 1979, pp. 67–74.

federal princes, then the judgement that this was 'revolution from above' seems to be confirmed.

But such an impression is superficial. In reality, along with the governmental forces of the pre-democratic, authoritarian monarchy, other powers influenced the creation of the German nation-state. Iron was not only the symbol for the superior military power of Prussia, it also stood for the power of industry. Economically, the small German union had long before become a reality. Already by 1834 most of the German states had come together to form the German Customs Union under Prussian dominance, and the rest, with two exceptions — the Hansa cities Hamburg, Bremen and Lübeck, and Austria — followed suit during the subsequent decades. Austria was prevented from becoming a member not only due to the cleverness of Prussian diplomacy, but due even more to its own old-fashioned interventionist and mercantilistic economic policies, which contradicted the liberal economic principles of Prussia. As a result, economic growth within the framework of the Customs Union started relatively late when compared to Western European countries, but caught up quickly, and since the 1850s the annual growth rate of the gross national product per capita was far ahead compared to the rest of Europe, whereas the gross national product in Austria–Hungary stagnated and actually, by comparison, declined.[17] A glance at the map showed by 1860 at the latest that in Austria–Hungary the concentration of railroad lines, of the telegraph network, of the banking system, and of the industrial sites south of the Saxon and Bavarian borders decreased rapidly. From the economic point of view, it was already obvious at this time that the Greater Prussian concept of Small Germany was a one-way street. And, contrary to earlier research, we know today that this development was possible in the first place *despite* the State's economic policies, not because of them. Where the State intervened, it usually hindered economic development, as is very evident in the case of railroad construction. The economic unity of Germany came into being not via intervention 'from above', but was basically caused by the initiative of liberal entrepreneurs.[18]

17. P. Bairoch, 'International Industrialization Levels from 1750 to 1980', *Journal of European Economic History*, 11, 1982, pp. 269–333; H. Böhme, *Deutschlands Weg zur Groß-macht*, Cologne, 1966, pp. 57–90.
18. W. Fischer, 'Industrialisierung und soziale Frage in Preußen', in Fritz Thyssen Stiftung (ed.), *Preußen — Seine Wirkung auf die deutsche Geschichte*, Stuttgart, 1985, pp. 223–59.

And, finally, only he who merely looks at the surface of political events and overlooks the effect of mass moods, mentalities and attitudes can cling to the theory of the 'revolution from above.' The fate of the anaemic German Confederation illustrates this very clearly. In the age of mass industrial societies, even a state which is not democratic cannot survive in the long run without the consent of its subjects. The concept of a nation state was the only form which could grant political legitimacy in the nineteenth century. In addition to the conflict between Prussia and Austria, this was the most important reason why the German Confederation remained a lifeless body. All political tendencies against the national movement were bound to remain ineffectual. It is true that the liberal and nationalistic bourgeoisie never managed to fulfil its dream of a democratic Greater Germany, but in cases of conflict, a compromise was always reached; that was the case in 1848, at a time when finally all German states had representative constitutions, and again in 1871, when Bismarck — with his eye on public opinion — introduced manhood suffrage.

Thus, the foundation of the Second German Empire can be described as an interplay of Bismarck and the national movement. Public opinion was so powerful by then that not only Bismarck, but every German government sought to win over this potential force of power and adjusted its own political stand accordingly. This became evident in the fact that since 1815 no medium-sized German state dared to enter an alliance with a non-German power, although the Act of the German Confederation of 1815 left this possibility open. The policy of a 'Third Germany', a federation of the smaller states with French support, which appeared repeatedly in German history, would have now posed unpredictable domestic risks for German rulers.

The model of 'revolution from above' must, therefore, be qualified. Without doubt, the German Empire was not created by speeches and majority decisions, but was united by 'blood and iron', but nothing which was directed against the nationalism of the masses had success. Bismarck himself expressed this: 'Even though the decisions of local parliaments, newspapers and riflemen's meetings could not bring about the union of Germany, liberalism exercises such a pressure on the princes, that they feel more inclined to make compromises in favour of the Empire'.[19]

It is true that Bismarck's politics mediatised the national movement, but the movement imposed its goal on him. Without the diffuse yet sole

19. O. v. Bismarck, *Gedanken und Erinnerungen*, vol. 1, Stuttgart, 1899, p. 293.

legitimising authority of the movement for union, not a German Empire but a Greater Prussia would have emerged. Bismarck knew very well that he played a dangerous game by making use of the nationalism of the masses. His successors, however, would no longer know how to tame this tiger.

DIETER DÜDING

The Nineteenth-Century German Nationalist Movement as a Movement of Societies

Hambach Castle in the Bavarian Rhineland Palatinate, 27 May 1832: in the guise of a national festival, the biggest political rally of *vormärzlich* Germany (the Germany of the years 1830–48) is taking place. The inaugural speaker of the festival is Philipp Hepp, a doctor from Neustadt in the Palatinate. He makes a stirring appeal to the participants, who number several thousand: 'You German men and brothers, join together [*vereinigt euch*] all of you who are true patriots'. Hepp repeats his appeal to his enthusiastically patriotic audience: 'join together! not in secret and in disguise, but . . . in the sight of the Fatherland, and work to ensure that the evil are resisted and the weak are supported — work to ensure that the undecided reach a decision, the faint-hearted gain courage and public opinion is truly expressed. Only in this way can the dear Fatherland be helped and saved.'[1]

Despite the semantic fuzziness of the verb 'vereinigen', the deeper meaning of Dr Hepp's patriotic appeal was not lost on his audience, most of whom came from the Rhineland Palatinate. It seems to me beyond doubt that Hepp wanted his cry of 'vereinigt euch' to be understood chiefly as a call to join political *Vereine*, or societies, and that this is indeed how his audience understood it. In the light of contemporary political events in the Bavarian Rhineland Palatinate, such an interpretation seems obvious.

In January 1832, a potent oppositional social force had been created

1. Described by J.G.A. Wirth, assisted by an editorial committee, *Das Nationalfest der Deutschen zu Hambach*, Heft 1, Neustadt a.d.H., 1832, p. 31.

19

in this part of Bavaria, which lay on the left bank of the Rhine close to France and was geographically separated from its Bavarian 'Motherland'. It had taken the form of the radical-democratic, antiparticularist and German nationalist Press- und Vaterlandsverein (Press and Fatherland Society). The society had already taken a number of important political initiatives against feudal conditions. For example, the idea of a celebratory national gathering at the ruined castle of Hambach had first developed among groups connected with the Press- und Vaterlandsverein, and some of its members had undertaken to organise the festival. Hepp himself was a registered member of the society. His appeal for unity should be regarded as a thinly veiled call to his audience to join one of its many branch committees in the Rhineland Palatinate, although the Press- und Vaterlandsverein had actually been made illegal by the Bavarian authorities.

On 10 June 1832 in Vienna, the Austrian Chancellor Metternich expressed his personal attitude towards nationalist opposition groups in the Bavarian Rhineland Palatinate. His approach, which was not made public, was virtually a counterpoint to Hepp's appeal for unity. In private correspondence, Metternich told his confidant and sympathiser in Berlin, Prince von Wittgenstein: 'With popular representation in the modern sense, with freedom of the press and *political societies* [author's emphasis], every state must be destroyed, monarchic as well as republican. Only anarchy is possible, no matter what the scholars at their desks say. At the end of scholarship there will be blows. . . . We in Germany will come to blows'.[2]

Dr Hepp, a bourgeois patriot, saw the existence of political societies as an essential prerequisite for the defeat of feudalism and state particularism in Germany; Klemens Prince von Metternich, symbolic figure of the old system of princely states, regarded free political societies as a fundamental evil which would bring the collapse of state authority there. He was convinced of the need to tackle them resolutely, along with modern parliamentarism and the free press.

Hepp's high estimation of the value of political societies was by no means unusual within the German bourgeois nationalist and freedom movement of the nineteenth century. After the French July Revolution, the democratic opposition movement arrived on the scene as an organised force in the Bavarian Palatinate and the south-west of Germany; societies were the focal points of this democratic opposition. Moreover,

---

2. Metternich to Prince von Wittgenstein, 10 June 1832; quoted by Veit Valentin, *Das Hambacher Nationalfest*, Berlin, 1932, pp. 144ff.

the establishment of societies played an important role in the modern movement for freedom and unity in Germany as a whole between the Wars of Liberation and the foundation of the Reich. Indeed, it is no exaggeration to claim that the establishment of organised groups — of societies — was an essential feature of the bourgeois nationalist freedom movement in nineteenth-century Germany — that is, for those highly motivated and active social groups who were committed to the creation of a national state.[3] The German nationalist movement manifested itself in such associations and activities. The movement gained stability and durability through these forms of social organisation. Societies, and the many different activities of their members, gave the movement its characteristic, multifaceted appearance, its typical forms of expression, its own symbols, metaphors, rites, etc. Dr Hepp's appeal for unity, seen in this light, is a classic example; it reflects an immanent tendency of the nationalist movement in Germany, a structural element of the German nationalist movement.

Paradoxically, Metternich's verdict on the system of societies in Germany is equally significant and symptomatic. He could never complain of a lack of allies within the German ruling elites for his efforts to halt the irresistible drive of German patriots towards association. And it was not only during this time as Austrian Chancellor and 'Régisseur' of the Frankfurt Diet of the German Confederation that German governments revealed an almost obsessive impulse to penalise and prohibit nationalist organisations, and — after they had been disbanded — to make sure that the prohibitions were observed. Long after Metternich had left the political stage, German regimes persisted with the persecution of the nationalist movement which had begun during the *Vormärz*. This long-term persecution and suppression of their societies had a considerable effect on the development of the German nationalist movement; it even brought it to a temporary standstill on a number of occasions.

3. The nineteenth-century German nationalist movement (of societies) played a major role in the development of the German people into a modern nation. Of course, this process of integration was also strongly influenced by a number of other factors which are not included in this article.

One such factor was the gradual rise of a national market, a national economic area produced by industrialisation and changing economic and customs policy. Another was the modernisation of transport routes and methods, caused by technological innovation; these resulted in the development of a national transport system. A third factor was provided by the extension of a national system of information, based on an increase in the production of books and magazines and growing literacy and interest in the printed word. Recently, these factors have been examined in a most stimulating, informative and thoughtful book by Hagen Schulze, *Der Weg zum Nationalstaat. Die deutsche Nationalbewegung vom 18. Jahrhundert bis zur Reichsgründung*, Munich, 1985.

The degree of persecution naturally fluctuated, but had its roots in an excessive fear of bourgeois political association on the part of the Establishment in the princely states. The interaction of this persecution with the impulse to associate exhibited by middle-class patriots, despite all the coercive measures to which they were subjected, gave the German nationalist movement of the nineteenth century its unmistakable features.

This essay contains an attempt to trace the development of the socially organised German nationalist movement during the years between the Wars of Liberation and the foundation of the *kleindeutsch* ('lesser German') Reich. It will show that the obvious turning-points of the period are due in no small measure to the prevailing treatment of the nationalist societies by the state authorities. I will also argue that there were *four phases of development* in the nationalist movement before the foundation of the Reich. However, these phases of development were not caused solely by *exogenous* factors (the attitude and measures taken by the states); the *four phase theory*, arrived at empirically, also depends considerably on *endogenous* factors, deriving from the autochthonous forces of development and motivation within the nationalist movement itself. For example, the gradual development of the organised nationalist movement to include new, broader social groups — a phenomenon with great significance for our theory of phases — can be explained primarily in terms of its internal potential and power. Both endogenous and exogenous factors were thus important in the development of the four phases of the German nationalist movement.

Phase I: 1811–1819. The Organised Nationalist Movement as a Youth Movement (of Opposition)

The earliest — admittedly relatively modest — origins of a German nationalist movement which organised itself in societies can be traced back to the period immediately preceding the Wars of Liberation against Napoleon (1813–14). For Germany, these were years of extreme national humiliation. Napoleon's policy of war, hegemony and exploitation had — like no other modern event — filled the Germans with deep contempt and even sheer hatred for their great western neighbour. But it had also awakened a powerful sense of national self-respect, and a passionate feeling of national pride.

The upsurge of nationalist sentiments in German society in the half-decade before 1813 is most clearly apparent in Prussia. There was good reason for this. Despite French occupation and control, a reformist civil service elite there still had some room for political manoeuvre, which enabled its members to set in motion a process of political and social modernisation. This process operated at a number of different levels (emancipation of the peasantry, introduction of freedom of trade, municipal self-administration, reorganisation of the army, school and university reform). The civil service reformers saw their policy of Prussian renewal as a prelude to a similar realignment in the whole of Germany.

Without the climate of reform in the Prussian *state*, the German nationalist upsurge in Prussian *society* would have been unthinkable. Who produced this upsurge, and in what way? German nationalist ideas were popularised by members of the educated bourgeoisie through the medium of the spoken and written word — by speeches, lectures, sermons and books. Their nationalism was linked with a German cultural consciousness which had been apparent since the last thirty years of the eighteenth century in educated circles, and which must be interpreted as a deliberate attempt at dissociation from the French (linguistic) culture which dominated the royal courts of Germany.[4] This cultural nationalism, based on a national German language and literature, received a strong ideological impetus directly before the outbreak of the Wars of Liberation. The idealist philosopher Johann Gottlieb Fichte was largely responsible for this development.

In the winter of 1807–8, Fichte delivered his 'Speeches to the German Nation' before a large audience in French-occupied Berlin. In these, he posited an ostensibly historical and irreversible antithesis between the German and French languages, amounting to a major difference in quality. Whereas the Germans possessed a natural, original language (*Ursprache*), a 'mother-tongue' which had grown from living roots, the 'neo-Latin' French people had only a 'derived', synthetic language which was superficially living but was actually dead at the roots.[5]

On the eve of the Wars of Liberation, middle-class intellectuals were propagating a national consciousness which contained, along with cultural–nationalist elements, a considerable degree of political nationalism. The main spiritual forefather of this approach was Friedrich Ludwig Jahn, teacher at a Berlin grammar school (*Gymnasium*). His book *Deutsches Volksthum*, published in 1810, revealed Jahn's cultural nationalism, but

4. H. Schulze, *Weg zum Nationalstaat*, p. 60.
5. Johann Gottlieb Fichte, *Reden an die deutsche Nation*, in idem, *Ausgewählte Werke* (ed.) Fritz Medicus, vol. 5, Darmstadt, 1962, pp. 422–54.

also firmly established his ideas in the sphere of political nationalism. The book contains the author's attempt to create a model for a future German national state, which Jahn envisaged as a constitutional monarchy with a constitution, representative body (estates), people's army, municipal self-administration and a free peasantry.[6]

However, Prussian society on the eve of the Wars of Liberation was not marked only by *individual* patriotism, articulated in speech and writing; the upsurge in German nationalism during those years was also manifested in the first *collective* German patriotic alliances, the foundation of the first nationalist associations. Friedrich Ludwig Jahn was deeply involved in this development, adopting a higly significant and innovatory approach.

In 1810 he founded the Deutsche Bund (German League) in Berlin. This was a private and conspiratorial society whose members — inspired by political nationalist ideas — made preparations for an insurrection against Napoleon. The Deutsche Bund was rapidly joined by a string of other societies — in Berlin by the Reimersche Kreis and the Fechtbodengesellschaft, and in Königsberg by the Tugendbund. All of these were secret German nationalist groups.

On the other hand, Jahn's Berlin Turngesellschaft (Gymnastic Society), established in 1811, was a completely new form of society. In the years immediately after the Wars of Liberation, the Turngesellschaft was exceptionally important for the development of the nationalist movement in Germany.[7]

Because of their secret organisations, the Deutscher Bund, Fechtbodengesellschaft. Reimerscher Kreis and Tugendbund all followed the tradition of the eighteenth-century political groups created by the protagonists of the German Enlightenment. In the princely states, the establishment of public societies with political objectives was illegal; as a result, closed and secret groups were created, in a provisional solution which was always less than ideal. By founding the Berlin Turngesellschaft, in which cultural and political nationalism was apparent from the outset, Jahn had made the decisive step from secret political forms of organisation to the creation of public associations with a political tendency.

As a consequence of their secrecy, the earlier conspiratorial nationalist societies had been numerically and socially exclusive and elitist.

6. Friedrich Ludwig Jahn, *Deutsches Volksthum*, Lübeck, 1810.
    7. The following observations on the Berlin Turngesellschaft and the patriotic gymnastic movement before 1819 are based on my book on the nineteenth-century German nationalist movement before the 1848 Revolution. Dieter Düding. *Organisierter gesellschaftlicher Nationalismus in Deutschland (1807–1848)*, Munich, 1984, pp. 50–139.

At most, they had gained a few hundred educated bourgeois members and a few members of the nobility. By organising publicly, the Berlin Turngesellschaft made it possible for the nationalist groups to recruit members. This now took place in an open and unimpeded manner, a development which was of critical importance for the establishment of a large, organised movement.

There are other reasons why Jahn's Turngesellschaft broke new ground for the nationalist movement. He had planned it as a recruiting area for male *youth*. The founder of the Turngesellschaft on the Berlin Hasenheide was thus combining his initiative with powerful educational objectives.

Jahn was strongly influenced by the pedagogic theory of his time. The Philanthropists, educators affected by the Enlightenment, had been influenced by Rousseau's educational novel *Emile* and had made gymnastics the focal point of their reforming theories.[8] Jahn associated himself with the educational reforms of the period, but with certain important changes: firstly, he carried them into new forms of organisation, into societies which were independent of the school system and recruited members on a voluntary basis; and secondly, he gave them a new theoretical justification, derived from his own nationalist ideals.

Where the Philanthropists had tried to integrate gymnastics into the school programme, and thus to achieve the best education of the *individual* through balanced concern for both body and mind, Jahn wanted to use gymnastics to influence youth towards *national* ideas. He was convinced that physical exercises, undertaken by young men in free communities, would help to awaken strong feelings of togetherness; he believed that the Turngesellschaft must appear to its members as a kind of preparatory course for defenders of the Fatherland; for Jahn, national educational work naturally included an intensive nationalist schooling of the mind, coupled with a strong emotional component. The *Turnvater* was determined to fill the *Turnerjugend* (young gymnasts) with his own national-cultural and national-political ideas.

Jahn had a great deal of success. The young proved very susceptible to the emotional patriotism of the Turngesellschaft. Crowds of young people, mainly from middle-class backgrounds, came to the Turngesellschaft on the Hasenheide even before the Wars of Liberation; they included schoolboys, students, and youths in vocational training. In March 1813 these same youths — or at least those who had reached military age — hastened to the colours, and particularly to the volunteer units.

---

8. See especially Hajo Bernett, *Die pädagogische Neugestaltung der burgerlichen Leibesübungen durch die Philanthropen*, 3rd edn., Schondorf, 1971.

However, Jahn's community had its finest hour after the Wars of Liberation, when the national aspirations of the patriots had been dashed. Before and during the war, German patriots had repeatedly emphasised the harmony between the princes and the German people — but after the overthrow of Napoleon this harmony was revealed as an illusion. The German rulers showed no willingness to keep the promises they had made 'in their hour of need'. Failure to establish a national and constitutional German state, and the widespread refusal to introduce basic rights, were greeted with dismay. The results of the Vienna Congress of princes and diplomats left the bourgeois patriots disillusioned. Among the young patriots, in particular, there was bitter disappointment at the turn of events. As a result, a middle-class opposition, committed to national unity and freedom, developed in Germany in the years after 1815; its main adherents were bourgeois youths organised in societies. It is true that a number of liberal journalists and university teachers also belonged to this opposition. Nevertheless, the social opposition of the post-Napoleonic era became a durable, collective movement — characterised by group loyalties and behaviour — because of its closely-linked net of patriotic youth societies.

Patriotic youth became the organised basis of the modern German nationalist movement in its early phase, partly because of the effect of the Wars of Liberation. The patriotic experience of these years made an immensely deep impression on young people, and had a lasting psychological and spiritual effect on them. In consequence, a number of liberal, patriotic intellectuals consciously took on the role of spiritual 'foster-fathers' to middle-class youth after 1815. Among them, however, Jahn remained the unchallenged protagonist. For a number of reasons, his Berlin Turngesellschaft became the model for other German patriotic societies founded in the years between 1815 and 1819.

The Berlin Turngesellschaft had won itself a secure place in the public consciousness as a result of its rejection of secret organisation. The longer it existed, the more it became a model to be copied by other young patriots who were inspired by the ideas of freedom. When Jahn adopted 'openness' (*Öffentlichkeit*) as a *conditio sine qua non* for the organisation of the society, he was creating the basis for the foundation of other gymnastic societies throughout almost the whole of Germany. 'Openness' became a motivating force behind the territorial expansion of the national gymnastic movement which began in 1815.

New societies were not founded simply because of the news spread by journalists and by word of mouth. Jahn himself worked vigorously to help establish many new gymnastic societies. Until 1819, he was the tireless organiser of the national gymnastic movement as well as its spiritual inspiration. Thus, for example, he helped to found many societies by sending a group of young Berlin gymnasts — mainly students — to the regions concerned, where they provided moral support and temporary leadership for new groups. Jahn had trained these young men to be capable gymnasts, but he had also imbued them with a passionate national consciousness. Their sentiments helped to trigger a genuine missionary fervour among young patriots.

Jahn's success in providing the young gymnastic movement with a cadre of highly motivated and committed leaders was due largely to his own talents and qualities: many young people came under the spell of his unaffected, robust manner, his unconventional and natural way of life and behaviour, his extreme emotionalism and obvious humanity.

In 1818 there were about 150 gymnastic societies in Germany, with some 12,000 members. One hundred of them were in Prussia, and most of the remainder in the rest of northern Germany, central Germany and Hesse. Nine gymnastic societies had been established south of the Main, but there were none at all in Austria.

Most of the patriotic gymnasts were schoolboys and students, but there was also a considerable number who were training for jobs in handicrafts or commerce. A small number of gymnastic groups also had young adult members: craftsmen, businessmen, teachers, advocates.

These 150 groups were not merely a series of unconnected local units. For the first time, there was an effective system of contacts between German patriots in many areas. Jahn had been eager to establish a communications structure between the gymnastic societies, and it was characterised by a multiplicity of bilateral and multilateral links.

The manifold contacts between the various groups created the conditions for the establishment of an organised movement with a considerable degree of homogeneity. Most of the 'daughter' groups were modelled on the Berlin Turngesellschaft, being run under the guidance of an older patriot who was often a teacher. Consequently, their structure was patriarchal and hierarchic.

The gymnastic movement was not the only organised form of bourgeois–national opposition in Germany in the post-Napoleonic era. After 1815 it developed alongside another movement, the national student movement of fraternities (the Burschenschaftsbewegung).[9] The two

9. A recent work on the student fraternity movement is Wolfgang Hardtwig, 'Protestformen und Organisationsstrukturen der deutschen Burschenschaft 1815–1833', in Helmut Reinalter (ed.), *Demokratische und soziale Protestbewegungen in Mitteleuropa*

groups developed an almost symbiotic relationship on issues of personnel, communication and ideology.

These youth movements were complementary components of the organised German national movement in its early phase. Like the gymnastic movement, the Burschenschaftsbewegung owed its establishment to a national, educational impulse; although Jahn was not the 'Father' of the student fraternities, he can still be regarded as the 'midwife' of the movement.

In 1812, before the Wars of Liberation, he had written a memorandum on the 'Arrangement and Foundation of the German Student Fraternities', advocating a reform of their unsatisfactory codes of behaviour (for example, control of duelling) in the German national spirit. Jahn believed that the national idea had a moral-inducing force. In place of the particularist state patriotism of the regional student clubs (*Landsmannschaften*) and the enlightened cosmopolitanism of the orders, he advocated the development at German universities of student fraternities, societies committed to German national ideas. During the Wars of Liberation, Jahn was a member of the Freikorps Lützow, in which highly educated young men from all the regions of Germany fought side by side; he used this opportunity to promote the *Burschenschaft* idea among them.[10]

One result of Jahn's agitation was the foundation of the Urburschenschaft ('original fraternity') by Jena students in 1815. The mentors of this fraternity in Thuringia were the university professors Heinrich Luden (history), Jakob Friedrich Fries (philosophy), Dietrich Georg Kieser (medicine), Lorenz Oken (natural sciences) and Christian Wilhelm Schweitzer (law). Before long, other groups joined it on the German university landscape: by 1818 there were student fraternities at thirteen other universities, in both north and south Germany (but not Austria). Like the Jena Urburschenschaft, they were non-secret, public societies. In that year they had managed to organise between 3,000 and 4,000 students out of a total of about 10,000.

What were the emotional and intellectual attributes of youthful patriotism in the post-Napoleonic era? What abstract and figurative references did the patriotism of the gymnasts and students make use of? How did they express their convictions and sentiments?

The most popular mode of expression for the nationalist ideas and

---

1815–1848/49, Frankfurt on Main, 1986, pp. 37f. There is still no comprehensive social and ideological investigation of the student fraternity movement.

10. See Günter Jahn, *Friedrich Ludwig Jahn und das deutsche Studentum 1798–1848*, phil. Diss., Göttingen, 1958, pp. 128ff., 144ff., 158ff.

opinions of the organised gymnasts and fraternity members was the patriotic song. They resorted to it at every available opportunity. Most of all, they sang the patriotic war songs of Ernst Moritz Arndt, Max von Schenkendorf and Theodor Körner, written in 1813–14. These were found particularly attractive because of their use of national metaphors and symbolism, redolent of the experience and mood of the Wars of Liberation. The young organised patriots were desperately anxious to cultivate and perpetuate this emotional experience, and thus welcomed the songs of the Wars of Liberation into their societies. Moreover, the gymnastic groups and fraternities who wrote their own songs after 1815 frequently plagiarised and drew on the special patriotic atmosphere of 1813.

The lyrics favoured by the youthful patriots reveal that emotionalism was a distinct feature of the birth of modern German patriotism. Two main sources shaped the patriotic feelings of the period and gave the movement its tone. The first of these consisted of negative feelings towards France, the powerful western neighbour, which clearly bore xenophobic traits. The second was an excessively powerful emotion towards their own nation and people, the German 'Fatherland', *Volk*, or *Volkstum*; it was marked by strong religious sentiments and pietistic devoutness. The German nation was perceived as a priceless asset with holy grandeur and divine qualities. In the patriotism of the era of the Wars of Liberation, nation and religion were not linked by any relationship based on reason, but by an intense emotional fervour.

Again and again, the songs referred to Germany as the 'holy Fatherland', or mentioned 'the ancient holy rights of the *Volk*'; they wanted to 'preach' about 'the holy German Reich' or to swear a 'holy oath' to the Fatherland, and to fight for its 'holy earth', its 'holy soil' or for 'Germany's holy cause', if possible in a 'holy sacrificial battle'.[11]

The songs of the gymnasts and students also show the German *culture*, the *Kulturnation*, was of great importance to organised patriots after 1815. The incessant stereotyped use of terms such as 'German mind', 'German nature', 'German diligence', etc., presumed a special cultural capacity of the Germans.[12]

As the basis of this cultural nationalism were two vital, inseparable convictions: first, the idea that, of all the modern peoples, the Germans had preserved most access to the forces of nature, to their natural originality; and second, the belief that the cultural advantages and

11. See for example Adolf Ludwig Follen (ed.), *Freye Stimmen frischer Jugend*, Jena, 1819, pp. 9, 16, 41, 52, 58, 76; and *Deutsche Lieder für Jung und Alt*, Berlin, 1818, pp. 60, 82.
12. Follen (ed.), *Freye Stimmen*, pp. 34, 36, 88.

achievements of the Germans were manifested most of all in their history.

Vivid and poetic metaphors of the 'green', 'tall oak tree' were used to convey the idea that the Germans were especially close to nature. The oak — with its associated concepts of natural strength, sturdiness and fertility — was awarded the status of a national symbol; people spoke of the 'Fatherland of the green oak tree' or the 'land of the oak', and their listeners knew that they were referring to Germany.[13]

If the oak was a national symbol from the world of nature, then Arminius, the legendary, warlike Germanic prince, became a national symbol from history. This tribal leader, whose struggles against the Roman Empire were regarded as a cultural act of enormous significance, appeared repeatedly in these songs as a symbol of national identity.[14]

In view of Fichte's theory of national languages, it is not surprising that the German language was a major symbol of national and cultural identity and greatness in the songs of the gymnasts and fraternity members. This was particularly obvious in Arndt's patriotic song 'Was ist des Deutschen Vaterland?', which was published in 1813 and was enormously popular in the early stages of the organised nationalist movement.

Arndt begins seven verses of his song with the same question: 'Was ist des Deutschen Vaterland?' (meaning: how far does it extend?). After each question, the poet names several states and regions, only to conclude vehemently that these alone cannot be the Fatherland of the Germans: 'Oh no, oh no, oh no! Its Fatherland must be greater than this'. In the seventh verse of the song, Arndt finally gives the answer to his question: 'As far as the German tongue rings out and praises God with songs! This it shall be, brave German, it shall be'.[15]

Arndt's criterion for identifying and defining the 'Fatherland' was thus provided by the German language; all those areas where German was the mother-tongue were seen as part of the German nation. This emphasis on the integral nature of the 'Fatherland', on the fellowship and unity of the German lands, was bound to awaken the idea of the political unity of the nation in a German state, and to fix it in the consciousness of singers and listeners alike. In this way, linguistic and cultural ideas of the nation were mixed with political concepts of

---

13. *Deutsche Lieder*, p. 84, and Follen (ed.), *Freye Stimmen*, p. 76.
14. Many examples can be found in the song collections circulated among the gymnasts and students.
15. *Deutsche Lieder*, pp. 31ff.

nationhood.

It is easy to understand how Arndt's song of the Fatherland came to be seen by contemporaries, after the Vienna Congress and the restoration of a confederation of states in Germany, as a proclamation of an oppositional political approach — even if in somewhat oblique form.

The oppositional character of the organised nationalist movement was even more apparent in other songs which were popular in the gymnastic societies and student fraternities. These were songs which were composed after 1815, mostly by the organised patriots themselves. They articulated two national grievances: the fact that the nation had yet to be united politically, and the lack of political liberties in the German territories. Some songs by the Giessen 'Unbedingten' ('Unconditionals') — a small, republican nationalist and revolutionary minority — also expressed revolutionary sentiments which merged ardour for liberty with attacks on the princes.

In the youth societies of the early German national movement, a remarkably cohesive patriotic community of feeling and conviction had been established. But this was no sworn society, closed to the public and shut away from it; exactly the opposite was the case. Because the societies had chosen 'openness' as their basic principle of organisation and action, their patriotic opinions and ideas were inevitably communicated to the surrounding society. The patriotism of the organised gymnasts and students was imparted to German society and left its traces there. These traces included its political opposition, its desire to alter the political status quo.

The patriotic youth societies made their biggest impact on German society with their publicly staged German patriotic festivals. The stimulus for them was provided by the French revolutionary festivals, which took on the style of national celebrations.[16] The German patriotic festivals provided an effective sounding-board for the emotional and intellectual patriotism of the societies. Patriotic songs could be heard by the general public, along with patriotic speeches which were designed to emphasise the political opposition of the festivals. There were rhetorical demands for a constitutional monarchy, a people's army and a German national state, along with freedom of the press and of speech, movement, and trade.

One of the most spectacular of these occasions was the Wartburg festival, held by the student fraternities on 18–19 October 1817 at

16. There is now exhaustive material on the French revolutionary festivals: Mona Ozouf, *La Fete révolutionnaire 1789–1799*, Paris, 1976; Marie-Louise Biver, *Fetes révolutionnaires à Paris*, Paris, 1979.

Eisenach (Thuringia). More than 450 students from almost every region of Germany took part, although none came from Austria.[17] This national festival made a lasting impression on contemporary opinion and on the governments of the princely states. Its impact was due less to the criticism of the princes made by speakers than to the dramatic symbolic gestures which were made there. In an *auto-da-fé*, festival members destroyed the writings of journalists who had opposed the idea of German national unity; a Prussian uhlan's laced corset, an Austrian corporal's baton and a military braid from Hesse were also consigned to the flames. The students were destroying the symbols of the absolutist princely states and emphasising their own symbol of the organised nationalist movement: the black, red and gold flag, which was given a special place in the events of the festival. Black, red and gold had been the tunic colours of the Prussian Freikorps Lützow, and the combination had had particular force as a symbol of nationhood and liberation ever since.

The oppositional student festival at the Wartburg was both the high point and the turning-point of the modern German national movement in its early phase. Its sudden change of fortune was brought about by concerted diplomatic pressure from Vienna and Berlin, masterminded by Metternich and brought to bear on Duke Carl August von Sachsen-Weimar, on whose territory the festival was taking place. There followed systematic observation and investigation of participants, student fraternities and gymnastic societies, linked with house searches and arrests, by government and police forces. The deputy Prussian Minister of Police, von Kamptz, spoke of 'a mass of degenerate professors and students who had been led astray', who were responsible for the 'vandalism of demagogic intolerance' at the Wartburg. And King Wilhelm III of Prussia saw a 'highly pernicious and highly criminal' 'spirit of licentiousness' at work.[18]

On 23 March 1819 the writer Karl August von Kotzebue, an opponent of the fraternities, was murdered by a fraternity member and gymnast, Carl Ludwig Sand. This crime was the result of a frenzy of patriotic feeling. In any case, it was an excuse for, rather than the cause of, the decision of the princely authorities to destroy the organised

17. On the Wartburg festival, see Günter Steiger, *Aufbruch. Urburschenschaft und Wartburgfest*, Leipzig, Jena and Berlin, 1967.
18. Quoted by Günter Steiger, 'Das "Phantom der Wartburgverschwörung" 1817 im Spiegel neuerer Quellen aus den Akten der preussischen Polizei', in *Wissenschaftl. Zeitschrift der Friedrich-Schiller-Universität Jena, Gesellschafts- u. Sprachwissenschaftl. Reihe*, no. 2, 1966, pp. 191f., 197.

nationalist movement.[19]

The Karlsbad Resolutions of August 1819 were initiated by Metternich and adopted by the Frankfurt Diet of the German Confederation. They contained a ban on the German student fraternities, whilst the gymnastic societies were prohibited by decrees issued by the governments of the individual states. The bans were quickly followed by the disbanding of the various societies. Jahn, who had been arrested in the middle of July 1819 because of 'demagogic intrigues', remained in prison until 1825. Any gymnastic societies that continued to exist after 1820 tended to concentrate solely on gymnastics, to be unpolitical, and to avoid national objectives and means of expression. The few student fraternities which operated in the 1820s did so in secret, had very few members and elicited no public response. The life of the national movement seemed to have been snuffed out.

Phase II: 1830–1847. The Organised Nationalist Movement of the *Vormärz* Period as a Mass Movement of Middle-Class Opposition

At the beginning of the 1830s it became clear that Vienna and Berlin had not succeeded in dealing a fatal blow to the German nationalist movement. Instead, it had fallen into a deep sleep, from which it was woken by the renewed 'crowing of the Gallic cockerel' (Heinrich Heine) and the powerful wingbeats of the Polish eagle (that is, by the July Revolution of 1830 in France and the November uprising in Congress Poland that same year).

On this occasion, the nationalist movement did not come to the fore in Prussia, which had remained without a constitution after 1815, but in the south-west of Germany. In the *Landtage* (state assemblies) of the constitutional states of Bavaria, Württemberg and Baden, a liberal opposition gained in strength immediately after the events in France and Congress Poland. It was concerned with the extension of existing constitutional rights (liberalisation of the franchise, extension of the powers of the *Landtage* to make laws and control the budget, etc.).

Uncompromising monarchical resistance to opposition requests in Bavaria changed the nature of this liberal protest. It helped to turn the parliamentary opposition, which had wanted reforms within the state,

19. On the Sand affair see the new study by Günther Heydemann, *Carl Ludwig Sand. Die Tat als Attentat*, Hof, 1985.

into an opposition which was organised outside parliament and pursued radical democratic and German nationalist objectives. As mentioned in the introduction, the Press- und Vaterlandsverein was created at the start of 1832 in the Bavarian Rhineland Palatinate, with a 'central committee' in Zweibrücken and a large number of filial committees throughout the region. The society also recruited members from Bavaria itself and from other south-west German territories (Baden, Württemberg, Grand Duchy and Electorate of Hesse, and Frankfurt on Main).[20]

The Press- und Vaterlandsverein saw itself as a support group for the opposition press in Germany. Through the spending power of its members, progressive organs of the press were to be made viable and sustained. In this way, the society would assist in the 'spiritual rebirth of Germany' as one of its founders, the journalist Dr Johann Georg August Wirth, claimed when describing the aim of the society in the radical democratic newspaper *Deutsche Tribüne* which he edited. In what amounted almost to a programme for the society, Wirth argued that its material assistance would help to convince all German citizens of 'the need for the organisation of a German Reich in a democratic manner'. If the 'spiritual rebirth of Germany' could be achieved, then 'material unification' would follow 'automatically' — through 'the power of public opinion'.[21]

The society thus attributed special significance to the moulding of public attitudes. It is scarcely surprising, therefore, that it was anxious to remove all forms of conspiracy from its own work and to adopt the maximum degree of transparency. 'Everything that happens should . . . happen publicly, in the sight of the authorities', advised another founder of the society, the journalist Dr Philipp Jakob Siebenpfeiffer. He added in explanation: 'We want works of the light, not the darkness!'[22]

The Press- und Vaterlandsverein was thus dedicated to the political goal of national unification in a democratic and republican manner. Its members, the overwhelming majority of whom were adults, were drawn from various levels within the German middle classes. Among them, petty bourgeois artisans and businessmen predominated, but

20. See Cornelia Foerster, *Der Press- und Vaterlandsverein von 1832/33. Sozialstruktur und Organisationsformen der bügerlichen Bewegung in der Zeit des Hambacher Festes*, Trier, 1982. Based on wide sources, this is a meticulous work which offers sound judgements on the organised nationalist democratic movement in the early *Vormärz*.

21. Quoted from Wilhelm Herzberg, *Das Hambacher Fest. Geschichte der revolutionären Bestrebungen in Rheinbayern um das Jahr 1832*, Ludwigshafen on Rhein 1908, p. 61.

22. Ibid, p. 59.

there was also a considerable number of educated and propertied citizens. Only about 20 per cent of the 5,000 members of the society were youths, mainly students belonging to associated secret fraternities.[23]

The social composition of the organised national movement had thus changed a good deal. After the Wars of Liberation it had been mainly a movement of schoolboys and students, but was now — at the start of the *Vormärz* — overwhelmingly a movement of employed men from almost every level of the middle class.

Despite changes in the membership structure of the resurgent nationalist movement in south-west Germany, it did not forget the traditions which dated from the years after 1815. The Press- und Vaterlandsverein did not confine itself to the financing of liberal newspapers. Among their other activities, members used public national festivals as a means of communication, and to mobilise national consciousness among wider sectors of the population. In so doing, they continued the old tradition of national festivals begun by the gymnasts and students between 1815 and 1819. The Wartburg festival in particular acted as a model for the organisers of the Hambach national festival.[24] But whereas the active participants at the Wartburg gathering had almost all been students — that is, young men — the Hambach festivities were attended mainly by adult men and women. Approximately 25,000 people went to the festival, making it into a genuine mass gathering.

The sheer size of the festival and the intense political commitment of its participants gave Metternich sufficient grounds to make another strike at the organised nationalist movement. He had already announced, in his diplomatic letter of 10 June 1832, that events would 'come to blows' in Germany; now he was to make his prophecy come true. On 5 July 1832 he persuaded the Frankfurt Diet of the German Confederation to introduce a catalogue of repressive measures against the nationalist movement, which was valid for the entire Confederation. It included the prohibition of all societies with political aims, along with a regulation banning political public festivals and gatherings.

Metternich, in league with Prussia, had also persuaded the Bavarian government to take drastic action in the Rhineland Palatinate. With the aid of police and military forces, the government initiated a wave of persecution, arrests and convictions against the activists of the national-

23. Important here is Foerster, *Press- und Vaterlandsverein*, pp. 156ff.
24. Important literary sources on the Hambach festival in the survey by Hans Fenske, '150 Jahre Hambacher Fest. Ein Blick auf dem Büchermarkt', *Zeitschrift für die Geschichte des Oberrheins 130* (1982), pp. 347ff.

ist and democratic movement. Some of these sought refuge by fleeing to France. The pressure of persecution meant that the legal and public existence of the Press- und Vaterlandsverein could not be maintained. It was forced to go underground and become a secret and conspiratorial organisation, a fact which automatically led to a dramatic loss of members.[25] In July, the Zweibrücken central committee disbanded itself. Several of its members became involved with the lamentably unsuccessful assault on the guard in Frankfurt on 3 April 1833, an attempt by about fifty students, craftsmen and intellectuals to trigger a German revolution. The Press- und Vaterlandsverein did not survive beyond 1833, even as a secret organisation.

However, the future of the German nationalist movement was not based on secret groups. Since the inauguration of the Hasenheide gymnastic arena by Jahn in 1811, 'openness' had been a characteristic feature of the nationalist movement in Germany, and one which had given it its extraordinary momentum. This was still to be the case after 1832. Certainly, a small minority of patriots — reacting to the escalation of state repression — did seek salvation in conspiratorial societies; however, the overwhelming majority of patriots remained loyal to the principle of public and open organisation, even in the very difficult internal conditions of the *Vormärz*. With flexibility and courage, they managed to obey the letter of the law banning political societies whilst finding ways to express their desire for national unity and political freedom in internal affairs through organised group activities. Even in the 1830s — immediately after Metternich had made his attacks — the organised national movement was neither dead nor in suspended animation.

In this decade, German patriotic men's choral societies sprang up in several southern and central German states.[26] These did not fall victim to the prohibitions because *superficially* they were pursuing non-political and artistic objectives — the study of four-part male voice harmonies.

The impulse behind the creation of this movement of organised German singers came from a Swiss music teacher, Hans Georg Nägeli of Zurich, who became the theoretician of German patriotic men's choral societies. Since 1810, Nägeli had energetically promoted the idea of such societies, in publications and by establishing an appropriate department in his Zurich Institute of Singing.

In the same way that Jahn had given a national educational role to

25. For this and the following see Foerster, *Press- und Vaterlandsverein*, pp. 43ff.
26. Sources used in this essay on the *vormärzlich* men's choral societies are given in Düding, *Organisierter gesellschaftlicher Nationalismus*, pp. 160ff.

gymnastics, so Nägeli (influenced by the teaching of Pestalozzi) believed that secular men's choral societies provided an excellent means of providing a national education. When he emphasised the national character of men's choral societies, Nägeli was not thinking of the Swiss people but of the German. His national consciousness was clearly influenced by Fichte, and was partly based on the idea that language had a nation-building force. If language was an important sign of nationality, then it was possible — as Nägeli did — to regard the German-speaking Swiss as belonging to the German nation.

Nägeli considered that only *men's* choral societies could have an educational effect of this kind, since he thought that the *male* articulation of the German language was more correct than the female. Because of their deeper, 'purer' and louder voices, men were more capable of articulating the words more clearly than women. Nägeli thought that women's voices were dominated by an 'undulatory quality'.

For Nägeli, linguistic articulation gave men's choral singing a genuine German national quality. But this itself was not enough to achieve his national educational objectives. In Nägeli's opinion, the content of the songs was even more important. He recommended songs about 'nature', 'love', 'conviviality', and folk traditions for the singers' repertoire. Above all, though, he advocated the patriotic songs of the Wars of Liberation, the texts of Arndt, Körner, and Schenkendorf. It was quite clear that Nägeli — greatly influenced by the occupation of his homeland by Napoleon — also intended his men's choral societies to have a national *political* task.

From the mid 1820s, a men's choral movement of considerable size grew up in German-speaking areas of Switzerland as a response to Nägeli's enthusiasm for the idea. At the same time, individual men's choral societies or *Liederkränze* (Song Circles) were founded in Württemberg, also under the influence of Nägeli. However, the further development of men's choral societies in Germany was exclusively the work of German patriots.

From the start of the 1830s the number of *Liederkränze* increased rapidly, and the movement spread from Württemberg to Baden, Bavaria, Hesse, Thuringia and Saxony. 'Openness' as a principle of organisation and action was a crucial precondition for the territorial expansion of the men's choral movement. The national singers' movement then grew dramatically during the 1840s, up to the time of the 1848 Revolution. First, many more societies were founded in those areas where the tradition was already established. Secondly, however, the movement expanded in the west and north of Germany, to Prussia,

Hanover, Mecklenburg and Danish-ruled Schleswig-Holstein. Groups were even established in German-speaking Austria, although the societies here remained few and far between. On the eve of the 1848 Revolution there were over 1,100 men's choral societies in Germany, with at least 100,000 members.

The singers' movement was not the only mass movement of societies in the late *Vormärz*. It was joined by another, albeit smaller, movement — the gymnastic movement, which had re-formed after 1842 as a movement of men's gymnastic societies.[27] The organised gymnasts made no mention of political and nationalist aims in their club rules, so that their official purpose was solely concerned with the physical training of members; in consequence, they generally managed to avoid being banned by the various German governments. The gymnastic movement of the *Vormärz* was strongest in south-west Germany, Saxony and west Prussia, but did not exist at all in Austria. By 1847 it consisted of about 250 societies and between 80,000 and 90,000 gymnasts.

These two mass movements — singers and gymnasts — together represented the organised nationalist movement in the late *Vormärz*. Their membership profile was very similar to that of the Press- und Vaterlandsverein, and thus to that of the organised national movement in the early *Vormärz*. Organised mass patriotism in the 1840s found its home in *men's* choral societies and *men's* gymnastic clubs. Thus, adult males formed the overwhelming majority of the organised national movement in the pre-revolutionary period; the number of students and grammar school boys was extremely small. The German national movement had left its youth phase irrevocably behind; it had, quite literally, grown up.

The social profile of the gymnasts' and singers' movement of the 1840s confirms the thoroughly bourgeois character of the national movement in the *Vormärz*. Like the Press- und Vaterlandsverein, the movement of singers and gymnasts was dominated by men from a wide range of middle-class groups. Members of the petty bourgeoisie were in a clear majority, but a reasonable number of middle-class academics also found their way into the societies.

As the German nationalist movement mutated from a youth movement into an organisation of adults, its structure also changed. Between 1811 and 1819, societies had been guided by older patrons with patriarchal styles of leadership. However, the nationalist movement of the late *Vormärz* was dominated by societies which were administered

27. On the *vormärzlich* gymnastic movement see ibid, pp. 219ff.

and run according to democratic principles. The patriarchal style of leadership had become obsolete now that an adult mass movement had developed with no need for the guidance of a small elite of committed mentors.

The process of change and renewal in the nationalist movement of the pre-revolutionary era did not rule out respect for tradition and for tried and tested methods. National festivals, cultivated by young patriots in the early years of the nationalist movement, now experienced something of a renaissance. Despite the ban on political festivals in 1832, the singers and gymnasts made the national festival into a vital institution for communication and integration. It became the most important way in which both movements could make possible declarations of faith.

During the 1830s, the singers' movement had already organised a series of festivals. Although taking place at regional level, they had clear national elements. In the years after 1832, understandably enough, the spirit of political opposition could only be expressed in an indirect and veiled manner in festival speeches and songs, in order to avoid further bans.

This political reserve was gradually dropped at national festivals in the 1840s. Political protest was articulated ever more frankly — without being answered by prohibitions from the authorities. Some of these political celebrations were truly national or all-German (*gesamtdeutsch*) in that they included singers or gymnasts from the whole of Germany. Or more correctly, from nearly the whole of Germany; Austrian patriots were still notable for their absence. Three festivals of the singers in particular from the 1840s can, because of the place of origin of their participants, be described as *gesamtdeutsch*, even more than the Hambach festival; those at Würzburg in 1845, Cologne in 1846 and Lübeck in 1847. The phenomenon was greatly encouraged by the development of two new methods of transport — railways and steamships — which enabled many patriots to travel to regional and central gatherings for the first time.

It is now time to make some observations on the intellectual and emotional make-up of organised patriotism in the 1830s and the pre-revolutionary 1840s (the *Vormärz* era). Were its terms, metaphors and symbols derived from the youth patriotism of the Napoleonic era? Did it reveal an intellectual and psychological continuity with the patriotism of that epoch?

Beyond doubt, *vormärzlich* patriotism was imbued with the *cultural* nationalist terms, symbols and metaphors of the early national movement; these provided its spiritual and emotional nexus. The songs of the Wars of Liberation, taken up by the Press- und Vaterlandsverein and later by the singers and gymnasts, were particularly important in this respect.

However, the repertoire of songs sung by *Vormärz* patriots was not restricted to the lyrics handed down from the founding period of the modern German nationalist movement. It also contained many texts created by political songwriters in the *Vormärz* period itself, by men such as Georg Herwegh, Hoffmann von Fallersleben, Ferdinand Freiligrath and Robert Prutz. Their lyrics frequently lacked the religious accent and anti-French trimmings which had been a feature of songs written during the Wars of Liberation. These facts support the theory that — in general — *Vormärz* patriotism was less affected by religiosity and francophobia. Such ideological changes did not mean that *Vormärz* patriotism had lost most of its emotionalism or was less loaded with feelings than youth patriotism had been during and after the Wars of Liberation. It was rather that the emotionalism had become more secular.

Strong patriotic emotions were produced at the Hambach festival and the national festivals of the 1840s, for example, by the use of rhetoric to awaken sentiments of national *brotherhood* among all the participants. Addresses such as 'brothers', 'brothers in song', 'brother gymnasts', 'German brothers', 'beloved brothers', 'my brothers'[28] contributed to the increase in emotional intensity. Feelings of brotherhood were also evoked by the festival rhetoric, which was frequently left vague and ill-defined as regards its political statements. In any event, these techniques helped to ensure that national fraternisation was not greatly damaged by ideological discord between patriots with different political beliefs. Arndt's song 'Was ist des Deutschen Vaterland?' also produced strong sentiments of national solidarity. In the *vormärzlich* nationalist movement, it was the most popular song for communal singing.[29]

Similarly, the oppositional political content of *Vormärz* patriotism contained elements inherited from youth patriotism as well as new features. The adult patriots identified just as closely with the black, red and gold tricolour which had been the symbol of nationhood and liberation for their youthful predecessors. At the Hambach festival it appeared in the form of flags, rosettes and sashes — in such quantity

28. Ibid, p. 264.
29. Ibid, p. 271.

that the Frankfurt Diet of the German Confederation was moved, in 1832, to forbid it to be displayed in public. However, this measure did not prevent the gymnasts and singers from displaying it openly at their festivals during the 1840s.

The political opposition of the organised singers did not usually extend beyond positions of political liberalism. Similarly, part of the gymnastic movement remained committed to liberal beliefs. They advocated political ideas which had been supported by the great majority of young patriots between 1815 and 1819.

However, another section of the gymnastic movement, as well as the Press- und Vaterlandsverein, was influenced by radical democratic and republican theories. In particular, the gymnasts of south-west Germany on the eve of the 1848 Revolution were — as their songs show — passionate supporters of the principle of sovereignty of the people; they were filled with the democratic and republican spirit. Their criticism of the princes and the system was massive, vitriolic and implacable. For the first time, these men were also making social criticisms of the system, diagnosing the contrast between the haves and have-nots as a typical cancer of German society. Frequently, they argued in favour of revolutionary acts. This ideological development was strongly influenced by craft journeymen, whose employment was nomadic and insecure. Such men had joined the gymnastic movement in large numbers, but were hardly represented at all in the men's choral societies. In contrast to the youth patriotism of the early national movement, republican and revolutionary sentiments had gained considerable ground in the adult patriotism of the *Vormärz* period. All in all, the organised national movement of the 1840s had grown into a powerful and effective force. Its existence was certainly a prerequisite for the outbreak of the Revolution in Germany.

Phase III: 1848–1849. The Structural and Political Split in the Bourgeois Nationalist Movement During the Revolution

The revolutionary spark from France lit the flame of the German Revolution in March 1848. There were speeches and deputations, public meetings and demonstrations, and — not least — fighting in the streets and on the barricades. With the aid of these events, the German bourgeoisie forced the acceptance of the 'March demands' by German authorities which had been paralysed by the

experience of the February Revolution in France. Their demands
included freedom of political association and assembly, freedom of the
press, establishment of jury courts, and convocation of a German
national assembly. When the German princes appointed liberal 'March
Ministers' to the cabinets of the individual states, the middle classes
felt that their objectives were within reach.

The events of March also introduced a period of open discord within
the German nationalist movement. The republican and democratic
patriots had no sympathy for the political complacency of the liberals.
After all, the March Revolution had not resulted in the breakthrough of
their principle of popular sovereignty. Germany had not become a
republic. The March Revolution had limited the power of the princes,
but not eliminated them. Even in the *Vormärz*, there had been ideological differences between democratic-republican and liberal-constitutional patriots; now, the March events turned these differences into a
deep political gulf, with grave consequences for the structure and
image of the bourgeois nationalist movement.

In the first and second phases of development of the nationalist
movement, there had been no consistent structural division along
political and ideological lines. Between 1815 and 1819 there had been
room for both liberal-constitutional and democratic-revolutionary patriots in the gymnastic societies and the student fraternities. In the
vormärzlich gymnastic movement, too peaceful coexistence between the
two political camps had been possible. Now, in 1848, the German
nationalist movement divided along political-ideological lines. After
April of that year, the various German states saw the development of
two rival middle-class political movements: on one side the movement
of *democratic* societies, and on the other, the movement of *liberal*
societies.[30] The local democratic societies did not all call themselves by
that name — they were also named people's societies, Fatherland
societies, societies for people's rights and people's freedom, or political
clubs — but they were united by their opposition to the authority of the
princely states. The local liberal societies — citizens' societies, German
societies, constitutional monarchist societies, national societies, constitutional clubs — were not, as they saw it, *opposition* organisations; their members advocated a national policy of conciliation with the old ruling elites.

30. See Wolfram Siemann, *Die deutsche Revolution von 1848/49* Frankfurt on Main, 1985,
particularly the chapter on political societies and bourgeois pressure-groups pp. 90ff.
Also Werner Boldt, *Die Anfänge des deutschen Parteiwesens. Fraktionen, politische Vereine und
Parteien in der Revolution 1848*, Paderborn, 1971; and Hartwig Gebhardt, *Revolution und
liberale Bewegung. Die nationale Organisation der konstitutionellen Partei in Deutschland 1848/49*,
Bremen, 1974.

The polarisation of the two movements was already manifest during the nomination of the delegate candidates to the National Assembly in May 1848 — in which process the democratic and liberal societies at local level played an active part. In September 1848 the liberal-constitutional societies established a federation at national level. This organisation — the 'National Society' — contained liberal societies from northern, central and southern Germany. After two unsuccessful attempts, the democratic patriots also succeeded in creating a large and effective parent organisation in November 1848, under the name 'Central March Society' (Zentralmärzverein). The initiative for its creation had come from democratic-republican delegates to the Frankfurt national parliament. In consequence, the Zentralmärzverein was the first official link in Germany between a political movement of societies and parliamentary delegates. The modern party had been born.

Austrian patriots were almost completely excluded from the network of communication and organisation established by the liberals and democrats. In this way, the tradition of the first and second phases of the organised national movement was maintained: Austrian patriots had played no part in the patriotic youth societies of 1815–19, and had been only minimally involved in the organised national movement of the *Vormärz*.

Apart from political and ideological dissension, the appearance of the national movement in the revolutionary era was changed in one further way: the national festival was no longer seen as a useful medium for communication and self-promotion. Its particular value, of acting as a bridge between different bourgeois opposition groups, was no longer relevant. Middle-class national brotherhood for the purpose of creating a united front against the feudal and princely authorities no longer seemed appropriate. It was replaced by political disagreement between the two camps of the nationalist bourgeoisie, a battle waged passionately in public declarations, manifestos, publicity campaigns, public meetings, etc. Consequently, *cultural* nationalism, which had been strengthened by *vormärzlich* national festivals and their songs and rhetoric and had been a common element linking liberal and democratic patriots, diminished in intensity during the revolutionary years.

Clearly, national festivals had lost much of their attraction for organised patriots. Those gymnasts' and singers' societies which continued to exist in the revolutionary era did not organise any festivals of genuine national significance. In the singers' movement, where membership fell dramatically, communications broke down over wide areas.

The democratic gymnasts, federated in the 'League of Democratic Gymnasts', followed in the wake of the democratic movement. Only the student fraternities, which no longer needed to work in secrecy after March 1848, held a national festival at the Wartburg at Whitsun in that year.[31] But this gathering did not deserve the name of national festival. Apart from its nostalgia for 1817, it resembled a student parliament for debating university issues rather than a festival with genuine national significance. The fraternity students had lost their role as the avant-garde of the nationalist movement.

The rapid victory of the Counter-revolution in Germany, which was emerging in October 1848 and was completed in spring 1849, cut the ground from beneath the liberal and democratic societies, and from all national societies with political tendencies. Reactionary laws on societies destroyed the freedom of association of the revolutionary period and shattered the structural foundation of the German nationalist movement once again. The nationalist movement of the revolutionary years was an exceptional case, of only ephemeral significance — although the revolutionary period itself continued to influence the thinking of German patriots during the foundation of the Reich.

Phase IV: 1859–1866. The Organised Nationalist Movement as a Mass Movement of Opposition Transcending the Classes

Inspired by the Italian nationalist movement and by the accession of a Prussian king who seemed to promise a more liberal 'new era', the German nationalist movement blossomed again at the end of the 1850s and the beginning of the 1860s. Almost overnight, patriotic societies sprang up throughout Germany, encouraged by a more restrained use of the existing laws on societies by the German governments.

The German nationalist bourgeoisie did not draw on the political societies of the revolutionary era for its inspiration, but on the tried and tested organisations of the *vormärzlich* singers and gymnasts. A third bourgeois nationalist mass movement was also established: the 'riflemen's movement' (Schützenbewegung). The existing riflemen's societies had lost their earlier citizens' militia elements and had become

---

31. See Karl Griewank, *Deutsche Studenten und Universitäten in der Revolution von 1848*, Weimar, 1949, pp. 31ff.

essentially social gatherings. However, infected by the general national
excitement and influenced by the national riflemen's traditions of the
Swiss, these now became increasingly receptive to ideas of nationhood
and freedom.[32]

Like the singers and gymnasts of the *Vormärz*, the singers, gymnasts
and riflemen of the foundation period of the Reich were involved in
highly democratic, not hierarchical, organisations. They attracted all
the various social groups within the bourgeoisie, although the predominance of petty bourgeois groups — already observable in the
Vormärz — seems actually to have increased.

In 1861, the riflemen's societies created a national parent organisation in the shape of the 'German Riflemen's League'. They were
followed by the choral societies and their 'German Singers' League' in
the following year. The gymnasts had already established a national
guiding authority, the 'Committee of the German Gymnastic Societies', in 1861.

As they adapted the organisations of the pre-revolutionary period,
the attention of these later German patriots was also drawn once again
to the concept of the national festival, an integral component of the
organised nationalist movement in the first half of the nineteenth
century before the Revolution. Almost inevitably, they breathed new
life into this well-tried institution. Singers, gymnasts and riflemen
organised several central, national mass festivals between 1860 and
1862. Leading representatives of the German National Society (Deutscher Nationalverein), a nationalist pressure group of about 25,000
members which advocated a Prussian–German national state[37], ap-
issue. The three biggest and most effective festivals during the 1860s
were the German Riflemen's festival in Frankfurt (1862), the German
Gymnastic Festival in Leipzig (1863), and the German Singers' Festival in Dresden (1865).[33]

---

32. Satisfactory investigations by academic historians of the national movements of
gymnasts, singers and riflemen in the decade before the foundation of the Reich have not
previously been available. For the gymnastic movement in this period, a substitute is
available in the form of the sporting history of Wolfgang Eichel, *Vom "Allgemeinen
Deutschen Turnerbund" zur "Deutschen Turnerschaft" — eine entscheidende Wende in der Geschichte
der deutschen Körperkultur (1849–1871)*, Habilitation thesis (MS), Deutsche Hochschule für
Körperkultur in Leipzig, Leipzig, 1965; on the singers' movement in this decade see the
older work by Otto Elben, *Der volksthümliche deutsche Männergesang. Geschichte und Stellung im
Leben der Nation*, 2nd edn., Tübingen, 1887, pp. 163ff.; on the riflemen, Hans Germann,
Der Ehrenspiegel deutscher Schützen, Leipzig and Berlin, n.d.

33. The following descriptions are taken from: *Das allgemeine deutsche Schützenfest zu Frankfurt
am Main, Juli 1862, Ein Gedenkbuch*, Frankfurt on Main, 1863; G. Hirth and E. Strauch (eds.),
Das dritte allgemeine deutsche Turnfest zu Leipzig, 2. bis 5. August 1863, Leipzig, 1863;
Das erste deutsche Sängerbundesfest zu Dresden, 22. bis 25. Juli 1865. Ein Gedenkbuch, Dresden, 1865.

Like the festivals of the *Vormärz*, the national festivals in the decade before the foundation of the Reich were highly emotional. As before, nationalist sentiments were evoked mainly through the rhetoric of brotherhood. At the riflemen's festival of 1862 in Frankfurt on Main, the organisers made special efforts to integrate scenes of brotherhood into the festival events: there were three cheers for the Swiss and American riflemen at the ceremony, who were seen as representatives of nations which had proved in exemplary fashion what could be achieved by a desire for national unity and freedom. The Stars and Stripes was granted a place of honour at the festival. This emphasis on solidarity with Swiss and American riflemen did not diminish German nationalist sentiments. Rather the reverse: the act of fraternisation gave added legitimacy to the participants' feelings for their own, German nation. The act was not based on an original idea by the organisers of the Frankfurt Festival, but had a precedent dating from the *Vormärz*: at the Hambach festival there had been a German–Polish ceremony of fraternisation.

The patriotic songs sung at the gymnasts', singers' and riflemen's festival reveal how much these men subscribed to a patriotism whose emotional and intellectual roots dated back to the youth and adult patriotism of the Wars of Liberation and the *Vormärz*. By adopting the songs of the Wars of Liberation (including, of course, Arndt's song to the Fatherland), the patriots of the 1860s were also adopting the cultural nationalist terms and images with which the organised patriots of preceding generations had been so familiar.

The progressive political tradition of the early and *Vormärz* nationalist movement was also maintained by the patriots of the 1860s. In their festival songs (which included *vormärzlich* and contemporary music), festival addresses, extempory speeches and toasts, the desire for the political unity of the nation was clearly apparent. Speakers were equally enthusiastic in their demands for political rights and freedoms. The creation of an all-German parliament was a central political demand, as was the arming of the people. The idea that national unity and freedom was a task to be achieved primarily by the German people, and not 'from above' by princes and governments, was a thread running through many speeches. The desire of the participants for unity and freedom — as at the festivals of the *Vormärz* — was optimistically underlined by a host of black–red–gold flags.

It was noticeable that festival speakers were not afraid to keep alive the memory of the German Revolution. Among them was the young historian and lecturer Heinrich von Treitschke, whose speech at the

German Gymnastic Festival in Leipzig (1863) attracted a great deal of attention. Some speakers demanded the restoration of the Reich Constitution of 1849, the other doubted the legality of the Frankfurt Diet, and individual speakers proclaimed sovereignty of the people as their political goal. Both liberal–constitutional and democratic–republican sentiments were expressed at the festivals of the gymnasts and riflemen, although the singers remained loyal to the ideas of liberal patriotism.

Despite the continuity between the national movement of the *Vormärz* and that of the 1860s, there were also significant differences between them:

(1) The organised national movement of the post-reaction period included substantial numbers of workers for the first time. Industrial and factory workers joined many gymnastic societies and riflemen's clubs, though very few choral societies.[34] At the national gymnastic festival in Leipzig there were even (democratic and liberal) workers' educational societies, though these did not belong officially to the gymnastic movement. The integration of workers into the nationalist movement turned it into a mass movement with the ability to transcend the classes even though it remained predominantly bourgeois in character.

(2) The number of organised patriots grew during the 1860s. In 1863, the gymnastic movement alone had 134,000 members, and increased its total to 167,000 by 1865.[35] The German Riflemen's Festival in Frankfurt (1862) was attended by 8,000 riflemen, 20,000 gymnasts went to the German Gymnastic Festival in Leipzig (1863), and 16,000 singers attended the German Singers' Festival in Dresden (1865). As the inhabitants of these cities and surrounding areas also came to the festivals in large numbers, each of them involved at least 100,000 people.

(3) For the first time, the organised nationalist movement of the 1860s contained a sizeable contingent of patriots from Austria. Gymnastic, riflemen's and choral societies in German Austria were now integral parts of the German nationalist movement. Their representatives took part in the establishment of the national parent organisations, whilst large groups of organised patriots from Lower Austria, the Steiermark and Tyrol attended the national festivals of the 1860s.

---

34. See for example *Statistisches Jahrbuch der Turnvereine Deutschlands* (ed.) G. Hirth, on behalf of the Committee of the German Gymnastic Societies, Leipzig, 1863, p. XLI; *Zweites Statistisches Jahrbuch der Deutschlands Turnvereine* (ed.) G. Hirth, Leipzig, 1865, p. LII.

35. *Statistisches Jahrbuch der Turnvereine*, p. XXXVIII; *Zweites Statistisches Jahrbuch der Turnvereine*, p. XLII.

Much attention was paid to the Austrians at these festivals, particularly to the lively Tyrolese. The other participants regularly flattered the Austrians, whom they saw as the 'problem children' of the German nation.[36] There were both historical and topical reasons for this attitude. The *kleindeutsch* (lesser German) decision of the German national parliament in 1849, and the failure to achieve a Prussian-led German national state because of the refusal of Friedrich Wilhelm IV, had reduced the sympathy which many patriots felt for Prussia and had awakened feelings of guilt towards the Austrian Germans. Moreover, these anti-Prussian and pro-Austrian sentiments had been increased by the Prussian constitutional conflict, which had been smouldering since 1862. Leading representatives of the German National Society (Deutscher Nationalverein), a nationalist pressure group of about 25,000 members which advocated a Prussian–German national state,[37] appeared at the various festivals but were unable to counteract this trend. But there was no support at the festivals for a German national state under Austrian Habsburg leadership. It may be that the idea of a national state which included Austria and had its political centre in the 'third Germany' — perhaps with Frankfurt as its capital — was attractive to a considerable number of festival participants. There were many rhetorical allusions to such a solution, and it may have been no accident that the great national festivals of the early 1860s were held outside both Prussia and Austria. Its national monarch could have been a minor German prince, the ambitious Ernst II of Saxe-Coburg, who was well-disposed towards the gymnastic, choral and riflemen's societies. He had written the tune for the popular patriotic song 'An die deutsche Tricolore' ('To the German tricolour'), was honorary president of the League of German Riflemen, and had made effective appearances at several national festivals.

The Prussian Minister-President Otto von Bismarck, who had sent a senior Prussian civil servant to observe the Leipzig gymnastic festival[38], was well aware of these attitudes. His final route to national unification, 'from above' and by means of a war against Austria, was not the solution that the organised patriots of the 1860s had wanted. In June 1866 the *Deutsche Turn-Zeitung*, the newspaper of the gymnastic movement, printed a candid leading article entitled 'The gymnasts and

---

36. *Das allgemeine deutsche Schützenfest zu Frankfurt am Main*, pp. 100f.
37. On the National Society see the older work by Richard Le Mang, *Der deutsche Nationalverein*, Berlin, n.d.
38. Central State Archive of the DDR, Department Merseburg, 2.4.1., Prussian Ministry for Foreign Affairs, no. 8252, pp. 367ff.

the war'. Its author claimed that the movement wanted 'nothing to do' with the 'sad fact of the German fratricidal war', 'with the struggle that leads German into the field against German'. The current conflict was 'not a struggle ignited by selfless true love of the German Fatherland', it was 'not a struggle in which the old battle songs of Körner, Arndt, Schenkendorf will ring out to the blithe fight!'[39]

With the Austro-Prussian War, which clearly set the course for the Prussian *kleindeutsch* solution, Bismarck took the wind out of the sails of the organised national opposition movement. They saw no real cause to hold festivals; their songs were no longer sung. Then, after a period of disorientation, the German patriots began to see the foundation of the Reich as such a vital act that it silenced their objections, which had been based on liberal or democratic conscience. Furthermore, they became reconciled to separation from the 'problem children' of the nation. The two concepts which had previously gone hand in hand in their hearts and minds — the cultural nation and the nation-state — were now separated. In future, the Austrian Germans were still regarded as belonging to the German cultural nation; Bismarck's power politics, however, had decided that they would not be part of the German nation-state.

39. *Deutsche Turn-Zeitung*, Blätter für die Angelegenheiten des gesammten Turnwesens. Organ der Deutschen Turnerschaft, 29 June 1866.

ADOLF M. BIRKE

German Catholics and the Quest for National Unity

Were a German Catholic to be faced with the alternative, then an 'infinitely closer tie' bound him to a Catholic Negro than to a German atheist.[1] This remark, made anonymously in the journal *Historisch-Politische Blätter* (an organ of political Catholicism), reflects the attitude of many Catholics in the era of nation-building. Liberals and nationalists always thought that international confession and national loyalty could not co-exist without inner tensions and a clash of principles. Indeed, until as late as this century, Catholics were reputed to be 'unreliable' in matters concerning the national interest — a stigma that was not fully removed until the establishment of the Federal Republic.

In what ways did Catholics participate in the German national movement? What significance did the German Question have for the ways in which Catholics thought and acted? When we try to answer these questions, misunderstandings easily arise, largely because of our present-day perspective. One difficulty is that we tend generally to underestimate the importance of religion and confession in the nineteenth century, concentrating instead on the factors that led to modernisation. No-one has yet written the history of political Catholicism in nineteenth-century Germany. However, Christianity and the Church were among the forces that shaped that century. They were not mere relics of an earlier age, destined to decline in a new world. 'Religion

---

1. Quoted in T. Nipperdey, *Deutsche Geschichte 1800–1866. Bürgerwelt und starker Staat*, Munich, 1983, p. 384.

and Church are a force, a self-evident power that determines the existence, the awareness and the behaviour of people. They continue to be of the greatest importance for the state, for society and for culture'.[2] They were an example of historical continuity that, in the process of finding a national identity and establishing a nation-state, combined traditional and new elements. We have become too accustomed to seeing the nineteenth century as the linear projection of a process of secularisation of many centuries' duration. This expresses only one aspect of the historical reality. The century of nation-building was also a period of religious fundamentalism. After the Napoleonic era, a broad religious revival took place in all social classes. This was a supra-national phenomenon that went beyond the established churches and strengthened the social basis of the confessions. Christianity held its own, remoulding itself in the course of its conflict with the factors leading to modernisation. The churches lost their feudal character, but gained in spiritual strength. The framework within which they oper-ated, the areas of conflict and their position within the process of nation-building were determined by many factors: spiritual and politi-cal liberalism; imminent industrialisation; the modernisation of the State and extension of its power (including that of the bureaucracy); as well as theological disputes and tensions within the churches them-selves.

As far as the religious revival is concerned, we can certainly find parallels between developments in Germany and Britain that in other respects followed a different course.[3] But the impact of the spiritual revival varied widely in the two countries. Not only religious and confessional factors, but also national, governmental and constitutional as well as social and economic preconditions in each case were of a completely different nature. The explosive issue of national identity was absent in Britain. The Established Church, with all its theological and organisational differences as well as regional variations in Eng-land, Scotland and Ireland, participated in the difficult process by which the British constitution was transformed in the nineteenth century. It was able to maintain its privileged position, despite the fact that Nonconformity, already a broad movement, continued to gain ground.

In Germany, a different situation prevailed. Here the confessional map had been essentially fixed since the Thirty Years War and it

---

2. Ibid., p. 403.
3. A. M. Birke, Introduction to *Church, State and Society in the 19th Century. An Anglo-German Comparison*, Prince Albert Studies, 2, Munich and New York, 1984, pp. 13ff.

remained unchanged under the new system of states created in 1815. The decisive point is that the confessional map, in all its diversity, was made up of homogeneous blocs: whole towns and villages tended to be of a single confession, even where the surrounding area was of a different one. Germany was divided between Protestantism — or, to be more precise, two major Protestant confessions — and Roman Catholicism, but the Roman Catholics formed the largest group.

The constitutional, social and economic position of the Catholic Church in Germany had changed radically since the beginning of the nineteenth century. The feudal nature of the Church was being undermined by secularisation and modernisation; this process accelerated in the aftermath of the French Revolution and the Napoleonic reforms. The Church lost most of its worldly possessions and was excluded from the social and economic system of the *ancien régime*. It took no further part in the exercise of worldly power. This placed it in a new relationship to the State. No longer protected by corporative rights, the Church was now exposed to the claim of modern states to exercise absolute sovereignty. The Church felt permanently threatened; it attempted to counter this threat initially by making concordats or treaties between itself and the State, and later by demanding constitutional safeguards for the Church.

But the loss of worldly power was not only a disadvantage to the Church. It was also an important precondition for spiritual renewal. Thus de-feudalisation and religious revival cannot be separated from each other. The attitude of Catholics to the German Question and the rise of political Catholicism were an integral part of the wider situation discussed here. Developments within the Church were also a decisive contributing factor.

After 1815 the Catholic Enlightenment continued to have an impact; as time passed, however, its significance decreased. Its aim was to make the Church less dogmatic and to do away with Baroque forms of piety. This legacy of the eighteenth century did not, however, determine the wider religious, ecclesiastical and political attitudes of German Catholicism, as might have been expected. The decisive factor was Ultramontanism — a form of Catholicism that rejected any enlightened tendencies in theology and, emphasising the primacy of the Pope, called for the autonomy of the Church. Politics and society, culture and learning were judged by how closely they agreed with Catholic doctrine. Ultramontanism offered a prescription for Catholic self-assertion in times that were perceived as hostile. Its main distinguishing features were unanimity, a strictly hierarchical structure, and beliefs and an organisation disciplined by reference to Rome and papal authority, all harking back to the spirit of the Counter-Reformation and Scholasticism.

Ultramontanism was an international phenomenon aimed at the Church as a whole. It found a brilliant justification in de Maistre's famous book, *Du Pape*.[4] Despite its traditionalist origins and decidedly anti-liberal bent, Ultramontanism could be turned into a populistic, even democratic, weapon in the hands of the de-feudalised Church. This happened when the State encroached on the authority of the Church in organisational and religious matters, thus provoking a political reaction.

Where the Catholicism of the religious revival formed part of the Romantic movement, which idealised the world of the Middle Ages, it was in accord with German national culture and the nascent movement for national identification. But the devout practices being revived were out of step with the times. Their association with the Counter-Reformation provoked Protestants and laid the basis for the *Kulturkampf* which shook German society after the foundation of the Reich. The boom in religious orders, pilgrimages (the Holy Coat of Trier), penances, cults of Mary and Joseph (dogma of the Immaculate Conception 1854), belief in miracles — the whole emotional and sentimental package irritated those of a liberal or dissenting outlook and widened the gap between the confessions. Catholic fundamentalism had many adherents among believers who saw it as providing a guideline in times which were out of joint and whose modernity they did not understand. Nevertheless, this Catholicism was not anti-national from the start, and it was certainly not unpolitical. It answered a need felt by ordinary church-goers as much as by the Church hierarchy. Political Catholicism was born when the traditional alliance between throne and altar broke down, at a time when the position adopted by the Church *vis-à-vis* the State had become a burning political issue. It may seem paradoxical, but it is true for all that: political Catholicism, which arose as a protest movement among Catholics against state interference in Church affairs, was a precursor of democratisation in Germany. It was in some respects even earlier and more comprehensive than modern liberalism and socialism.

After 1815 individual journals and a few organisations and societies

4. J. de Maistre, *Du Pape*, Lyon, 1819.

were already voicing new demands relating to ecclesiastical policy. In the *Landtage* (state diets) of south Germany small groups of Catholic deputies joined forces. But the start of a new era was signalled by the disturbances that took place in Cologne in 1837–8, when the Archbishop of Cologne, von Droste-Vischering, and the government of Prussia had a dispute about the issue of marriage between Catholics and non-Catholics.[5] The Archbishop, who was of fundamentalist persuasion, insisted on following to the letter the canon law relating to mixed marriages, and would allow them to take place in his diocese only if the partners promised to bring up any children they might have as Catholics. The less strict practice previously followed of allowing such marriages to take place without this promise was discontinued. The case had wider implications, but to discuss them here would take us beyond the scope of this article. What is important is that this conflict spread beyond the Church hierarchy. After the Archbishop's arrest, a broad Catholic protest movement arose. It encompassed the nobility of the Rhineland and Westphalia and large sections of the Catholic middle classes, as well as ordinary church-going people, and it evoked a response all over Germany. The eloquent journalist Görres popularised the legal issues at stake in his book *Athanasius*,[6] presenting them with great pathos as a conflict of principle between faith and worldly power. For the first time, Catholic public opinion found a voice. One factor assisting at the birth of political Catholicism was anti-Prussian feeling on account of the events in Cologne, despite the fact that since the time of Frederick the Great, Prussia, which had incorporated the large Catholic areas of the Rhinelands and Westphalia after 1815, had maintained a relatively conflict-free relationship with the Catholic Church.

With the accession to the throne of Frederick William IV, who cooperated with the Catholic Church on important issues, the situation calmed down. The festival held in 1842 to celebrate the resumption of building on Cologne cathedral turned into a demonstration of a national desire for unity. It was also a celebration of reconciliation between Church and State. At this time, German national feeling was not yet a one-sided Protestant affair. However, this was soon to change.

From the start, political Catholicism incorporated the whole spectrum of political views. It included both conservative and liberal elements. The real integrating factor was the need to defend the right of

---

5. R. Lill, *Die Beilegung der Kölner Wirren*, Düsseldorf, 1962, pp. 50ff.
6. E. R. Huber, *Deutsche Verfassungsgeschichte seit 1789*, vol. 2, 2nd edn., Stuttgart, 1968, pp. 253ff.

the Church to exist; this overshadowed secular concerns. But political Catholicism was not exclusively a matter for the elite. Ordinary church-goers: peasants, artisans, domestic servants and other of the common people, all participated. For them, the threat posed to the Church signified a direct threat to their spiritual existence and to their way of life. The important sociological fact that Catholicism was based pre-dominantly in the agrarian and small-town regions of Germany (well-known exceptions being the Rhinelands and Upper Silesia), shaped the way in which Catholics thought of themselves. From this perspective, modernism, liberalism and individualism could be seen as the result of human hubris, as a 'turning away from God' and the 'natural order' — to use the language of contemporary Catholicism. The fundamentalist orientation of political Catholicism also led to a revival of the old opposition between the confessions (with disastrous consequences for a unified Germany), and it intensified the contrast between the Catholic and the Protestant milieu. In all this, however, Catholicism was mostly on the defensive.

In 1848 — and this too has often been overlooked — many Catholics initially supported a pragmatic liberalism.[7] A similar combination of political Catholicism and liberalism also existed in other countries. In Belgium, Poland and Ireland, for example, Catholics wanted to achieve independence from foreign domination; national aims were intertwined with a desire for religious freedom.

This amalgam of religion and national feeling was different in Germany. Nevertheless, when liberalism and Catholicism attacked absolutism together, the combined impact could be strong enough to force agreement on important constitutional demands. The liberal demand for fundamental rights — freedom of association and as-sembly, freedom of the press, self-government and restrictions on the power of the State, the rule of law — could be applied to the position of the Church.

The assembly that gathered in the Paulskirche in Frankfurt contained many Catholic deputies who, unlike the conservative Catholics of the *Vormärz* period, welcomed the Revolution. They did not stand alone, but enjoyed wide support throughout the country. Catholic newspapers were founded, assemblies and conventions were held and associations set up, and 1,142 petitions were addressed to the Frankfurt Parliament. Membership of the four hundred Piusvereine für religiöse Freiheit (Pious Associations for Religious Freedom) increased to 100,000. The

7. Cf. A. M. Birke, *Bischof Ketteler und der deutsche Liberalismus*, Mainz, 1971, pp. 15ff.

first German *Katholikentag* (general meeting of Catholics) took place in Mainz. These activities show that Catholics did take part in the national and constitutional movement of the day.[8] Catholic deputies of various political persuasions met in the Catholic Club to develop a strategy for achieving the freedom of the Church in the State and from the State. Their efforts were extremely successful. Many of their demands were incorporated in the list of fundamental rights compiled by the assembly in the Paulskirche. At this early stage it also became apparent that the radicals were aiming to liberalise and democratise the Church from without; this threat was successfully fended off.

In 1848 the majority of Catholics were naturally in favour of a *großdeutsch* solution to the German question. Their traditional partiality for Catholic Austria had been strengthened by developments in ecclesiastical policy in Prussia. The attitude to this question of Wilhelm Emmanuel von Ketteler, deputy for Westphalia and later to become Bishop of Mainz, is representative of that of many Catholics. Ketteler was to become one of the leading figures of German Catholicism in the nineteenth century. He firmly opposed the idea of a 'North German monarchy under the Prussian throne'. With great reluctance, he voted against accepting the Malmö armistice. He 'could not bear to let arch-Prussianism off the hook'. Ketteler, as a deputy, could see that in the contemporary climate the Catholic Club as an ecclesiastical lobby was not capable of developing a convincing political line on the national question. The fact that a Prussian, Radowitz, was the chairman of the club necessarily dampened the Catholic deputies' commitment to a *großdeutsch* solution. Ketteler was disgusted by the club's moderation in the national question. 'If I were not a man of the cloth', he wrote to his brother, 'I would definitely support a political party from parts of the Rhineland, Westphalia and Bavaria, because our political indifference is almost unendurable'.[9]

Aversion to 'Prussianism' and a 'Prussian solution' did not, however, result in clear opposition to Prussia. Indeed, the 'Christian-Germanic' ideas held by the circle around Frederick William IV, who had settled the Cologne disturbances, were received with sympathy. The Frankfurt Constitution's provisions for settling the question of the Church in terms of fundamental rights within the framework of general political freedoms did not meet all the expectations of Catholics, but they could live with them. Most liberals were prepared to grant the Catholic

---

8. K. Repgen, *Märzbewegung und Maiwahlen des Revolutionsjahres 1848 im Rheinland*, Bonn, 1955.
9. Printed in O. Pfülf, *Bischof von Ketteler (1811–1877)*, vol. 1, Mainz, 1899, p. 158.

Church the status of a free, non-privileged association, without decisively reducing its influence in society. There was no desire to jeopardise universal rights *vis-à-vis* an all-powerful state by making an exception in law of an institution they disapproved of. Most had little time for the Catholic Church. An understandable anticlericalism in some cases developed into open contempt, and on the left there was a clear inclination to fight the Catholic Church with all the means available to the State. Ultimately, the attempt to unify Germany failed, and with it failed the project of introducing a constitution. At the same time, the likelihood of a constitutional movement uniting liberals and Catholics dwindled: its potential political strength cannot be over-estimated. What seemed possible in 1848 was out of the question in 1866.

After the Revolution, political Catholicism remained a powerful — if latent — force, despite the fact that most governments during the period of reaction were so cooperative that a specifically Catholic party seemed superfluous. The situation was particularly advantageous in Prussia, where the constitution imposed by the throne granted the Catholic Church such a high degree of internal and external freedom that Bishop Ketteler called it a Magna Carta of religious peace that could serve as a model for other settlements.[10] During the 1850s the responsibility for voicing Catholic demands seemed to have passed to the institutionalised church, the episcopate and the clergy. In several German states, reactionary governments concluded treaties and concordats with the Church. In the Prussian chamber of deputies a Catholic faction came into being in 1852 in order to defend religious–Catholic rights. It was made up chiefly of Rhenish dignitaries, and in the constitutional conflict, too, it by no means represented the majority of Catholic voters.

Not until the 1860s did a change come about that subjected the relationship of Catholics to liberalism and nationalism to a new test and, at the same time, lifted the conflict between the Church and the State out of the provincialism of the small state milieu into a national context.[11] In 1866 the German Confederation was dissolved and Austria, the dominant Catholic power and embodiment of continuity with the old Reich, was excluded. These events put paid to any Catholic hopes of a *großdeutsch* solution to the national question. Catholics were now in an

10. On this cf. A. M. Birke, 'Bischof Ketteler und die Anfänge der Zentrumspartei', in F. Quarthal and Wilfried Setzler (eds.), *Stadtverfassung — Verfassungsstaat — Pressepolitik* Sigmaringen, 1980, pp. 339–48.
11. On this cf. J. Becker, *Liberaler Staat und Kirche in der Ära von Reichsgründung und Kulturkampf*, Mainz, 1973.

overall minority: in the North German Confederation, they were in a minority of 8 million to 20 million Protestants. They were among the losers of 1866. Their immediate reaction was one of disappointment and pessimism, especially as the politically dominant National Liberals interpreted Prussia's victory over Austria in terms deriving from the *Kulturkampf,* and celebrated it as a triumph of the 'Protestant' over the 'Catholic principle'. The intensity with which liberals drew on arguments originating in the *Kulturkampf* to justify the new development ideologically, suggested that a new quality would be injected into the struggle with Ultramontanism. It was no longer a matter simply of acknowledging the situation that had been created by Austria's defeat; this situation was now justified and presented as 'necessary'. Heinrich von Treitschke described the unification of north Germany as an 'act of historical necessity' that followed the 'trend of history', while Ludwig Rochau lauded Prussia's reshaping of Germany as in harmony with a 'necessary law of nature' that could not be judged by individual morality.[12] From seeing what had happened as an essential prerequisite for a natural development it was a small step to glorifying the outcome for setting a moral standard. In some cases views such as these acquired an eschatological perspective: the events of 1866 were celebrated as a 'confirmation of the will of God'. Droysen wrote of a 'triumph of the real German spirit of 1517 and 1813 over the Roman one'.[13] According to J. C. Bluntschli, the 'task of Protestantism' was to save Germany from the impact of the 'military-hierarchical spirit of Ultramontanism'.[14] Interpretations such as these frequently culminated in a demand for a German national Church. Faced with the rising tide of liberalism — often Protestant in orientation — the majority of Catholics retreated into a totally defensive position in which their comprehension of the demands of the day, 'of modern culture and industrial development could not grow'.[15]

Bishop Ketteler was one of the few Catholics who recognised the danger of isolation that threatened them after Prussia's victory. It was several months before he could judge the political situation calmly. In his famous book, *Deutschland nach dem Kriege von 1866* (published in 1867), he accepted the outcome of the war as the basis for a future

12. Examples in K.-G. Faber, *Die nationalpolitische Publizistik Deutschlands von 1866 bis 1871,* 2 vols., Düsseldorf, 1963.
13. R. Hübner (ed.), *Johann Gustav Droysen. Briefwechsel,* vol. 2, Berlin and Leipzig, 1929, p. 871.
14. K.-G. Faber, *Die nationalpolitische Publizistik Deutschlands,* pp. 52f.
15. W. Bußmann, 'Preußen und das Jahr 1866', *Aus Politik und Zeitgeschichte. Beilage zur Wochenzeitung 'Das Parlament',* 24, 1966, p. 21.

solution to the German Question. Ketteler now considered the best option for Germany to be an idea proposed by Heinrich von Gagern as long ago as at the Frankfurt Assembly: his solution had envisaged a federal state to be led by the King of Prussia while 'the legal autonomy of the German princes and states would be safeguarded. A close and indissoluble alliance with Austria would exist'.[16] Ketteler suggested that the south German states should quickly be affiliated to the North German Confederation. While he did not refrain from criticising Prussia's attitude in his presentation of the causes of the war, he did not want to absolve Austria from all responsibility for starting the war. There were three main reasons for his support of the *kleindeutsch*, Prussian solution. Firstly, he was convinced that Austria could only regain its position in Germany by defeating Prussia in another civil war. Secondly, he came to the historically significant conclusion that in its current form, the multinational Habsburg Empire could not head a German national state. And finally, it was the chance of the articles in the Prussian constitution protecting the Church being adopted in all the states of the future Reich that made him overcome his traditional preference for Austria in favour of the new solution to the German question; he could see an opportunity of constitutionally removing the basis of the *Kulturkampf*, which was already showing signs of starting in some of the south German states.

Most Catholics neither shared nor welcomed Ketteler's support for the *kleindeutsch* solution. His own diocese and cathedral chapter disagreed with him on this issue. But as time passed, Ketteler's assessment was increasingly accepted. There were a few adherents of political Catholicism among the deputies elected to the newly constituted Reichstag of the North German Confederation. While remaining critical, they had to accept the realities of the situation. No Catholic faction existed, but Catholic deputies, in alliance with several conservative Protestants, moved that religious freedom be given the status of a basic right by adopting the Church paragraphs of the Prussian Constitution into the Constitution of the North German Confederation. This was by no means a simple matter; any initiative in the area of basic rights that applied only to religious freedom and excluded other human rights would necessarily appear opportunistic. Further, any central settlement relating to religion and the Church contravened Bismarck's constitutional ideas, which provided for federal regulations to be

---

16. W. E. v. Ketteler, *Deutschland nach dem Kriege von 1866*, Mainz, 1867, repr. in idem, *Sämtliche Werke und Briefe* (ed.) E. Iserloh, part I, vol. 2, *Schriften, Aufsätze und Reden 1867–1870*, Mainz, 1978, p. 49.

introduced only where the rights of member states were adequately protected. Leading Catholic deputies like Mallinckrodt and Windhorst appreciated this. They attempted, albeit unsuccessfully, to avoid a later repeat of the debate on fundamental rights.[17]

If the defeat of Austria in 1866 had been celebrated by many liberals as a victory of the 'Protestant' over the 'Catholic principle', then the victory over France was an even clearer instance of the triumph of the 'Germanic' over the 'Roman spirit'. What could be more natural than to secure this victory domestically against growing Ultramontane movements. The Vatican Council had increased the distance separating it from modern culture and liberalism. With the rise of Old Catholicism in reaction to the doctrine of Papal Infallibility, there seemed to be a prospect of freeing Catholics from 'the domination of Rome'. The national state which had grown out of the *kleindeutsch* solution was seen as a Protestant affair; the *Kulturkampf* became a national concern. As Constantin Rößler wrote, it was a matter of 'incorporating the Roman Catholic Church into the German state', of 'banishing the power of the papacy, in all its forms, from the face of the modern state'.[18]

The *Kulturkampf*, starting with the foundation of the Reich, was conducive to the establishment of a Catholic political party, and provided the conditions under which it became an important political factor in the Kaiserreich. 'If we have no power and no influence in public life', wrote Bishop Ketteler, 'then we have everything to fear from our adversaries, all the more so as the exclusion of Austria from the German Reich means that we have lost 10 million Catholics and now make up only one-third of the total population, whereas we previously made up more than half of it'.[19]

The controversy about the Reichstag's address to the Kaiser in 1871 was the occasion of the first major clash between the Catholic Centre Party and German liberalism in the national parliament. But it was no more than a prelude to the more significant debate about the Centre Party's motion that the Church paragraph of the Prussian Constitution be adopted in the Constitution of the Reich. After a fierce and polemical debate, the Catholic party was defeated by a large majority. Thus its plan to anchor parity between the confessions in the Constitution failed; it was also the failure of national reconciliation. From now on,

17. A. M. Birke, 'Bischof Ketteler und die Anfänge der Zentrumspartei', p. 347.
18. C. Rößler, *Das deutsche Reich und die kirchliche Frage*, Leipzig, 1876, pp. 432 and 436.
19. W. E. v. Ketteler, *Die Katholiken im Deutschen Reich*, Mainz, 1873, repr. in idem, *Sämtliche Werke*, p. 91.

Catholics were — and felt themselves to be — treated as second-class citizens in the *kleindeutsch* nation-state. The Centre Party was politically isolated, but it emerged from the dispute with increased inner strength. The fact that it united Catholics of all social classes behind the goal of strengthening the position of the Church gave it great political weight. But it also from the start carried within itself the danger of narrowing its political outlook to concentrate unduly on the interests of the Church.

In conclusion: the situation in which the Catholic Church found itself in nineteenth-century Germany was still shaped by traditional divisions between the confessions, and the secularisation and defeudalisation of the Church. Its loss of worldly power altered the relationship of the Church to the State, which for its part tried to bring a newly-acquired claim to sovereignty to bear *vis-à-vis* the Church. This led to new tensions. But the Church's loss of worldly power was, at the same time, an essential precondition for its spiritual renewal. The religious revival can only be understood if it is also seen as an attempt made by believers to find traditional guidelines in the age of modernisation. But, at the same time, it reactivated the opposition between the Catholic and the Protestant milieu, with dire consequences for the development of the German nation-state. Ultramontanism was not a movement restricted to the Catholic elites of the Church hierarchy; it encompassed the full range of church-going people. This meant that ordinary believers participated in the struggle for the rights of the Church — this struggle was democratised. Political Catholicism was born out of the Cologne disturbances. During the *Vormärz* period it was not yet at variance with German national culture and a growing national feeling. In the revolution of 1848, Catholics and liberals made common cause; this pragmatic cooperation failed, however, and with it failed the attempt to anchor the freedom of the Church in the Constitution as a basic right. As early 1848-9 it became clear what the *großdeutsch–kleindeutsch* alternative meant for the confessions. At the beginning of the era of reaction, the Prussian Crown voluntarily conceded the Church freedom in the Constitution it imposed. In the mid 1860s political Catholicism, which had revived and now appeared in the form of a political party, wanted to have this Magna Carta of religious peace in states of mixed confession adopted in the Reich — all the more so as with the exclusion of Austria in 1866 Catholics were in an overall minority. This was an attempt to ensure their integration into the nation-state, which was increasingly seen as a Protestant concern. The Centre Party's attempt in the Reichstag to have the freedom of the Church guaranteed as a basic right did not, however, result in national reconciliation. It failed, inaugurating the *Kulturkampf*, with the result that well into the twentieth century Catholics were placed — and placed themselves — in a position of inferiority.

ALEXANDER SCHWAN

German Liberalism and the National Question in the Nineteenth Century

I do not approach this subject using the methods of an historian. As a political scientist I am concerned to look at it from the perspective of political theory, and I am particularly interested in its significance for the theory of democracy. Of course, political theorists must be careful to observe strict objectivity when dealing with historical evidence. However, they regard all descriptions of historical events as interpretations which cannot be divorced from the particular preoccupations and interests of those studying the subject. Indeed, such a divorce would not normally be desirable. As a result there can exist for them no simple historical truths, but only arguments about the past which should certainly be based on carefully sifted evidence, but which must constantly be adapted to the changing perspectives of their protagonists.

Therefore I intend to tackle this subject by presenting a number of mildly provocative theses, which I shall attempt to elucidate in the limited space at my disposal. My fundamental proposition is that German liberalism did not only fail because it could not solve the 'national question' — i.e. the task of unifying Germany in the nineteenth century — but that it failed above all because it allowed itself to be drawn into a national question which was insoluble without violating liberal principles. By its commitment to national unification it largely gave up the original ingredients of its liberal faith. As German liberalism developed, so nationalism increasingly overshadowed constitutionalism; the interest in a liberal constitution and liberal political

65

practices were pushed into the background by concern for national unity and power. However, in the absence of national unification carried through in a liberal spirit, liberal policies in general were largely a spent force.

While liberalism in Western Europe after the First World War widely joined with conservative and democratic–socialistic movements and, especially in this way, considerably influenced the final foundation of a democratic and political culture, it almost totally disappeared from sight in Germany. This occurred even though the left-liberal splinter party, the DDP (Deutsche Demokratische Partei, from 1930 on the Staatspartei) was associated with the SPD and the Catholic Centre Party in the first Weimar coalition. Without real political weight and especially without any influence over the conservative right, German liberalism was not able to do anything to prevent the rise of National Socialism and the establishment of a totalitarian system. The foundation of a stable democracy in West Germany after 1945 is, so to say, the result of Western liberalism and not of German liberalism.

German liberalism — upon which the development of an original democratic culture might have been expected to depend — was actually ruined between 1867 and 1871 by its own ill-conceived nationalism. The causes of this lie not only in the superior political skill of Bismarck but also in its own tradition. The beginning of this tradition can already be seen in 1848, even in the period of *Vormärz*, and before that in the time of the *Freiheitskriege* (the Wars of German Liberation), the *Reformen*, and even during the 1790s. This chronology helps to explain the historical stages of a separate path which hindered liberalism in Germany. It prevented the possibilities gained by liberalism elsewhere in the West (in Western Europe, in the United States and even to a certain extent in Italy) which enabled, in spite of all setbacks, the establishment and consolidation of free, constitutional and pluralistic democracies.

The nationalism, however, which was finally brought about in Germany as a result of Bismarck's politics (Bismarck himself was, as is well known, not a 'nationalist') was in its substance illiberal. During the twentieth century it worked itself up into one of the deadliest threats to democracy throughout the world. When today here and there in the Federal Republic certain tendencies towards a resurrection of nationalism can be discerned — tendencies which are parallelled in the German Democratic Republic, although there they owe more to the political calculation of party and state authorities — and when a new German patriotism has been proclaimed, it seems not inappropriate to remember the decline of German liberalism through nationalism. Even if these tendencies at the present time are far removed from the excesses of earlier nationalism, they are still rooted in an alarmingly illiberal, and basically anti-Western attitude. Keeping this in mind, the historical burden concerning the relationship between nationalism and the national question, on the one hand, and democracy and liberal politics, on the other, should be recognised by all Germans.

In order to explain my theses I would like to start with a description of the Founding Programme of the National Liberal Party of 12 June 1867. With this programme the separation from the Deutsche Fortschrittspartei, founded in 1861, was confirmed. This was supported by a majority, especially among the North German liberals who, after the military victory of Prussia over Austria in 1866, now saw that the best way to national unification lay in Bismarck's policy; so that basically they were prepared to support that conservative statesman in spite of their reservations about him.

The latter resulted from the serious conflict, which had only just ended, concerning the reform of the Prussian military. Bismarck had governed since he came into office as Prussian Prime Minister and Foreign Minister (1862) with the rights of only a royal (and explicitly not of a parliamentary) minister, without a budget and against the Prussian House of Representatives. He suppressed the freedom of the press, he placed the civil servants of the Prussian administration under sharp pressure, and with the Alvensleben Convention (1863), he assisted Russian despotism in its persecution of Polish rebels. At the same time he had provocatively declared that the great questions of the day would not be decided by speeches and majority decisions, but by iron and blood.

After victorious wars against Denmark (1864) and Austria (1866), which were carried through using the same anti-liberal methods, he gave in and sought an 'indemnity'. Against the opposition of Conservatives, who had more or less supported him, he applied for the belated parliamentary authorisation of expenditures without a normal budget. Impressed by his successful policy, but also hoping to be able to influence that policy in the future, the Liberals approved the indemnity proposal by a large majority. They thereby became involved in an extremely dubious compromise. On the one side, they agreed to support the military reform and the unconstitutional hold of the monarchical government over the military; they even agreed belatedly to approve the entire policy of the previous five years. On the other hand, they got the right of the parliament over the budget confirmed — but only in principle.

The compromise led to a *de facto* 'coalition' — but of rather short duration — in which Bismarck, however, took over the leading role. Prussian influence was decisive in the shaping of the North German Confederation, and with National Liberal support, a constitution was decided which called for a Reichstag (Imperial Diet) with general and equal suffrage and — according to the wishes of the National Liberals and against Bismarck's original intention — a secret ballot. There was no bill of rights. The Reichstag, however, was balanced by the Bundesrat (Federal Council); this was an assembly of the princes and the free cities, a legislative organ of equal status with the Reichstag, organised in a federalistic, and absolutely undemocratic way. Nevertheless the National Liberals had brought about the accountability of the Bundeskanzler (Federal Chancellor), the later Reichskanzler (Imperial Chancellor), whose office was run in personal union with the Prussian Foreign Minister and for the most part also together with that of the Prussian Prime Minister. This accountability, however, consisted only of the duty to report to the Reichstag and the countersigning of directives and decrees of the Präsidium (Presidency) which was identical with the person of the Prussian King, later to be the German Emperor. It did not mean, for instance, dependence upon parliamentary majority rule of the sort already established at Westminster, in the Belgian Constitution and later in France's Third Republic.

In short: the National Liberals liked to entertain the hope that they had gained and could consolidate a few constitutional assurances, but they were operating completely in the shadow of their former opponent. At least for the moment they turned their backs on liberal goals in favour of the national politics of unification which Bismarck was practising. They did not do this, however, without being alarmed at their own daring although, correctly speaking, they should have been dismayed by their own timidity.

This policy choice and the atmosphere in which it was made, are significantly expressed in the National Liberal Party's Founding Programme of 1867.[1] The programme boasts of greater rights for the National and Prussian Parliaments. It criticises the still existing obstruction of the press, the restrictions on the right to assemble and to

1. On the following see Wilhelm Mommsen (ed.), *Deutsche Parteiprogramme*, Munich, 1960, pp. 147ff.

organise, the class structure of the Prussian municipal, county and provincial councils, the continued existence of privileges for land-owners, the stunted development of the principles of law and jurisprudence in general and the ever-increasing demands of the military. The National Liberals claimed to have 'plentifully provided' the military with resources and to have 'supported' the armament which made the Prussian victories possible, and they insisted that in the future for 'the honour and the position of power of the fatherland' they would be prepared 'to act in the same way', again. Concerning the basic question of the past conflict (three-year military service) they insisted upon the idea that 'the reduction of military service assured by the Constitution of the North German Confederation' would be quickly realised.

Although the programme provided a liberal critique of the political situation in Prussia and the North German Confederation, and although it did not try to conceal the great dangers and difficulties, it did declare that it was willing to support the Prussian government principally because of its efforts to bring about unification. The liberal powers should cooperate to bring this work to a successful conclusion and, thereby, to realise the demands for freedom by the people. Within the programme, however, unification was placed before freedom; the power of the State was set before the question of the Constitution. This implied, but none the less very significant and fateful, accentuation of the national issue resulted from the experience that not everything could be obtained at once: 'that it is not allowed to fight in every period for the same goals with the same weapons'. What mattered was to do away with the 'conventional phrases' of the 'simple and easy tradition', and to pay attention to the 'signs of the times'. They should devote their energies to hard and continuous work to achieve fully the com-mon goal of unification. This meant that they should defer attainment of all other liberal objectives, however much these were to be kept in mind for the long run. 'The final goals of liberalism are lasting, but its demands and methods are not locked away from life and do not exhaust themselves in dogma.' Flexibly adapting itself to the situation, the liberal movement should support concrete steps to unification in anticipation that these were at the same time advances 'in the areas of freedom' or that they could at least carry with them some impulse in that direction. And because the left–liberal minority clearly did not want to recognise the meaning of the 'great question of the times' and the 'correct choice of the methods', it therefore justified the founding of a National Liberal Party.

Hagen Schulze commented that the establishment and programme of the National Liberal Party at the same time marked the end of the German National Movement.[2] This is true, and moreover they bear witness, fundamentally, to the end of German liberalism as an independent and dominant political force.

The result of the parliamentary elections, however, seemed to demonstrate that the National Liberals were right. The Deutsche Fortschrittspartei which, in 1861, had immediately become the strongest party during the elections to the Prussian House of Representatives with 104 mandates, and which increased its representation in 1862 to 133, and in 1863 to 141 seats, had in 1866 — on the day of the Prussian victory at Königgrätz — sustained substantial losses in favour of the Conservatives (the Liberals obtained only 95 seats). The National Liberal secession and the arrangement with Bismarck now paid off: during the elections to the constituent Reichstag of the North German Confederation, on 12 February 1867, the National Liberals became the strongest party with 79 seats, while the remaining left–liberals of the Fortschrittspartei received only 19 mandates. Together with the Free Conservatives (Freikonservative), a parallel pro-Bismarck secession on the right which controlled 39 seats, a majority group was able to form. With the establishment of the Kaiserreich and the Reichstag elections in 1871, this line of victories continued until 1877, but it came to an end in 1878. From then on, the number of seats held by the National Liberals as well as the Fortschrittspartei, later Freisinn, continually decreased. In 1912 the Social Democratic Party (SPD) finally reached approximately the parliamentary position of the National Liberals in the 1870s. Developments in the Prussian House of Representatives were also very similar. The only exception was that after the gradual defeats of all liberal parties, including the National Liberals, from 1879 on, it was not the Social Democrats, but the Conservatives who gained. This was due to the three-class electoral system and other special features in Prussia.

But even when we examine the apparent upsurge of the National Liberals from 1867 to 1878–9, which corresponded with a dramatic weakening of the other liberal parties, it is clear that the circumstances of their foundation heralded the end of truly independent liberalism in Germany. Contrary to their demands and hopes, the National Liberals showed themselves to be unable to exert appreciable influence over Bismarck's unification policies. The union of the North German Confederation with the southern German states to the Reich was the result,

---

2. See Hagen Schulze, *Der Weg zum Nationalstaat. Die deutsche Nationalbewegung vom 18. Jahrhundert bis zur Reichsgründung*, Munich, 1985, p. 168.

as is well known, of the war against France. The founding of the Reich was through and through 'from above'. With the proclamation of the Kaiser in Versailles, the Princes and Bismarck placed themselves in fact above the Reichstag and the representative assemblies of the states, and, more importantly, the National Liberals contributed no liberal modifications to the Imperial Constitution (*Reichsverfassung*) of 1871. The *Reichsverfassung* meant an almost total acceptance of the Constitution of the North German Confederation which had been clearly criticised in the Founding Programme of the National Liberals. It restricted itself to mere technical modifications and to the codification of a few federalistic, special privileges for the southern states which enjoyed no liberal character.

It is true that Bismarck supported his policies in the 1870s with the 'coalition' between the National Liberals and the Free Conservatives. Their economic and politico-cultural interests were similar. Bismarck let them have a virtual free hand for the *Kulturkampf* against the Catholic Church. In this way the impression could be given that the National Liberals had been able to play a key role in completing the task of unification. It is true that the *Kulturkampf* was not least nationally motivated. After all, the Catholics and their organisations, their associations and their parties were blamed as being enemies of the Reich and 'ultramontane', which means that they were supposed to be willing to obey a foreign power, the papacy.

But aside from the fact that the militant and intolerant behaviour towards the Church did not, indeed, contribute to the inner liberality of the National Liberals, it is even more important to note that it greatly furthered their partiality for a powerful state. Yet, during this time, the National Liberals under Bismarck had almost nothing to say on constitutional matters. The new press legislation of 1874 turned out to be totally ambivalent. Bismarck did not try to hide the fact that he planned restrictive association and coalition laws which anticipated his struggle with the rising force of social democracy. More than anything the National Liberals had to draw back in the old struggle about the military budget; in the end they even capitulated. The renewed and serious confrontation over this question resulted in the truly unhealthy compromise of the 'Septennat', which determined the force levels of the military for seven years, so that the most elementary parliamentary control over the army was taken away for a long period. It was now confirmed that the military should remain a state within the State and that the formally constitutional monarchy, supported by the military, should keep its strong, autocratic characteristics.

   With this, Germany's special constitutional development as opposed
to that of Great Britain, France, Italy, the United States and other
Western countries was confirmed. It was not least those authors who
understood themselves to be 'liberal', who were in fact violently
nationalistic and even thought in imperialistic terms, like Heinrich von
Treitschke or later the young Max Weber; they supported this decidedly non-Western, undemocratic special development in Germany's
political system and found ideological reasons to justify it. When in
1879, with Bismarck's change to a policy of protective duties and the
ending of the *Kulturkampf*, the unequal alliance was formally with-
drawn, the National Liberals lost the last remnants of their influence.
During the following period — except for very brief phases of more
positive activity — they remained completely sunk in their nationalistic
ideology.

   During the Weimar Republic which had to carry the burdens of the
World War which the Empire had lost, the successor party to the
National Liberals, the Deutsche Volkspartei (DVP), dominated by
nationalistic motives, rejected the new republic. This situation indicated an illiberal spirit, but it was quite consistent with the decades of
continuous decay of the National Liberals before 1918. When in the
early 1920s, the DVP's chairman, Gustav Stresemann, showed his
outstanding political judgement by throwing off those ties to the old
regime, he remained nearly isolated within his party. In fact, he made
many bitter enemies. After 1930, the DVP was pulverised just like its
left–liberal companion, the DDP, later renamed the Deutsche Staatspartei, which was the only one among all German parties to accept the
Weimar Republic without reservation, but which, because of its
quantitative unimportance, was not able to do anything to prevent the
onset of the Nazi Dictatorship. The triumph of nationalism, which had
become significant in 1867, was completed in 1933 under the swastika,
the symbol of the extreme perversion of German politics. This fatal
development did not necessarily have to happen, but the ground was
prepared for it in 1867 and events finally brought it to fruition. The
failure of German liberalism is certainly not the only reason for Hitler's
triumph, but it remains an important contributory factor.

What led to this result, we have to ask now: not just to the fatal end of
1933, but to the basic decision by the majority of liberals in 1866, 1867
and 1871, to yield out of national considerations to their former enemy,
Bismarck, who thereby became in no way their political friend but

who, on the contrary, effectively broke the spine of German liberalism? Does the year 1867 mean a sharp break in the history of German liberalism, i.e. an interruption in its historical development? Could this have resulted perhaps because of a purely opportunistic idolisation of success and power? Or was it in fact an important decision, to which there could have been alternatives, but a decision which nevertheless was based on attitudes which had developed over a long time? Was this, therefore, a form of continuity, a decision which was surely not necessary but which obviously increased the gravity of the situation?

I would argue for the last version which, naturally, can refer only to the dominating and not the exclusive tendencies of the preceding development. The main reason for this continuity, as I have pointed out, was, in substance, the long-term preoccupation of the liberal movement with the 'national question': a problem that in Germany was so complicated as to be fundamentally insoluble for the liberals. For that reason the connection between liberalism and nationalism must be appraised as a tragic historical mistake, but one surely unavoidable in view of the spirit of the age in Europe.

The growth of this burden on German liberalism, involving specific factors which came to a head in this problem, went through several stages which I am only able to outline. I can identify five stages in the period before 1867:

(1) The beginning of this account is rooted in the fact that German liberal politics, in the narrow sense, were first brought into being by the impetus of the French Revolution. At the same time they first became imaginable as a reaction to the power and ambitions unleashed in France. Prussian philosophers of the Enlightenment, such as Immanuel Kant and Moses Mendelssohn, had already taken up the ideas of anti-absolutist freedom in a cautious way. They had accepted these ideas from a moralistic standpoint but, at the same time, had limited and restrained them. During the 1790s the young Wilhelm von Humboldt on the one hand had emphatically advocated the right of individuals to determine the development of their own personalities, in other words, the right of self-determination more in a philosophical than a political sense. For this purpose he reduced the 'activity of the State' to the narrow borders of superficial legal protection of individual affairs, the State being completely stripped of all social functions. But combined with this view Humboldt, on the other hand, is ready to accept the State which arose from the enlightened absolutism of Frederick the Great, a state which Kant and the Berlin Rationalists had also found satisfactory.

When dealing with this state, Humboldt felt that it was only necessary to fence off and protect the individual's private sphere, and it was not important to achieve the active participation of the citizens in politics. This first liberal concept dispenses completely with the element of democracy. Humboldt distances himself emphatically from the rational thinking of French constitutionalism about natural rights, in favour of the specific historicity of each people. He calls this in his *Ideen über Staatsverfassung, durch die neue französische Konstitution veranlaßt*, of 1791 'the more powerful coincidence'. With this there appears the first national, at the same time somewhat anti-Western, anti-rationalistic component in German liberal thinking, which at this time was in any case limited to a small circle of intellectuals.

It seems to me to be characteristic that Humboldt's more famous writing from his youth, *Ideen zu einem Versuch, die Grenzen der Wirksamkeit des Staates zu bestimmen* of 1792, published in its entirety for the first time in 1851, appeared to many German liberals, who at that time — after 1848 — found themselves in deep despair about the political outlook, as a revelation and as a timely credo. Humboldt himself, also as a later diplomat and politician, remained true to his early liberal writings from his youth to the extent that he argues in his *Denkschrift über die deutsche Verfassung* of 1813 and in other works not for a liberal constitution but only for a confederation of states as a union of the princes. Quite rightly, he regarded as illusory the idea of total German unity under constitutional rule in view of the dualism of Prussia and Austria. His views are followed to a great extent during the construction of the Germanic Confederation of 1814 — the same confederation which liberals were later to criticise so fiercely.

(2) Next, during the first fifteen years of the nineteenth century, the national idea develops into a broad appeal in Germany as an expression of resistance against Napoleon. As a result of this it is shaped by anti-French emotions. The animosity against France involves especially the rejection of the French Revolution, including its liberal phase when it still had a moderate constitution, and even the Declaration of Human and Civil Rights, which were felt to be extremely individualistic.

Concerning this phase, it is typical that the protagonists of the national idea, for instance Johann Gottlieb Fichte or Ernst Moritz Arndt, are not to be qualified exactly as liberal or conservative. To them the freedom of the Germans is important, not primarily as individuals but as members of their oppressed and, thanks to the machinations of politics — Napoleon's, but also the German princes'

— divided people. Here the repeatedly virulent, idealistic understanding of freedom in Germany is accentuated. This views the freedom of the individual as something only to be realised as a part of the moral whole, of the unified nation. The People as a collective must gain its freedom and its unity; then the individuals too will win their share — more moral than political — of freedom. It is most important that the *Volksfreiheit* (freedom of the People) must be fought for outwardly, and then after that it may be achieved within. In doing so it remains very unclear under which prerequisites of the State and within which limitations this should occur.

More and more attention was focused on 'das deutsche Wesen' (the German being) in the 'heart' of Europe. The German People, with its ancient Reich history which was to be popularised once more, was regarded as the *Urvolk* which possessed all the highest human qualities. Although temporarily hidden, it can be revealed again by regaining its unity and freedom for the good of all Peoples. Especially as a result of the German People's alienation, its outstanding intellectual and cultural elite felt themselves even more challenged to expand. They had to be politically transformed for the good of a new Reich which should in any case stand for the perfection of the intellect and culture. The world shall be made better again by the creation of Germany.

From these mental attitudes the great paradox can be explained that Prussia, and also other German states, during the time of deep political humiliation, could still embark on impressive programmes of reforms. The reformers, who also could not be sorted precisely into conservatives and liberals, were able to make great gains in a very short time and at least lay the foundations for an effective change in the areas of communal and state administration, the laws of agriculture, the military and the entire field of education. But significantly, Stein, Boyen, Scharnhorst, Gneisenau, Humboldt, Schleiermacher and even the long ruling Chancellor Hardenberg were not able to clear the path for an efficient constitutional reform; in spite of their respective endeavours in this field, they failed.

At the end of the German War of Liberation against Napoleon, the chief German powers, Prussia and Austria, were still without a constitution. In their inner structure, they were quite happy to usher in the epochs associated with the Restoration and Holy Alliance. Ironically we find that it was the principalities which had been at Napoleon's mercy, such as the Kingdoms of Bavaria and Württemberg and the Grand Duchies of Baden and Hesse-Darmstadt, which opposed this reactionary development. They felt themselves forced for the sake of their own consolidation to come to an understanding about acceptable constitutions or at least constitutions that could be imposed on the people. After 1823, Prussia had only assemblies of the estates on the provincial level. All German states retained their sovereignty, founded on the monarchical principle. With the German Confederation they built only a *Staatenverein* à la Humboldt without any parliamentary basis.

(3) Since in 1814–15 neither national unification nor political freedom had been achieved, a broad liberal and, in a more limited sense, a radical–democratic movement appeared, whose development cannot be gone into more closely here. The epoch of the Restoration merges more and more, at the same time, into one of *Vormärz*. The oppositional tendencies take on an organisational character, first as social groups (students' societies, gymnastic clubs, rifle associations, choirs, reading societies, etc.), and then in the form of the first political clubs or even political parties. At the same time freedom and unity and the liberal and national interests are listed, as a rule, equally and at the top of the programme. This meant, however, that already the liberal movement in Germany was prevented from concentrating on the questions of the Constitution in the sense of a liberal design and political modification of an existing state (as in Great Britain or in France), but in striving for inner freedom it bound itself together with an integral, exalted and, during the Romantic period, an increasing desire for unity.

The demand for unification, however, clashed immediately with the interests of both Great Powers, Prussia and Austria: the authors of the Restoration, both to a certain extent border states without a homogenous population, and competitors for supremacy in Germany (whereby their own interest in power, not the national interest, was uppermost). For that reason the liberal movement could not align itself, as in Italy, with the open-minded government of a dominating state (Piemont–Sardinia) and make itself a representative of a Risorgimento against absolutism based on foreign rule. It stood in Germany against all relevant 'particularist' powers, doomed to play the role of an internal opposition. Its majority tried, as time went by, more and more to free itself from the helplessness caused by this — by turning to the state which seemed politically and constitutionally the lesser evil, and which promised strength in the power struggle: namely Prussia. Against the opposition of some — but by no means all — southern German liberals and democrats, the northern German course was pushed through under the intellectual leadership of Friedrich Christoph Dahlmann and Johann Gustav Droysen, who viewed Prussia as the only lever for the unification of Germany. Because they disregarded, as a result, the old Imperial Habsburg power, this became the (at that time) still un-wanted beginning of a development which in the end led to the expulsion of Austria from Germany — with the short-sighted approval of the liberals. At the same time, we find here the beginning of that *realpolitischen* orientation which caused the liberals to forget their reser-vations against the strongly conservative, even authoritarian Hohen-zollerns in order to gain national unity.

Dahlmann, Droysen and the other liberals surely desired to per-meate a Germany unified by Prussia with a liberal spirit and the rule of law. But they also felt a need to stress the special situation of Prussia. This was seen to be the result of the history of its people, or of the German tradition in general interpreted from a pro-Borussian viewpoint. They claimed that to suit Germany's supposedly stronger organic and less rationalistic idea of the State, a parliamentary monarchy or all the more a republic could not be contemplated, but only a constitutional monar-chy with pronounced prerogatives for the Crown. Karl von Rotteck's and Robert von Mohl's constitutional-theoretical references to the French Revolution — limited as they were — were not able to revise this notion. Even the South-West German liberals in their First Party Programme (Heppenheim, 1837) placed unity before freedom and pinned all of their national hopes on Prussia.

(4) In 1848–9, in the year of the Revolution, the dilemma of the German liberals became brutally clear. It is true that after months of (much too long) debates the Frankfurt National Assembly passed an exemplary liberal constitution, containing the codification of basic rights and parliamentary sovereignty. But of course the perceived need to unify Germany led to a turn towards Prussia, together with the Erbkaiser Party under the leadership of Heinrich von Gagern, as well as a tendency to hope for help from the Prussian monarchy. The Imperial crown was offered to Friedrich Wilhelm IV, although at this late point in time as it happens (in April 1849), he had already provoked the liberals by the imposition of the Prussian Constitution (December 1848). The Erbkaiser Party tried to prevent this, but in the end it succumbed so as not to jeopardise the hoped-for work of unification under Prussian leadership. And previously it turned against a liberal reform of the Prussian Landtag (State Assembly) in order to prevent every form of rivalry to the projected National Parliament. By so doing, it gave the idea of unification preference over a consistent liberal strategy.

Because the liberals chose the national option and at the same time committed themselves to Prussian leadership in 1848, the majority of them ruled out two alternative possibilities: on the one hand, the founding of a German republic (according to the model of the United States or of Switzerland) which would have been able to clear away the claims of the princes by means of a fundamental revolution or, on the other hand, giving priority to the liberal reformation of the individual states by tying them into liberal–constitutional, parliamentary monarchies. The consistent fulfilment of this task could only have led to national unification much later, if at all. The first way would have tied unification to a type of freedom which, in those times, seemed too radical. Only in this way, could Prussia have 'submerged' itself in Germany, as so many liberals vainly hoped. The second way would have put the achievement of freedom before the goal of unification (which in those times, however, was not regarded as something which could be postponed). Both choices were (taking into account the political atmosphere in Germany) obviously unrealistic. But the way of the middle course, decided by a majority at the Paulskirche, proved to be impracticable too. It failed. It meant unification — but even then an only partial unification — under the leadership of the quite illiberal state of Prussia; it also meant wanting to strive for a freedom which was not sufficiently well established in the individual German states, especially Prussia itself. This policy was, viewed from the standpoint of liberal principles, a complete failure. The loss of political freedom was already clear as the result of its confusion with the national question. For this question there was no solution, however, either in a constitutional or at the same time in a political sense, because there could be no consensus between liberals and princes, or between Prussia and Austria.

(5) In the decade after the failure of 1849, German liberalism tended towards political resignation, but at the same time it strengthened itself economically and culturally. But it was only able to take hold of the *Besitz-und Bildungsbürgertum* (the property owning and educated middle classes) as a nationally oriented and at the same time pragmatic movement. The journalist August Ludwig von Rochau gave, in 1853, an account of the pervading atmosphere in his book *Grundsätze der Realpolitik, angewendet auf die staatlichen Zustände Deutschlands*. Johann Gustav Droysen, and then Heinrich von Sybel and Heinrich von Treitschke, formulated in an ever more intense manner the idea of the powerful State, which was now regarded as the unavoidable requirement for the realisation of unification and freedom — even an important content of that realisation and an end in itself. They related this thought once more to Prussia, which had so disappointed the liberals in

1849, but which at the same time had let it be known that it was going to lay claim to the leadership in Germany.

With the 'new era' of Wilhelm I, new hopes were aroused, based on such notions of so-called *realpolitik*. The liberals unwisely believed that they would be able to form a government in Prussia and through Prussia in Germany. In 1859, the year of the grave defeat of Austria in Italy, the Deutsche Nationalverein was founded. It wanted, as it stated in its Declaration of Eisenach, the achievement of national unification, and in the meantime it demanded that military leadership and the diplomatic representation of Germany should be put wholly in the hands of the Prussian Government. It placed national independence and unity plainly higher than the rights of the party. Its ideas about the Constitution were based not so much on the structure of freedom as on the need to centralise the Germany which was to be unified. The Deutsche Fortschrittspartei did not go this far in its founding programme two years later. But for it also, only a strong central power in the hands of Prussia could create the liberal rule of law that it was striving for. For this reason Prussia's existence, might and honour were to be supported.

The conflict between the liberals, Wilhelm I and Bismarck over the military budget led, of course, to the great struggle between the Prussian liberals and their *Machtstaat*. Yet the liberals had accepted the State to such an extent that the battle for parliamentary rights could not seriously endanger the State's power. As a result of this, the struggle had already been lost right from the start. The compliance of the majority which formed the National Liberal Party in 1867, under the impression of the wars and victories of Bismarck and acceptance of his politics of unity 'from above' is, for that reason, only consistent with earlier developments. The new party could appeal to the major part of the German liberals who supported the long-developing, national-political, pro-Prussian orientation. Their principles of freedom were always limited, dominated and distorted by the national question.

For us Germans at the present time the 'national question' is posed in a fashion which is both different and yet similar. It is different because the liberals do not stand in opposition to two opposing, more or less autocratically governed and nationally mixed Great Powers, for the purpose partly of working against them and partly collaborating with them to make a unified Germany within unclear boundaries. Today a democratic and a Communistic State with opposing structures and with set established borders (strengthened by the Berlin Wall) face one another. To that extent the situation concerning the national question is clear, but even more difficult.

Nevertheless, the 'national question' still has similarities with that of the nineteenth century because once more it contains a tension between the relationship of freedom and unification. And again the danger could arise that the essential differences between these concepts will not be recognised. The German liberals did not sufficiently grasp the contradiction. This had to do with their hope of being able to effectuate the unification of Germany in freedom with the help of authoritarian powers — or even to have the authoritarian powers carry it out for them. Today a consensus in favour of reunification fails because of the contradiction between the established systems of freedom and dictatorship. But the urge for unification is in certain circles already so strong that they are very tempted, once more, to ignore the differences in the systems or at least to play these down. And again it remains unanswered under which exact constitutional and political preconditions unity could be brought into being. Unification threatens once more to be placed above freedom; freedom once more could be sacrificed for the priority of unity.

HUBERT KIESEWETTER

Economic Preconditions for Germany's Nation-Building in the Nineteenth Century

To Sir Karl Popper on his 85th birthday

> The unity of the nation is the fundamental condition for lasting national prosperity.
>
> *Friedrich List, 1841*

The nineteenth and twentieth centuries witnessed a German Empire and German nationalism which were responsible for two world wars, the last one even more disastrous than the first.[1] Both wars were fought under the assumption that Germany's economic strength would at least be sufficient to win a rather short and intensive battle in the field. In trying to explain the underlying economic developments, we must examine the economic suppositions of this nation which, belatedly and incompletely united, seemed to be economically so dominant in Europe at the end of the nineteenth century.[2] To put this question

1. See Louis L. Snyder, *German Nationalism: The Tragedy of a People. Extremism Contra Liberalism In Modern German History*, 1952, 2nd edn., Port Washington, 1969; idem, *Roots of German Nationalism*, Bloomington and London, 1978; Gordon A. Craig, *The Politics of the Prussian Army, 1640–1945*, Oxford, 1955; J.C.G. Röhl, *From Bismarck to Hitler: The Problem of Continuity in German History*, London, 1970; Hubert Kiesewetter, *Von Hegel zu Hitler. Eine Analyse der Hegelschen Machtstaatstheorie und der politischen Wirkungsgeschichte des Rechtshegelianismus*, Hamburg, 1974; Michael Geyer, *Deutsche Rüstungspolitik 1860–1980*, Frankfurt on Main, 1984.
2. Tom Kemp, *Industrialization in Nineteenth-Century Europe*, 1969, ninth impression, London, 1980; Charles P. Kindleberger, 'Germany's Overtaking of England, 1806 to 1914', in *Economic Response. Comparative Studies in Trade, Finance, and Growth*, Cambridge, Mass., 1978, pp. 185–236; Clive Trebilcock, *The Industrialization of the Continental Powers 1780–1914*, London and New York, 1981.

81

another way, how was it possible that within a little more than four decades after the establishment of the German Empire in 1871 a previously disjointed economy was capable of so much progress and growth? Is the assumption that the economic roots for Germany's nation-building lay in the first two-thirds of the nineteenth century reasonable? And if so, what were the economic preconditions and how did they influence the process of Germany's nation-building? Can we say, as Berdahl did, 'that nationalism is generated among a people by the growing awareness of its economic backwardness and by the desire for a modern economy'?[3] These are some of the questions I posed to myself while preparing this paper. But before I dig deeper into the economic background, especially for the period between 1815 and 1871, let me make some introductory remarks.

One reason for dealing nearly exclusively with Germany's nation-building, and not with that elsewhere in continental Europe, is the political and economic complexity and singularity of the territory, which was later called Germany. One can hardly understand Germany's economic history during the nineteenth century without keeping the political preconditions of German particularism in mind.[4]

In 1800 the continental states, with the exception of Italy and Poland,[5] were politically united and rather homogeneous in their territories but not in their ethnic composition. France, Spain, the Netherlands, Sweden, Russia, Austria and Switzerland are good examples of this. Within the territory of Germany, however, there were 350 sovereign dominions, 51 imperial towns and 61 ecclesiastical territories, principalities and counties. As a result of the Napoleonic Wars most of them were dissolved in 1803 by the so-called *Reichsdeputationshauptschluß*. The territorial winners were Baden, Bavaria, Prussia and Württemberg. In 1806 the Holy Roman Empire, which still existed formally, was liquidated under pressure from Napoleon, and in the same year the Confederation of the Rhine was founded, consisting mainly of the newly established Kingdoms of Württemberg, Bavaria, Saxony, West-

---

3. Robert M. Berdahl, 'New Thoughts on German Nationalism', *The American Historical Review*, vol. 77, 1972, p. 72; similarly Alexander Gerschenkron, *Economic Backwardness in Historical Perspective. A Book of Essays*, Cambridge, Mass., 1962.

4. Some recent introductory books are: Manfred Görtemaker, *Deutschland im 19. Jahrhundert. Entwicklungslinien*, Opladen, 1983; Thomas Nipperdey, *Deutsche Geschichte 1800–1866. Bürgerwelt und starker Staat*, Munich, 1983; Michael Stürmer, *Das ruhelose Reich. Deutschland 1866–1918*, Berlin, 1983; Reinhard Rürup, *Deutschland im 19. Jahrhundert 1815–1871*, Göttingen, 1984; Hagen Schulze, *Der Weg zum Nationalstaat. Die deutsche Nationalbewegung vom 18. Jahrhundert bis zur Reichsgründung*, Munich, 1985.

5. There were, of course, some other smaller states not yet united; see Peter Alter, *Nationalismus*, Frankfurt on Main, 1985, p. 100, Table 1.

phalia, the Grand Duchies Baden, Hesse, Berg and others.[6] The end of the Holy Roman Empire 'had its roots in an entirely singular nation-building process'.[7]

The economic consequences of the Continental Blockade (21 November 1806–20 March 1813) on Germany[8] are difficult to assess and attempted estimations have been subject to much controversy. In terms of production and trade, for example, the textile industry in the Kingdom of Saxony gained much by this form of artificial protectionism, i.e. the exclusion of English competition. Forty-eight factories were founded there during this period.[9] On the other hand, however, the Continental Blockade forced England to conquer new foreign markets, which damaged the less developed textile industries in Saxony, in the Rhineland and in Silesia after 1813. One can say, as Lütge[10] does, that the effects of the Continental Blockade were of fundamental importance for Germany's entire social and economic structure. Its effects on East Prussia were devastating. Grain exports to England were stopped almost entirely; the ground lost here was not recovered until after the repeal of the British Corn Laws in 1846. Although the Continental System and the Blockade had been erected in order to destroy, or at least seriously damage, England's industrial supremacy, and to help France attain political, military and economic hegemony in Europe, the opposite happened.[11] After 1815 England's economic and political power was greater than ever before and British industrial exports flooded into the

6. See Elisabeth Fehrenbach, *Traditionelle Gesellschaft und revolutionäres Recht. Die Einführung des Code Napoléon in den Rheinbundstaaten*, Göttingen, 1974 (*Kritische Studien zur Geschichtswissenschaft*, vol. 13); and Helmut Berding, *Napoleonische Herrschafts- und Gesellschaftspolitik im Königreich Westfalen 1807–1813*, Göttingen, 1973 (*Kritische Studien zur Geschichtswissenschaft*, vol. 7).
7. Heinrich Otto Meisner, 'Staats- und Regierungsformen in Deutschland seit dem 16. Jahrhundert', in H.H. Hofmann (ed.), *Die Entstehung des modernen souveränen Staates*, Cologne and Berlin, 1967, p. 339; similarly Heinrich Lutz, *Die deutsche Nation zu Beginn der Neuzeit. Fragen nach dem Gelingen und Scheitern deutscher Einheit im 16. Jahrhundert*, Munich, 1982.
8. See Roger Dufraisse, 'Französische Zollpolitik, Kontinentalsperre und Kontinentalsystem in Deutschland der napoleonischen Zeit' in H. Berding and H.-P. Ullmann (eds.), *Deutschland zwischen Revolution und Restauration*, Königstein/Ts. and Düsseldorf, 1981, pp. 328–52.
9. Rudolf Forberger, *Die Industrielle Revolution in Sachsen 1800–1861*, vol. 1/1: 'Die Revolution der Produktivkräfte in Sachsen 1800–1830', Berlin (East), 1982, pp. 508–19.
10. Friedrich Lütge, *Deutsche Sozial- und Wirtschaftsgeschichte. Ein Überblick*, Berlin, Göttingen and Heidelberg, 1952, p. 343.
11. For detailed interpretations: see Eli F. Heckscher, *The Continental System. An Economic Interpretation*, Oxford, 1922, pp. 257–363; François Crouzet, *L'économie britannique et le blocus continental* (1806–1813), 2 vols., Paris, 1958, esp. vol. II, pp. 421–82; Glenn R. Hueckel, *The Napoleonic Wars and their Impact on Factor Returns and Output Growth in England 1793–1815*, New York and London, 1985; for a case-study, Geoffrey Ellis, *Napoleon's Continental Blockade: The Case of Alsace*, Oxford, 1981.

German territories which could not stem the tide because they were so divided.

While Napoleon's Continental System had effectively divided Germany as a nation, the war against France brought an upsurge of national feeling against French oppression. But Johann Gottlieb Fichte's 'Speeches to the German Nation' (*Reden an die deutsche Nation*, 1807–8), Ernst Moritz Arndt's song 'What is the German's Fatherland?' ('Was ist des Deutschen Vaterland?', 1813), and Friedrich Ludwig Jahn's national gymnastic movement (Turngesellschaft) were extraordinary expressions of a short reform period and stood along with other propaganda for a united Germany in sharp contrast to the political and economic situation. They were, of course, legitimations of the claim to national unity but not the prime causes of it. It was not Germany as a whole but mainly Prussia which fought with England, Russia, Sweden and Austria against Napoleon. Ironically enough Saxony, whose territory had been heavily damaged by these military activities, felt too much loyalty towards the Emperor to side with her former German enemy.[12]

The Congress of Vienna remodelled the territorial map of continental Europe completely. But neither England nor any other of the major powers were interested in a united Germany which could perhaps again emerge as a competitor on European and foreign export markets. In addition, the already existing political dualism between Austria and Prussia led to their territorial expansion at the expense of many other German states and Germany as a whole.[13] The political construction resulting from these diplomatic quarrels was the German Confederation, consisting of an empire, five kingdoms, eighteen grand duchies and duchies, eleven principalities and four Free Cities (see Table 1).

Compared to the hundreds of territories in the Holy Roman Empire the reduction to thirty-nine members in the German Confederation, thirty-five of them sovereign states, can be seen as an advantage. But in fact the Confederation could work neither as a political nor as an economic mediator of German interests. England was linked in per-

12. The main reason for Saxony's attitude was the rivalry with Prussia, stemming at least since the Seven Years' War, 1756–63; see Rudolf Kötzschke and Hellmuth Kretzschmar, *Sächsische Geschichte. Werden und Wandlungen eines Deutschen Stammes und seiner Heimat im Rahmen der Deutschen Geschichte*, 3rd edn., Frankfurt on Main, 1977.

13. Austria gave up the southern Netherlands (Belgium), and Vorderösterreich in favour of Galicia, northern Italy and Dalmatia. Prussia could not annex the Kingdom of Saxony totally — 'only' 58.2 per cent of her territory — but was compensated with the Rhineland and Westphalia. Of the other German states it was Bavaria which extended her territory by annexing the Palatinate.

sonal union with Hanover, Denmark with Holstein, and the Netherlands with Luxemburg; not to mention the fact that more than half of
Austria's territory and nearly a third of Prussia's lay beyond the
borders of the German Confederation and were never integrated into it.
Therefore, almost every effort to find a common base for economic
decisions at the German Diet in Frankfurt on Main was condemned to
failure, as we shall see later.[14] In the following I will try to outline three
economic spheres which were closely connected with Germany's
nation-building: (1) the freedom to engage in trade or industry (*Gewerbefreiheit*); (2) the development of the German Zollverein; and (3)
railway construction.

The freedom to engage in trade or industry (*Gewerbefreiheit*)[15] with the
exception of a very few has often been considered responsible for
Germany's industrialisation as well as a precondition of her nation-
building. Let me quote Sartorius von Waltershausen: 'The introduction of *Gewerbefreiheit* was, with regard to the formation of a centralised
economy in Germany, a historical necessity'.[16] There is no doubt that
the guild system, especially in its ossified form at the end of the
eighteenth and the beginning of the nineteenth centuries, severely
hindered the spread of industrial enterprises, as Adam Smith so clearly
pointed out.[17] And, of course, the guild system resulted in the backwardness of some handicrafts.[18] But the various German states handled
the matter in different ways and, as one must add, between a liberal
concession system and complete *Gewerbefreiheit* there were many possibilities of promoting industry without interfering with the handicrafts

14. See L. Fr. Ilse, *Geschichte der deutschen Bundesversammlung, insbesondere ihres Verhaltens zu den deutschen National-Interessen*, 3 vols., repr., Hildesheim, 1971–2.
15. See Karl Heinrich Kaufhold, 'Gewerbefreiheit und gewerbliche Entwicklung in Deutschland im 19. Jahrhundert', in *Blätter für deutsche Landesgeschichte*, vol. 118, 1982, pp. 73–114.
16. A. Sartorius von Waltershausen, *Deutsche Wirtschaftsgeschichte 1815–1914*, 2nd edn., Jena, 1923, p. 22 (my translation); similarly Georg Adler, *Uber die Epochen der Deutschen Handwerker-Politik*, Jena, 1903, p. 56; Hagen Schulze, 'Die Stein-Hardenbergschen Refor-men und ihre Bedeutung für die deutsche Geschichte', in *Preußen: Seine Wirkung auf die deutsche Geschichte*, Stuttgart, 1985, p. 216.
17. Adam Smith, *An Inquiry Into the Nature and Causes of the Wealth of Nations*, London, 1776, book II, chap. X. But one can also find the view of a textile manufacturer of the Lower Rhine 'that Adam Smith's doctrine of commercial freedom would work upon Prussia like moonlight on tropical plants'. Quoted in Carl Brinkmann, 'The Place of Germany in the Economic History of the Nineteenth Century', *The Economic History Review*, vol. IV, 1932–4, p. 131.
18. In 1831 out of 1,088 master joiners in Berlin 640 could not pay any duties. See F. Lütge, *Deutsche Sozial- und Wirtschaftsgeschichte*, p. 333.

Table 1. Population and area of the Germanic Confederation's members in 1816[1]

States[2]	Inhabitants	Area in km[2]	Inhabitants per km[2]	% of total area
Empire and Kingdoms				
Austria[3]	9,482,227	195,228.44	48.6	31.15
Prussia[4]	8,042,562	185,460.25	43.4	29.59
Bavaria	3,560,000	76,395.75	46.4	12.19
Hanover	1,328,351	38,568.43	34.4	6.15
Württemberg	1,410,327	19,506.66	72.3	3.11
Saxony	1,192,789	14,958.15	79.7	2.39
Grand Duchies and Duchies				
Baden	1,005,899	15,307.23	65.7	2.44
Mecklenburg-Schwerin	308,166	13,260.65	23.2	2.12
Holstein-Lauenburg	360,000	9,580.44	37.6	1.53
Hesse-Cassel[5]	567,868	9,567.78	59.4	1.53
Hesse-Darmstadt	587,995	8,414.82	69.9	1.34
Oldenburg	221,399	6,339.06	34.9	1.01
Nassau	301,907[11]	4,765.44	63.4	0.76
Brunswick	225,273	3,729.21	60.4	0.60
Saxe-Weimar	193,869	3,640.57	53.3	0.58
Mecklenburg-Strelitz	71,764	2,724.92	26.3	0.43
Luxemburg	154,000[10]	2,587.82	59.5	0.41
Saxe-Meiningen	115,000[12]	2,549.28	45.1	0.41
Saxe-Gotha[6]		1,422.75		
Saxe-Coburg	111,989	586.39	55.7	0.32
Saxe-Altenburg	95,855	1,330.80	72.0	0.21
Anhalt-Dessau[7]	52,947	894.17	59.2	0.14
Anhalt-Bernburg	37,046	827.55	44.8	0.13
Anhalt-Köthen	32,454	662.92	49.0	0.11
Principalities				
Waldeck-Pyrmont	52,557	1,202.51	43.7	0.19
Lippe-Detmold	78,900	1,129.83	69.8	0.18
Hohenzollern-Hechingen[8]	50,060	1,148.00	43.6	0.18
Hohenzollern-Sigmaringen				
Schwarzburg-Rudolstadt	53,937[11]	958.04	56.3	0.15
Schwarzburg-Sondershausen	45,125	852.33	52.9	0.14
Reuss-Gera	69,333	834.16	83.1	0.13
Schaumburg-Lippe	24,000	443.23	54.2	0.07
Reuss-Greiz	30,293	345.78	87.6	0.06
Hesse-Homburg[9]	23,000	262.09	87.8	0.04
Liechtenstein	7,000	159.67	43.8	0.03
Free Cities				
Lübeck	36,600	364.50	100.4	0.06
Hamburg	146,109[11]	351.83	415.3	0.06
Bremen	50,139	263.19	190.5	0.04
Frankfurt on Main	47,850[11]	100.76	474.9	0.02
Total	30,174,590	626,725.40	48.1	100.00

Sources: Carl von Rotteck and Carl Welcker (eds.), *Staats-Lexikon oder Encyklopädie der Staatswissenschaften*, 15 vols., Altona, 1834–43; Friedrich W. von Reden, *Deutschland und das übrige Europa. Handbuch der Bodens-, Bevölkerungs-, Erwerbs- und Verkehrs- Statistik; des Staatshaushalts und der Staatsmacht. In vergleichender Darstellung*, Wiesbaden, 1854; Hugo F. von Brachelli, *Deutsche Staatenkunde. Ein Handbuch der Statistik des Deutschen Bundes und seiner Staaten, mit Einschluß der nichtdeutschen Provinzen Österreichs und Preußens*, Vienna, 1857; Georg von Viebahn (ed.), *Statistik des zollvereinten und nördlichen Deutschlands.* Part One, *Landeskunde*, Berlin, 1858; *Quellen zur Bevölkerungs-, Sozial- und Wirtschaftsstatistik Deutschlands 1815–1875*, vol. I, *Quellen zur Bevölkerungsstatistik Deutschlands 1815–1875*, compiled by Antje Kraus. Boppard a.Rh., 1980.

1. In the original source, F. W. von Reden, 1854, the area of the different states is declared in square miles. Here they are computed from one square mile = 55.06 square kilometres.
2. The states are arranged by political status and area.
3. Only the inhabitants or area of the empire which belonged to the Germanic Confederation.
4. Without the provinces West and East Prussia and Posen, which did not belong to the Germanic Confederation.
5. Electorate (Kurhessen).
6. By the partition of inheritance at Hildburghausen, 12 November 1826, the duchy Gotha came to Coburg.
7. The Köthen dynasty died out in 1847, the Bernburg dynasty in 1863. Both territories went to Anhalt-Dessau.
8. Both principalities of Hohenzollern ceded their sovereign rights to Prussia on 7 December 1849.
9. Hesse-Homburg became a member of the Confederation in 1817.
10. In 1834.
11. In 1817.
12. In 1818.

too much. This was done in many German states during the first half of the nineteenth century.[19]

The opinion that *Gewerbefreiheit* is so closely linked with Germany's industrialisation and nation-building is obviously deduced from the Prussian case. Let me make some remarks on this Prussian dominated view. To students of German economic history, and to social and political historians as well, Germany's nation-building was of such an overwhelming character that for a period of nearly one hundred years the process of regional industrialisation did not attract much interest.[20] There is, of course, a well established tradition of historiography of the German *Länder*, but the study of their economic conditions was neglected until the early 1960s, partly because of a lack of quantitative material.[21] Comparative studies of regional industrialisation in Germany have only emerged in recent years.[22]

Gewerbefreiheit in Prussia was introduced as early as October 1807 in conjunction with the great reform movement of Stein and Hardenberg but was further specified by the trade tax reform of 28 November

19. See, for example, Wolfram Fischer, 'Government Activity and Industrialization in Germany (1815–70)', in W.W. Rostow (ed.), *The Economics of Take-Off into Sustained Growth*, London, 1963, pp. 83–94; Alexander Dorn, *Pflege und Förderung des gewerblichen Fortschrittes durch die Regierung in Württemberg*, Vienna, 1868; Wilhelm Ullmann, *Die hessische Gewerbepolitik von der Zeit des Rheinbundes bis zur Einführung der Gewerbefreiheit im Jahre 1866*, Darmstadt, 1903; Rudolf Bovensiepen, *Die Kurhessische Gewerbepolitik und die wirtschaftliche Lage des zünftigen Handwerks in Kurhessen von 1816–1867*, Marburg, 1909; Wolfram Fischer, *Der Staat und die Anfänge der Industrialisierung in Baden 1800–1850*, vol. I: *Die staatliche Gewerbepolitik*, Berlin, 1962; Hubert Kiesewetter, 'Staat und regionale Industrialisierung. Württemberg und Sachsen im 19. Jahrhundert', in H. Kiesewetter and R. Fremdling (eds.), *Staat, Region und Industrialisierung*, Ostfildern, 1985, pp. 108–32.

20. This was not the case in the decades before 1870 when many statistical works were based on regional differentiations: see C.A. von Malchus, *Statistik und Staatenkunde. Ein Beitrag zur Staatenkunde von Europa*, Stuttgart and Tübingen, 1826; C.F.W. Dieterici, *Statistische Übersicht der wichtigsten Gegenstände des Verkehrs und Verbrauchs im Preußischen Staate und im deutschen Zollverbande*, 6 vols. for the period 1831 to 1853, Berlin, Posen (Poznań) and Bromberg, 1838–57; Fr. W. von Reden, *Deutschland und das übrige Europa. Handbuch der Bodens-, Bevölkerungs-, Erwerbs- und Verkehrs-Statistik; des Staatshaushalts und der Streitmacht. In vergleichender Darstellung*, Wiesbaden, 1854; Hugo F. Brachelli, *Deutsche Staatenkunde. Ein Handbuch der Statistik des Deutschen Bundes und seiner Staaten, mit Einschluß der nichtdeutschen Provinzen Österreichs und Preußens*, Vienna, 1857; Georg von Viebahn, *Statistik des zollvereinten und nördlichen Deutschlands*, 3 vols., Berlin, 1858–68; Adolf Frantz, *Österreich, Preußen, Deutschland und die Schweiz. Handbuch der Statistik nach den neuesten und besten Quellen bearbeitet*, Breslau (Wrocław), 1864.

21. See Wolfgang Zorn, 'Ein Jahrhundert deutscher Industrialisierungsgeschichte. Ein Beitrag zur vergleichenden Landesgeschichtsschreibung', in *Blätter für deutsche Landesgeschichte*, 108, 1972, pp. 122–34; P. Fried (ed.), *Probleme und Methoden der Landesgeschichte*, Darmstadt, 1978, with a useful bibliography.

22. Frank B. Tipton, *Regional Variations in the Economic Development of Germany During the Nineteenth Century*, Middletown, Conn., 1976; Klaus Megerle, *Württemberg im Industrialisierungsprozeß Deutschlands. Ein Beitrag zur regionalen Differenzierung der Industrialisierung*, Stuttgart, 1982; Hubert Kiesewetter and Rainer Fremdling (eds.), *Staat, Region und Industrialisierung*, Ostfildern, 1985.

1810.[23] The industrial code for the whole Prussian territory was first realised in 1845, by which time the economic development in the industrialising regions — Silesia, the Rhineland, Westphalia, and Brandenburg with Berlin — had made such progress that the restrictions on the commercial law four years later could not stop the growth process. These restrictions were partly a result of the revolutionary uprising in 1848, which was heavily supported by unemployed journeymen. It is quite interesting to note that one of the journeymen's political goals was the restoration of the guild system, e.g. to prevent the growth of an industrial system.[24] The point I want to make here is that the early introduction of *Gewerbefreiheit* in Prussia strengthened the view that this freedom, industrialisation and nation-building went hand in hand. That this is incorrect can be easily seen by looking at the development of a Prussian neighbour, the Kingdom of Saxony.[25]

Again Saxony is a good example of the importance of comparative regional studies in trying to explain the economic roots of Germany's nation-building. *Gewerbefreiheit* was introduced in Saxony in 1861, at a time when this country had the highest percentage of industrial employment and the lowest percentage of agricultural employment of all the various German regions and states.[26] As late as 1830 it was argued, that in Saxony 'the most wicked spirit of guilds prevails and the blue Monday prospers with all its negative consequences, in spite of the fact that the advanced date demands absolute *Gewerbefreiheit*'.[27] But how did the Saxon government manage to support industrial development,

23. See Barbara Vogel, *Allgemeine Gewerbefreiheit. Die Reformpolitik des preußischen Staatskanzlers Hardenberg (1810–1820)*, Göttingen, 1983 (*Kritische Studien zur Geschichtswissenschaft*, vol. 57), pp. 165–87.
24. See Gustav Schmoller, *Zur Geschichte der deutschen Kleingewerbe im 19. Jahrhundert. Statistische und nationalökonomische Untersuchungen*, Halle, 1870; Ernst Friedrich Goldschmidt, *Die deutsche Handwerkerbewegung bis zum Sieg der Gewerbefreiheit*, Ph.D. Munich, 1914; D. Dowe and T. Offermann (eds.), *Deutsche Handwerker- und Arbeiterkongresse 1848–1852. Protokolle und Materialien*, Berlin and Bonn, 1983; Jürgen Bergmann, 'Soziallage, Selbstverständnis und Aktionsformen der Arbeiter in der Revolution von 1848', in H. Volkmann and J. Bergmann (eds.), *Sozialer Protest*, Opladen, 1984, pp. 283–303; Karl Heinrich Kaufhold, 'Handwerkliche Tradition und industrielle Revolution', in K.H. Haufhold and F. Riemann (eds.), *Theorie und Empirie in Wirtschaftspolitik und Wirtschaftsgeschichte*, Göttingen, 1984, pp. 169–88.
25. Of the many books and articles let me just mention Heinrich Bodemer, *Zur Beurtheilung des Entwurfs einer Gewerbe-Ordnung für das Königreich Sachsen*, Leipzig, 1859; Hermann Rentzsch, *Die Reform der sächsischen Gewerbegesetzgebung*, Dresden, 1862; Paul Horster, *Die Entwicklung der Sächsischen Gewerbeverfassung (1780–1861)*, Ph.D., Heidelberg, 1907; Albert Herzog zu Sachsen, *Die Reform der sächsischen Gewerbegesetzgebung (1840–1861)*, Ph.D., Munich, 1970, pp. 666–1141.
26. See Hubert Kiesewetter, 'Bevölkerung, Erwerbstätige und Landwirtschaft im Königreich Sachsen 1815–1871', in S. Pollard (ed.), *Region and Industrialisation. Studies on the Role of the Region in the Economic History of the Last Two Centuries*, Göttingen, 1980, pp. 89–106.
27. *Aphoristische Bemerkungen über Sachsen*, Zerbst, 1830, p. 76 (my translation).

and at the same time uphold craftsmen's rights? One possibility existed in giving privileges and concessions to newly developing industries, especially in the area of cotton textiles. On the other hand the government gradually extended the rights of industrial enterprises. It even called upon its envoy at the London court in 1816 to make enquiries about the economic successes of the industrial freedom of trades in Great Britain,[28] unfortunately without any result. Ten years later, in 1827, the government was criticised by industrialists in Chemnitz, later called the 'Saxon Manchester', who spoke of an eternal war within the guilds which should be transformed into an eternal peace by introducing *Gewerbefreiheit*.[29] The Saxon government was, however, not willing to take a stand on the inevitable conflict between the crafts and industry, and the Estates (*Landstände*) postponed dealing with the whole issue in 1833.

It was not until 1840 that the Saxon government allowed some manufacturers and handicrafts to settle in the countryside, because the growing population could not be sufficiently supplied by the town craftsmen. The last great subsistence crises in the middle of the 1840s, and the subsequent revolutionary activities placed renewed emphasis on the necessity of a modern industrial code. But many craftsmen were already protesting against the *idea* of *Gewerbefreiheit* and informed the National Assembly at Frankfurt on Main of their dismay.[30] On 27 July 1848 ten master craftsmen from Crimmitschau wrote to the Saxon government arguing that the introduction of *Gewerbefreiheit* would give the capitalists complete control over the workers, and would thereby ruin the country. The capitalist, they said, had no interest in training workers but rather only wanted to subjugate them.[31] The devastating results of this freedom could be seen in Prussia, where one could find extensive poverty, especially among the weavers. Consequently they were against the introduction of *Gewerbefreiheit* in Saxony or in Germany as a whole.

The political restoration of the early 1850s put an end to the discussion concerning *Gewerbefreiheit* in Saxony for many years. In the

28. Dresden Archive, Loc. 31 695, p. 1, Acta, 'Die in Vorschlag gekommene Aufhebung oder Modification des Innungszwangs so wie die neue Gewerbe-Ordnung betr., 1817–1828'.
29. See *Die Biene. Wöchentliche Mittheilungen für Sachsen und angrenzende Länder*, vol. I, 1827, no. 11, March 18, p. 84.
30. This movement has been described in great detail by Heinrich Best, *Interessenpolitik und nationale Integration 1848/49. Handelspolitische Konflikte im frühindustriellen Deutschland*, Göttingen, 1980 (*Kritische Studien zur Geschichtswissenschaft*, vol. 37).
31. Dresden Archive, Ministry of Interior, No. 1336 a, p. 170, Acta, 'Die Verbesserung der Lage der arbeitenden Klassen betr., 1847–49'.

ensuing period economic growth strengthened the political influence of industry as compared with that of the handicrafts. In 1856 the government submitted a draft law, but again the guilds protested rigorously.[32] The main argument was that, if a new industrial code was inevitable, it should not infringe upon the hereditary rights of the guilds, otherwise an economic catastrophe would follow. Meanwhile Austria had submitted a draft law, and introduced *Gewerbefreiheit* in December 1859. Now Saxony found herself between two large territories, Prussia and Austria, which both had comparative advantages in industrial production and better chances in the competition to sell their products on foreign markets. After lengthy debates the Saxon government decided to introduce *Gewerbefreiheit* by 1 January 1862.[33]

Germany's rapid economic growth after 1850 and the liberal influence on free trade by the Congress of German Economists[34] led to the introduction of *Gewerbefreiheit* in many other German states and cities after 1860.[35] Following the establishment of the German Empire the Industrial Code of 1869 was accepted by all German states. Delays in granting *Gewerbefreiheit* had little hindered regional industrialisation in Germany, and the granting of the freedom itself was by no means a precondition of her nation-building. It did away with many or nearly all of the outdated guild rights. Indirectly it accelerated the dynamics of industrialisation by reducing the barriers for factor mobility.

The founding and development of the German Zollverein has, alongside the nation-building itself or Bismarck's policy, traditionally attracted the historian's interest.[36] There can be no doubt that this

32. See Dresden Archive, Ministry of Interior, No. 1385 b, Acta, 'Den Entwurf zu einer neuen Gewerbeordnung betr., 1846–1856'; and No. 1385 c, Acta, 'Die neue Gewerbe-Ordnung betr., Entwurf von 1857, 1856–1859'.

33. See Albert Herzog zu Sachsen, *Die Reform der sächsischen Gewerbegesetzgebung*, pp. 900–1141.

34. See Volker Hentschel, *Die deutschen Freihändler und der volkswirtschaftliche Kongreß 1858 bis 1885*, Stuttgart, 1975 (*Industrielle Welt*, vol. 16).

35. These were as follows: Nassau, 1 July 1860; Bremen and Oldenburg, 4 April and 23 July 1861 respectively; Württemburg and Baden, 1 May and 15 October 1862 respectively; Saxe-Weimar-Eisenach, Saxe-Meiningen and the principality of Waldeck, 1 July 1863; Frankfurt on Main, 1 May, Brunswick, 3 August, and Schwarzburg-Rudolstadt, 1 October 1864; Schwarzburg-Sondershausen, 1 January 1866; Lübeck, 1 January 1867; and, finally, Bavaria, 1 May 1868.

36. In so wide a field it is difficult to select a short list of good books, but for an overview see C.F. Nebenius, *Der deutsche Zollverein, sein System und seine Zukunft* (1835), repr. Glashütten im Taunus, 1970; Wilhelm Oechelhaeuser, *Der Zollverein. Seine Verfassung, sein handelspolitisches System und die Entwicklung der Tarifsätze seit 1818*, Frankfurt on Main, 1851; Wilhelm Ditmar, *Der Deutsche Zollverein. Ein Handbuch für Zoll- und Steuerbeamte, Kaufleute und Gewerbetreibende*, 2 vols., Leipzig, 1867–8; Hermann von Festenberg-

German customs union was of the utmost importance for the economic, social and political *coherence* of the German states. With regard to its effect on Germany's nation-building the opinions are not so clear-cut. While Henderson, for example, states that the Zollverein 'helped to prepare the way for the subsequent political unification of Germany',[37] Fischer believes 'that the rise of the Zollverein had nothing to do with the subsequent national unification'.[38] Who is right? To answer this question I shall analyse some of the economic milestones in the nation-building process during the formation and growth of the Zollverein. I am not going to retell the well-known history of the German Zollverein but I will try to question the view that this customs union helped to pave the way for Germany's nation-building. My doubts are even greater concerning the proposition that it can be used as a model for the European Economic Community,[39] but this is quite another field of research.

The formation of larger German states at the beginning of the

Packisch, *Geschichte des Zollvereins mit besonderer Berücksichtigung der staatlichen Entwickelung Deutschlands*, Berlin, 1869; Wilhelm Weber, *Der deutsche Zollverein, Geschichte seiner Entstehung und Entwicklung* (1869), repr. Glashütten im Taunus, 1972; A. Adler, *Die Entwickelungsgeschichte des deutschen Zollvereins*, Leipzig, 1879; K. Sturmhoefel, *Der deutsche Zollverein. Ein geschichtlicher Rückblick*, Berlin, 1906; *Gedenkschrift zum hundertsten Jahrestag der Errichtung des Deutschen Zollvereins*, Berlin, 1934; William O. Henderson, *The Zollverein* (1939), 3rd edn., London, 1984; Arnold H. Price, *The Evolution of the Zollverein. A Study of the Ideas and Institutions Leading to German Economic Unification between 1815 and 1833* (1949), repr. New York, 1973; Rolf Horst Dumke, *The Political Economy of German Economic Unification: Tariffs, Trade and Politics of the Zollverein Era*, Ann Arbor and London, 1977; *Als die Schranken fielen. Der deutsche Zollverein. Ausstellung des Geheimen Staatsarchivs Preußischer Kulturbesitz zur 150. Wiederkehr der Gründung des deutschen Zollvereins 1834*, Berlin–Dahlem, 1984; Hans-Werner Hahn, *Geschichte des Deutschen Zollvereins*, Göttingen, 1984.

37. W.O. Henderson, *The Zollverein*, pp. XIII, XIX. Similarly, Eugen Franz, 'Ein Weg zum Reich. Die Entstehung des Deutschen Zollvereins', in *Vierteljahrschrift für Sozial- und Wirtschaftsgeschichte*, vol. 27, 1934, pp. 105–36.

38. Wolfram Fischer, 'Der Deutsche Zollverein nach 150 Jahren — Modell einer erfolgreichen wirtschaftspolitischen Integration?', *List Forum*, vol. 12, no. 6, Sept. 1984, p. 350 (my translation). Theodore S. Hamerow, *Restoration, Revolution, Reaction, Economics and Politics in Germany 1815–1871*, Princeton, N.J., 1958, p. 11, even states: 'While economic and political motives were thus intertwined in the negotiations leading to the Zollverein, their ultimate growth cannot be overstated'.

39. Jacob Viner, *The Customs Union Issue*, New York, 1950 (*Studies in the Administration of International Law and Organization*, no. 10), p. 97, writes: 'The German Zollverein was the pioneer and by far the most important customs union, and generalizations about the origin, nature, and consequences of unification of tariffs tend to be based mainly or wholly on the German experience'. See also Günter Schmölders, 'Der deutsche Zollverein als historisches Vorbild einer wirtschaftlichen Integration in Europa', in *Aspects financiers et fiscaux de l'intégration économique internationale*, La Haye, 1954, pp. 137–48; see also Adolf Weber, 'Der deutsche Zollverein als Präzedenzfall für die Bildung eines freien europäischen Marktes', in *Schmollers Jahrbuch für Gesetzgebung, Verwaltung und Volkswirtschaft*, vol. 78, 1958, II. Halbband, pp. 45–63; Wolfram Fischer, 'The German Zollverein. A Case Study in Customs Union', *Kyklos*, vol. XIII, 1960, pp. 65–89; Erich Kordt, 'L'integration d'états souverains au XIXe siècle: Le Zollverein. Leçons pour l'actualité',

nineteenth century necessitated the abolition of the former system of internal tariffs and the erection of a customs system controlled by the government. Bavaria introduced new tariffs in 1807, Württemberg in 1808, Westphalia in 1811, and Baden in 1812. But the political and economic situation changed after 1815. The Federal Constitution declared on 8 June 1815 in Article XIX that 'the Confederated States reserve to themselves the right of deliberating, at the first meeting of the Diet at Frankfurt, upon the manner of regulating the commerce and navigation from one State to another, according to the principles adopted by the Congress of Vienna',[40] but nothing happened. The German Confederation was paralysed by veto powers, by the multiplicity of monetary systems and commercial codes, and last but not least by huge disparities in regional industrialisation.[41]

When the Prussian government promulgated the new Tariff Law on 26 May 1818, it was soon confronted with severe criticism from many sides. In fact this tariff was the only solution to the huge economic and fiscal problems with which Prussia was confronted after the Napoleonic Era. The main aim of this law lay in a reduction of the fiscal and administrative burden of a kingdom of about 10 million inhabitants and an area of more than 100,000 square miles. The national debt amounted to 217 million Prussian thalers by 1818.[42] Moreover, Prussia had to integrate rather different parts of an incontiguous territory: the economically more advanced and Catholic western provinces Rhineland and Westphalia with the predominantly agricultural and Protestant East and West Prussia, Posen (Poznań), and Pomerania as well as the annexed former Saxon territory. Apart from Prussia's decision to treat the twenty-two enclaves like her own territory, the new tariffs

in *Chronique de Politique Etrangère*, vol. XIX, no. 2, 1966, pp. 185–202; Emmanuel N. Roussakis, *Friedrich List, the Zollverein, and the Uniting of Europe*, Brügge, 1968 (*Studies in contemporary European issues* 1); Ragnvald Christiansen, *Vom Deutschen Zollverein zur Europäischen Zollunion*, Bonn, 1978 (*Schriftenreihe des Bundesministeriums der Finanzen*, no. 26); Sidney Pollard, *The Integration of the European Economy since 1815*, London, 1981; W.O. Henderson, 'The Zollverein and the European Economic Community', in *The Zollverein*, pp. 345–69; Rolf H. Dumke, 'Der Deutsche Zollverein als Modell ökonomischer Integration', in H. Berding (ed.), *Wirtschaftliche und politische Integration in Europa im 19. und 20. Jahrhundert*, Göttingen, 1984, pp. 71–101.
   40. Quoted by W.O. Henderson, *The Zollverein*, p. 25. See I.I. Eichhoff, *Betrachtungen über den XIX. Artikel der Deutschen Bundesakte nebst Andeutungen, wie im Gefolge desselben dem Handelsverkehr zwischen den verschiedenen Bundesstaaten Erleichterung zu verschaffen*, Wiesbaden, 1820.
   41. See F.B. Tipton, *Regional Variations in the Economic Development of Germany*, pp. 17–38.
   42. In 1815, after the war had ended, the public debt was 287.5 million thalers. Austria even had 744 million guldens debt in the same year: see F. Lütge, *Deutsche Sozial- und Wirtschaftsgeschichte*, p. 315.

were designed to solve internal problems.

The other German governments as well as public opinion regarded the Prussian tariffs as detrimental to Germany's common economic interests, and as disregarding the legal tasks of the German Confederation which was politically dominated by Austria. In April 1819 a Commercial and Industrial Union was constituted to restore national trade and industry. Friedrich List, one of the leaders of the Union and a spokesman for national industry, wrote a petition to the Federal Diet and complained bitterly about the hundreds of internal customs barriers all over Germany, which should be removed by a tariff reform.[43] Alas, all his efforts resulted in failure, because he had no common sense with regard to political realities and was obsessed with his own ideas. The Diet declared on 24 May 1819 that it would refuse to take notice of the petition. While the Prussian system was at least in the beginning based on low duties, List propagated a protectionist system in order to develop a national economy which could compete with England's. Again German particularism was too strong to find a way out of this dilemma. The agrarian North and the Free Cities favoured free trade, others preferred low duties, and the small businesses of Germany's south and south-west mainly desired a protective system. The Austrian government was afraid of every movement outside the institutional Metternich system, whereby her industry feared competition from the industrialising German regions, especially the Rhineland and Saxony. By 1821 the Commercial and Industrial Union was a rather lack-lustre group of tradespeople and entrepreneurs, whose idea of a national customs union was gradually dying.

The decade after 1818 saw the establishment of three separate customs unions in Germany, an obvious sign that narrow-minded political particularism had triumphed over economic necessities. The economic demand for nation-building seemed to be out of sight, and the political dualism between Austria and Prussia blocked any advancement in the direction of unification. Two matters forced many German states to join the Prussian customs union in the early 1830s.[44]

43. See Friedrich List, *Schriften/Reden/Briefe*, vol. I, (eds.) K. Goeser and W. von Sonntag, Berlin, 1932, pp. 67–81; Fritze Borckenhagen, *National- und handelspolitische Bestrebungen in Deutschland (1815–1822) und die Anfänge Friedrich Lists*, Berlin and Leipzig, 1915; Hans-Peter Olshausen, *Friedrich List und der Deutsche Handels- und Gewerbsverein*, Jena, 1935; Hans Gehrig, *Friedrich List und Deutschlands politisch-ökonomische Einheit*, Leipzig, 1956; William O. Henderson, *Friedrich List*, London, 1983.

44. The best documentation of archive material for the period 1815–33 is still *Vorgeschichte und Begründung des Deutschen Zollvereins 1815–1834. Akten der Staaten des Deutschen Bundes und der europäischen Mächte*, 3 vols., (eds.) W. von Eisenhart Rothe and A. Ritthaler, Berlin, 1934.

Firstly, there were financial problems. The agricultural situation of the 1820s led to devastating income losses by the peasants, and the existing customs unions outside Prussia were too small and heterogeneous to work satisfactorily. Administrative costs accounted, on the average, for the expenditure of nearly 50 per cent of the customs revenue, and in Hesse-Darmstadt even 91 per cent. Moreover, the economic fundaments of many German states were too weak to produce positive trade balances. Secondly, there were the consequences of the revolution in 1830. Two of the states most reluctant to contemplate economic unification were deeply involved. In Saxony far-reaching constitutional, political and agrarian reforms had been introduced in 1831 and 1832.[45] Constitutions were also given in Hanover, Brunswick, and Hesse-Cassel. In Hesse-Cassel the exalted elector, William II, retired and his son started a radical departure from the old economic policy.[46] Nearly all members of the German Confederation, especially Austria and Prussia, feared an encroachment of revolutionary ideas upon Germany. They saw in the Hambach manifestation on 27 May 1832 the first signs of an overthrow of the neatly balanced political system. As a result the German Diet suppressed all freedom of the press and of assembly.

The founding of the Zollverein, whatever glorious phrases have been used to describe it,[47] was nothing more or less than an emergency measure at a time when grave economic and political problems had to be solved, in Germany as well as in Europe. And, of course, it was a convincing victory for the diplomatic skills of the Prussian bureaucracy. 'The States concerned', says Henderson in his still valuable work on the Zollverein, 'fought for their own narrow interests and many of them joined the Zollverein only when economic depression and empty exchequers made further resistance to Prussia impossible'.[48] When this German customs union took effect on 1 January 1834, it had

45. See Gerhard Schmidt, *Die Staatsreform in Sachsen in der ersten Hälfte des 19. Jahrhunderts. Eine Parallele zu den Steinschen Reformen in Preußen*, Weimar, 1966 (*Schriftenreihe des Staatsarchivs Dresden*, vol. 7).
46. See Hans-Werner Hahn, *Wirtschaftliche Integration im 19. Jahrhundert. Die hessischen Staaten und der Deutsche Zollverein*, Göttingen, 1982, pp. 97–108 (*Kritische Studien zur Geschichtswissenschaft*, vol. 52).
47. Especially Heinrich von Treitschke, *Deutsche Geschichte im Neunzehnten Jahrhundert* (1890), vol. IV, Leipzig, 1927, pp. 342–96.
48. W.O. Henderson, *The Zollverein*, p. 95. F. Lütge, *Deutsche Sozial- und Wirtschaftsgeschichte*, p. 352, believes that 'Prussia consciously saw the first step to political unity in this Zollverein' (my translation). A.J.P. Taylor, *The Course of German History. A Survey of the Development of Germany Since 1815*, new edn., London, 1951, p. 63 says: 'The Zollverein was an "ersatz", an economic substitute for national unification; as the danger grew greater, the Prussian rulers were driven to offer in the Bismarckian Reich a political "ersatz" as well'.

23.5 million inhabitants, and nearly all of the larger German states, with the exception of Austria, Hanover, Baden, Mecklenburg-Schwerin, Oldenburg, Nassau and Brunswick belonged to it. These twenty-one German states accounted for 53 per cent of the total area of the German Confederation including Austria and 77 per cent of its total area without Austria. Such a great domestic market of course stimulated economic development to a great extent, but it didn't have much effect on Germany's nation-building. The difficulties of bridging the gap between economic necessities and political interests can be easily demonstrated by looking at the example of the European Economic Community today.[49] The Zollverein's difficulties were even greater. Mentioning a few of them serves to show that the pressures to build a coherent trade area resulted more from external than from internal influences.[50]

The economic growth effects of the Zollverein in its first phase were rather modest, though the agricultural situation was much better than in the 1820s. Dumke has shown that the benefits of joining the Zollverein amounted in Bavaria, Württemberg and Baden to 1.06 per cent of their total income.[51] This is not at all an impressive figure. And German per capita exports were on the average 7 per cent lower between 1840 and 1850 than between 1834 and 1840.[52] The reason why the new Zollverein treaties in 1841 were not strongly opposed by any member lay in the steadily growing customs receipts of which over 60 per cent resulted from colonial goods. The customs receipts grew from 14,815,723 thalers in 1834 to 22,255,204 thalers in 1841, that is over 50 per cent,[53] while the administrative costs sank to nearly 10 per cent.

The revolutionary unrest in 1848–9 and the National Assembly at Frankfurt could not solve the German Question, and the Zollverein

49. See, for example, Hans Kasten, *Die europäische Wirtschaftsintegration. Grundlagen*, Munich, 1978; Dieter Menyesch and Henrik Uterwedde, *Europa im Vergleich. Daten zur Wirtschafts- und Sozialstruktur der EG-Länder*, Berlin, 1980; Hermann von Berg, *Die Analyse. Die Europäische Gemeinschaft — das Zukunftsmodell für Ost und West?*, Cologne, 1985.

50. For an overview see C. Tilly (ed.), *The Formation of National States in Western Europe* Princeton, N.J., 1975 (*Studies in Political Development*, vol. 8); Theodore Schieder, *Staatensystem als Vormacht der Welt 1848–1918*, Frankfurt, Berlin and Vienna, 1977 (*Propyläen Geschichte Europas*, vol. 5); Hugh Seton-Watson, *Nations and States. An Enquiry into the Origins of Nations and the Politics of Nationalism*, Boulder, Col., 1977; Lothar Gall, *Europa auf dem Weg in die Moderne 1850–1890*, Munich and Vienna, 1984 (*Oldenbourg Grundriß der Geschichte*, vol. 14).

51. Rolf H. Dumke, 'Die wirtschaftlichen Folgen des Zollvereins', in W. Abelshauser and D. Petzina (eds.), *Deutsche Wirtschaftsgeschichte im Industriezeitalter*, Königstein/ Ts., 1981, p. 260.

52. Calculated on the basis of Gerhard Bondi, *Deutschlands Außenhandel 1815–1870*, Berlin, 1958, p. 76.

53. See H.-W. Hahn, *Geschichte des Deutschen Zollvereins*, p. 98.

was virtually untouched by these quarrels.[54] The situation changed rapidly when in June 1850 all the Habsburg dominions were organised into a single customs area, and Bruck's concept of an Austro-German customs union was presented to the Zollverein General Congress at Cassel in July. Now Prussia felt that the Zollverein had not even established economic unity, because some of the German middle states supported the Austrian plan.[55] But these states could not agree on the appropriate political and economic strategy and discussions ended in complete deadlock. By 19 February 1853, Austro-Prussian negotiations ended with the signing of a commercial treaty which was to be effective for twelve years. Again Prussia triumphed over German particularism, and the Zollverein was extended for a further twelve years on 4 April 1853. Nevertheless unity could not be reached, instead the first Zollverein crisis made very clear that Prussia's economic hegemony was inadequate to settle the political disputes.

The industrial take-off in Germany since the early 1850s had two important economic consequences. On the one hand, it led to two decades of rapid economic growth, interrupted only slightly by the crises after 1857 and 1865. The production of hard coal, for example, rose from 5.5 million tons in 1850 to 26.5 million tons in 1870; the production of pig-iron from 214,600 tons in 1850 to 1,390,500 tons in 1870; and the production of the cotton industry — spinning and weaving — from 48,655 tons in 1850 to 138,362 tons in 1870.[56] At the same time the economic integration of the Zollverein made irreversible progress, as W. Zorn and others have so lucidly demonstrated.[57] The German free-traders, on the other hand, gained a lot of ground, thereby inadvertently strengthening Prussia's economic and political lead over Austria. In the first half of the 1860s Prussia signed commercial treaties with the most important industrial states in Europe: with France in 1862, with Britain and Belgium in 1865. Austria's economic position was, therefore, steadily becoming weaker, as compared to that of the

54. See Günter Wollstein, *Das "Großdeutschland" der Paulskirche. Nationale Ziele in der bürgerlichen Revolution 1848/49*, Düsseldorf, 1977; D. Langewiesche (ed.), *Die deutsche Revolution von 1848/49*, Darmstadt, 1983 (*Wege der Forschung*, vol. 164).
55. Thomas F. Huertas, *Economic Growth and Economic Policy in a Multinational Setting. The Habsburg Monarchy, 1841–1865*, New York, 1977.
56. See Wolfram Fischer, Jochen Krengel and Jutta Wietog, *Sozialgeschichtliches Arbeitsbuch*, vol. I: *Materialien zur Statistik des Deutschen Bundes 1815–1870*, Munich, 1982, pp. 44–103.
57. Though the quantitative material is not very good, Wolfgang Zorn enabled us to see the interrelations much clearer. See his essays, 'Wirtschafts- und sozialgeschichtliche Zusammenhänge der deutschen Reichsgründungszeit (1850–1879)', *Historische Zeitschrift*, vol. 197, 1963, pp. 318–42, last repr. in H. Böhme (ed.), *Probleme der Reichsgründungszeit 1848–1879*, Cologne and Vienna, 1968, pp. 296–316; 'Wirtschaft und

Zollverein. Her defeat on the Italian battlegrounds in 1859 resulted in a financial and political crisis, and the beginning of a free-trade movement in Western Europe left Austria in an even worse position. To avoid economic isolation within the German Confederation, and perhaps a military confrontation with Prussia, she was unable to offer an economically satisfactory solution to the other German states.

The economic capitulation of the South German states to Prussia when the renewal of the Zollverein's treaty was at stake did not, as one might believe, favour the Prussian desire for political unification under her leadership. Only two months earlier, on 11 April 1865, the Zollverein and Austria had signed a commercial treaty which meant, regarding the political circumstances, that the idea of an Austro-German customs union had met its demise. Despite the free-traders' arguments that commercial and economic integration must render military activity impossible, Austro-Prussian dualism led to a civil war in June 1866. Hanover, Saxony, Bavaria, Württemberg, and the Hesse states fought with Austria against Prussia, without success. Prussia, after a triumphal victory in the Seven Weeks War annexed Hanover, Hesse-Cassel, Nassau, Schleswig-Holstein and Frankfurt on Main, binding these states together through the establishment of the North German Confederation. Immediately it was clear that the Zollverein was unable to unite the German nation, however one defines it, politically. Some months earlier, on 5 April 1866, Franz Ziegler wrote to Karl Rodbertus: 'People want to trade, earn, enjoy, and get along; they want not a state but a trading company'.[58]

The period between 1867 and 1870 could not solve the national problem by economic means either, but German–French rivalries united North and South Germany. Prussia's politics and her military and economic strength paved the way for a German Empire. There was no 'identity of economic interests between South and North

---

Gesellschaft in Deutschland in der Zeit der Reichsgründung', in T. Schieder and E. Deuerlein (eds.), *Reichsgründung 1870/71. Tatsachen, Kontroversen, Interpretation*, Stuttgart, 1970, pp. 197–225; 'Die wirtschaftliche Integration Kleindeutschlands in den 1860er Jahren und die Reichsgründung', *Historische Zeitschrift*, vol. 216, 1973, pp. 304–34; 'Zwischenstaatliche wirtschaftliche Integration im Deutschen Zollverein 1867–1870. Ein quantitativer Versuch', *Vierteljahrschrift für Sozial- und Wirtschaftsgeschichte*, vol. 65, 1978, pp. 38–76. Also Michael Kerwat, *Die wechselseitige wirtschaftliche Abhängigkeit der Staaten des nachmaligen Deutschen Reiches im Jahrzehnt vor der Reichsgründung*, Ph.D., Munich, 1977; Klaus Megerle, 'Okonomische Integration und politische Orientierung deutscher Mittle- und Kleinstaaten im Vorfeld der Reichsgründung', in *Wirtschaftliche und politische Integration in Europa*, pp. 102–27.
58. Quoted in Theodore S. Hamerow, *The Social Foundations of German Unification 1858–1871. Ideas and Institutions*, Princeton, N.J., 1969, p. 43.

Germany',[59] as Böhme assumes. It was not economic policy but economic pressures which were making for the economic unification of the country. The economic entanglements of the Zollverein did not lead to nation-building but did prevent a relapse into the former particularism which had for such a long time made any hopes for progress illusory. It is not correct to say, as Marxist scholars do, that Germany's nation-building was an economic and political necessity.[60] Rather, economic unity could be established without political unity.[61] The political unification of Germany ended the history of the original Zollverein by building a customs union of its own kind. The following decades were economically overshadowed by the 'Great Depression',[62] but when Hamburg and Bremen joined the new Zollverein in 1881 and 1884 respectively one great economic system was established which led to Germany's leading economic position in Europe.

German railway development coincided with the foundation of the Zollverein.[63] Again it was List who suggested a German railway system, based on the main trade routes of the eighteenth and early nineteenth centuries.[64] But railway construction was opposed by many critics.[65] They feared amongst other things that the sanitary effects would be disastrous or that commerce on the roads would be ruined.

59. Helmut Böhme, *Deutschlands Weg zur Großmacht. Studien zum Verhältnis von Wirtschaft und Staat während der Reichsgründungszeit 1848–1881*, Cologne and Berlin, 1966, p. 249–50 (my translation); and R.H. Dumke, *The Political Economy*, p. 328, even states: 'The identity of economic interests in the Zollverein states, then, proved to be the basic force which broke the bonds of German "particularism"'. Theodore S. Hamerow, *The Social Foundations of German Unification 1858–1871. Struggles and Accomplishments*, Princeton, N.J., 1972, p. 426, says: 'National unification was the achievement of a determined, influential, prosperous, intelligent, and indefatigable minority'.

60. Ernst Engelberg, *Deutschland von 1849 bis 1871. (Von der Niederlage der bürgerlich-demokratischen Revolution bis zur Reichsgründung)*, 2nd edn., Berlin, 1965, pp. 69–74; Heinz Wolter, 'Bismarck und die preußisch-deutsche "Revolution von oben"', in *Preußen. Legende und Wirklichkeit*, 3rd edn., Berlin, 1985, p. 158.

61. The reverse has been claimed by Wolfgang Sauer, 'Das Problem des deutschen Nationalstaates', in H.-U. Wehler (ed.), *Moderne deutsche Sozialgeschichte*, Cologne and Berlin, 1966, p. 420.

62. See Hans Rosenberg, *Große Depression und Bismarckzeit. Wirtschaftsablauf, Gesellschaft und Politik in Mitteleuropa*, Frankfurt on Main, Berlin and Vienna, 1976; S.B. Saul, *The Myth of the Great Depression, 1873–1896*, London, 1969.

63. The last publication on the occasion of the 150th anniversary of the first German railway line is *Zug der Zeit — Zeit der Züge. Deutsche Eisenbahn 1835–1985*, 2 vols., Berlin, 1985.

64. Friedrich List, 'Über ein sächsisches Eisenbahnsystem als Grundlage eines allgemeinen deutschen Eisenbahnsystems und insbesondere über die Anlegung einer Eisenbahn von Leipzig nach Dresden' (1833), in *Schriften/Reden/Briefe*, vol. III, part 1, Berlin, 1929, pp. 155–95.

65. See, for example, Rolf Peter Sieferle, *Fortschrittsfeinde? Opposition gegen Technik und Industrie von der Romantik bis zur Gegenwart*, Munich, 1984, pp. 87–117.

Before planning the construction of the first German railway line between Nuremberg and Fürth, which was only about four miles long, the number of the passengers on the post-chaises was counted.[66] The line was opened on 7 December 1835 more than ten years after the first railway between Stockton and Darlington. Soon other lines followed, like the Berlin–Potsdam railway in 1838, the Brunswick–Wolfenbüttel line in the same year. The first long-distance railway, the seventy-mile-long line from Leipzig to Dresden, was completed and opened on the 7 April 1839.[67] By the end of 1845 there were 2,143 kilometres of line open in Germany.

What was the effect of railway construction on Germany's nation-building? Johann Wolfgang von Goethe and Wilhelm Raabe, the German poets, were quite optimistic. They hoped and wished that the railways would unite Germany.[68] Others did not. They thought that 'political particularism was a severe hindrance to emerging railway construction'.[69] And indeed, German particularism led to a rather peculiar railway system. Different German states had different ideas as to whether the lines should be built by private companies or by the State, e.g. railway ownership varied from state to state.[70] The Prussian government did not, in the beginning, support railway construction for two reasons. First of all, the State had financed over 482 miles of public roads between 1816 and 1831 and feared a loss of revenue and of invested capital.[71] Secondly, in 1820 a law of national debt reduced the ceiling on the public debt. Not before the early 1840s, did state ownership of the railways in Germany multiply, partly because the lines proved to be a great financial success, partly because the private

66. See Edwin Kech, *Geschichte der deutschen Eisenbahnpolitik*, Leipzig, 1911, p. 35.
67. See *Die Leipzig–Dresdner Eisenbahn in den ersten fünfundzwanzig Jahren ihres Bestehens. Denkschrift zur Feier des 8. April 1864*, Leipzig, 1864; Udo Becher, *Die Leipzig–Dresdner Eisenbahn-Compagnie*, Berlin, 1981.
68. See the quotations in W.O. Henderson, *The Zollverein*, p. 147. And Jakob Vennedey said in 1835: 'In a completely different way and a much more perceptible fashion than is so often boasted of the Zollverein, the railroads will bring down all the internal borders in Germany. Ten years after all the large and capital cities are linked together by the railroad, Germany will be a completely different country, and the prejudices which have so splintered the German people up to now, which have so facilitated the rule of its oppressors, will have ceased to exist'. Quoted in R.M. Berdahl, *New Thoughts on German Nationalism*, p. 79.
69. A. Sartorius von Waltershausen, *Deutsche Wirtschaftsgeschichte*, p. 98 (my translation).
70. See Edwin Kech, *Geschichte der deutschen Eisenbahnpolitik*, Leipzig, 1911; Hans-Herbert Wilhelmi, 'Staat und Eisenbahnen. Die Entwicklung der Eisenbahnverfassung in Deutschland', *Archiv für Eisenbahnwesen*, 73, 1963, pp. 377–459; Hellmuth St. Seidenfus, 'Eisenbahnwesen', in *Deutsche Verwaltungsgeschichte*, vol. 2, Stuttgart, 1983, pp. 227–57.
71. See Paul Thimme, *Straßenbau und Straßenbaupolitik in Deutschland zur Zeit der Gründung des Zollvereins 1825–1835*, Stuttgart, 1931.

companies could not raise the investment capital. In 1847 Prussia decided to build the first State railway from Berlin to East Prussia. In Saxony the situation was similar. Not before the private companies had financial difficulties completing the lines did the State intervene. The southern German states Bavaria, Württemberg and Baden had contradictory territorial and commercial interests, therefore they could not find a common procedure. While Bavaria left the building of railways to private companies until 1844, Württemberg, Oldenburg and Baden had state railways from the beginning. The Baden government was in fact so short-sighted that it built a special gauge track, and had to rebuild the whole system after a few years using standard gauge track.[72] The King of Hanover is claimed to have said: 'I don't want railways in my country, I don't want every shoemaker and tailor travelling as fast as I do'.[73] Nearly every German state had a different opinion on how railways should be built, and one might suppose that this reduced the possibility of, or even prevented, the building of a suitable network. Up until 1850 this was indeed the case.

Two developments changed the situation rapidly. On the one hand many German states feared the diversion of trade routes and a resulting loss of income if the neighbouring state had a better railway system. This led to growing competition to build more railways linking one state to another. The combination of private and state railways on the other hand, made it possible to build and maintain less profitable routes which were needed for industrial or agricultural purposes. Regional competition or, if you like, the catching up of the industrialising regions, can be clearly seen when one compares the growth of railways between 1850 and 1871. While the railway lines grew during this period in Saxony by 146 per cent, and in Prussia by 254 per cent, the percentage for Württemberg was 311 per cent, for Bavaria 397 per cent, for the Rhineland 420 per cent, and for Hesse-Darmstadt an amazing 508 per cent.[74] Not only were communications improved, but the agricultural regions could supply the industrial regions with food more easily, while the industrial regions experienced a greater demand from agriculture. We can say that the competition and the imitative effects between the individual German states as well as the necessity of a railway network gave strong impulses to German unification. By

72. See Karl Müller, *Die badischen Eisenbahnen in historisch-statistischer Darstellung. Ein Beitrag zur Geschichte des Eisenbahnwesens*, Heidelberg, 1904.
73. Quoted by Kurt Martin, *Die Deutsche Lokomotivenbauindustrie*, Ph.D., Münster, 1913, p. 17, note 6 (my translation).
74. Calculated on the basis of G. Stürmer, *Geschichte der Eisenbahnen. Entwickelung und jetzige Gestaltung sämmtlicher Eisenbahnnetze der Erde*, Bromberg, 1872, pp. 54–61.

1871 Germany had after Belgium, Great Britain and the Netherlands the densest railway network per square kilometre in the world.

The economic effects of the German railway system and its forward and backward linkages to different industrial branches are well known.[75] We are not so well informed about the effects of the regional distribution of engine and carriage producing enterprises, etc. Between 1851 and 1871 the stock of engines in Germany rose from 681 to 5,701, e.g. 5.5 times. In the same time period the percentage of foreign engines fell from 37.1 per cent to 3.8 per cent.[76] This import substitution was made possible by a regional locomotive industry which was a result of German particularism. Nearly all of the larger German states tried to build up their own works. For example, Borsig, Wöhlert and Schwartz-kopff in Berlin (Prussia), Henschel & Sohn in Cassel (Hesse-Cassel), Hartmann in Chemnitz (Saxony), Maffei in Hirschau near Munich and Krauss in Munich (Bavaria), Egestorff in Linden near Hanover (Hanover), Kessler in Karlsruhe (Baden), or the engine works in Esslingen (Württemberg).

In my view, the economic interdependencies resulting out of this development were more effective in promoting political unity than any other economic or fiscal measure.[77] As soon as a better railway system reduced transport costs, etc. Germany became more and more independent of political pressure from outside. And the claims of sovereignty which had so many negative results on the Zollverein's attempts at nation-building did not matter much when coal, iron or grain were transported. Though the railways were thought to have separated the German states in the beginning, they unwittingly united the German nation in the end. In 1850 the German railways transported 782.7 million persons, in 1870 4,446.8 million. The total of kilometre tons (i.e. kilometres driven × tons carried) rose during the same period from 302.7 to 5,875.9 million tons.[78] 'It was symptomatic of an early stage of industrialism that before 1871 the most important area of investment was not in production but transportation'.[79]

75. See Rainer Fremdling, 'Germany', in P. O'Brien (ed.), *Railways and the Economic Development of Western Europe, 1830–1914*, London, 1983, pp. 121–47.
76. Calculated on the basis of *Deutsche Eisenbahnstatistik für das Betriebs-Jahr 1851 and 1871*, Stettin, 1853, and Berlin, 1873.
77. See also W. Zorn, 'Wirtschaft und Gesellschaft in Deutschland', p. 202.
78. Rainer Fremdling, *Eisenbahnen und deutsches Wirtschaftswachstum 1840–1879. Ein Beitrag zur Entwicklungstheorie und zur Theorie der Infrastruktur*, 1975, 2nd edn., Dortmund, 1985, p. 17 (*Untersuchungen zur Wirtschafts-, Sozial- und Technikgeschichte*, vol. 2).
79. T. S. Hamerow, *The Social Foundations of German Unification*, vol. I, p. 24.

Without having time to present extensive research into the economic basis of Germany's nation-building, let me just summarise the most important features of this process. The economic consequences of industrialisation were manifold, and we are unable to attribute the corresponding political effect to every economic development. The rapid growth of the population, the expansion of communication systems and economic infrastructures, the exploitation of mineral resources, the availability of sufficient industrial capital, the mass of technological innovations, the shift of employment from agriculture to industry, etc., within a rather short period gave the states much greater material and military power than had existed in the past. In Germany only one state had the political vigour and economic strength to impose her ideas upon the whole nation: Prussia. I agree with Pflanze that 'Bismarck helped to make the war of 1870 a popular national crusade in Germany'.[80] But stating this I do not claim that Germany's nation-building was a historical inevitability, either on political or on economic grounds.[81] Human beings as well as governments or institutions always have alternatives at their disposal, although they often do not have the ability to foresee the future or to decide according to their own principles. What we have to ask in the end is whether the economic preconditions developed an *internal logic* so that all the other German states, with the exception of Austria, felt compelled to accept the Prussian solution to the national question. I think this is true.

In 1815 the territory which was later called Germany lagged economically far behind England and even France.[82] Silesia, the Kingdom of Saxony and the Rhineland showed only few signs of economic growth and these mainly in mining and in the textile industry. Within five decades the picture changed. Though the United Kingdom still produced over four times more hard coal than Germany in 1870, Germany outranked France by 2:1.[83] At the same time the output of iron ore was comparable in France and Germany, while the United Kingdom produced over five times more. In 1873 the production of pig-iron (in thousands of metric tons) was 6,566 in the United King-

80. Otto Pflanze, *Bismarck and the Development of Germany. The Period of Unification, 1815–1871*, Princeton, N.J., 1963, p. 474.
81. See, for example, Nicholas M. Hope, *The Alternative to German Unification. The Anti-Prussian Party, Frankfurt, Nassau and the two Hessen 1859–1867*, Wiesbaden, 1973.
82. William O. Henderson, *The Industrial Revolution on the Continent. Germany, France, Russia 1800–1914*, London, 1961; David S. Landes, *The Unbound Prometheus. Technological Change and Industrial Development in Western Europe from 1750 to the Present*, Cambridge, 1969.
83. B. R. Mitchell, *European Historical Statistics 1750–1970*, London and Basingstoke, 1978, pp. 186–8. United Kingdom 112,203,000 metric tons, Germany 26,398,600, France, 13,330,000 tons.

Table 2. Levels of industrialisation of German states and regions in 1871

State/Region	Area in km^2 (1)	Percentage of Persons Employed[1] (2)	Density of Population[2] (3)	Order Column (2) (4)	Order Column (3) (5)
Saxony[3]	14,992.9	49.5	170.5	1	1
Rhineland[4]	27,000.2	41.1	132.6	2	2
Westphalia[4]	20,219.6	40.2	87.8	3	10
Württemberg[3]	19,507.3	39.8	93.2	4	7
Baden[5]	15,070.3	38.7	97.0	5	6
Saxony[4]	25,267.3	35.2	83.2	6	11
Brandenburg[4]	39,842.3	35.1	71.9	7	14
Hesse[5]	7,688.4	33.2	110.9	8	3
Silesia[4]	40,335.1	32.4	91.9	9	8
Hesse-Nassau[4]	15,708.0	32.1	89.2	10	9
Oberfranken[6]	7,001.6	31.4	77.3	11	12
Mittelfranken[6]	7,559.6	30.8	77.2	12	13
Palatinate[6]	5,939.2	29.7	103.6	13	5
Oldenburg[5]	6,429.1	29.0	49.0	14	24
Schwaben[6]	9,496.4	28.4	61.4	15	16
Schleswig-Holstein[4]	19,018.8	26.4	52.4	16	19
Alsace-Lorraine[7]	14,521.8	26.3	106.7	17	4
Hanover[4]	38,509.4	25.4	50.9	18	21
Oberbayern[6]	17,052.6	24.4	49.4	19	23
Oberpfalz[6]	9,668.2	23.2	51.5	20	20
Pomerania[4]	30,131.4	21.5	47.5	21	25
Unterfranken[6]	8,401.4	21.8	69.8	22	15
Niederbayern[6]	10,771.4	19.2	56.1	23	17
Mecklenburg-Schwerin[5]	13,126.9	18.8	42.5	24	26
Prussia[4]	62,556.7[8]	17.6	50.2	25	22
Posen[4]	28,991.5	17.5	54.6	26	18
Bremen	263.2	42.3	466.1	—	—
Hamburg	351.8	39.7	963.5	—	—
Lübeck	364.5	32.0	143.1	—	—

Sources: Statistik des Deutschen Reichs, vol. XIV/II, 1876, pp. vi, 132–56; and
Statistik des Deutschen Reichs, vol. II, 1874, pp. 153–65.

1. Mining and metallurgy, industry and building.
2. Inhabitants per square kilometre (I/km^2).
3. Kingdom.
4. Prussian province.
5. Grand Duchy.
6. Bavarian administrative district.
7. Reichsland.
8. East Prussia with 37,002.0 km^2 and 49.3 I/km^2, and West Prussia with 27,554.7 km^2 and 47.7 I/km^2.

dom, 2,241 in Germany and 1,382 in France.[84] A comparison of the length of the railway lines shows that after the annexation of Alsace-Lorraine in 1871 the United Kingdom had only 87 kilometres more than Germany (21,558 to 21,471), and France had only 15,632 kilometres at that time. By 1913 the ratios were 63,378 (Germany), to 40,770 (France), to 32,623 kilometres (United Kingdom).[85] How can we explain this rapid growth in Germany?

If one looks at Table 2 where twenty-six German states and regions are compared one gets some idea. The regional competition between the larger German states was of major importance for the industrialisation of Germany. The levels of industrialisation, measured by the percentage of persons employed in industry and the density of the population per square kilometre, indicate that there was a mixture of rather highly industrialised and purely agricultural German regions even within one state, for example Prussia. We can, therefore, distinguish three types of industrialisation, with greater or lesser variations' in nineteenth-century Germany.[86] This 'division of labour' of course influenced nation-building. By 1871 it was already so highly developed that in the following period, that is until 1914, German industry mainly had to concentrate mainly on technological improvements and increases in production. To be precise, regional industrialisation and economic disparities did not inevitably force Germany's nation-building, but they rendered any other alternative a costly adventure. In this respect regional industrialisation reduced the political opposition of particularism to Germany's nation-building in an age when nation-states seemed to be the only political solution to the problem of national self-determination, as we have experienced again so widely after the Second World War.[87]

---

84. D. S. Landes, *The Unbound Prometheus*, p. 194, Table 4.
85. B. R. Mitchell, *European Historical Statistics*, pp. 317–18.
86. For a detailed discussion see Hubert Kiesewetter, 'Regionale Industrialisierung in Deutschland zur Zeit der Reichsgründung. Ein vergleichend-quantitativer Versuch', in *Vierteljahrschrift für Sozial- und Wirtschaftsgeschichte*, vol. 73, 1986 pp. 38–60.
87. See, for example, Gavin Kitching, *Development and Underdevelopment in Historical Perspective. Populism, Nationalism and Industrialization*, London and New York, 1982; M. Bienefeld and M. Godfrey (eds.), *The Struggle for Development. National Strategies in an International Context*, Chichester et al., 1982.

HARM-HINRICH BRANDT

The Revolution of 1848 and the Problem of Central European Nationalities

To gain a vantage-point for evaluating the problems of nationalities and nation-building in Central Europe, let me begin with some theoretical and general remarks. Constitutional questions should be discussed within the concepts of modernisation, participation and integration. In the most general way Talcott Parsons and his followers developed the theoretical concept of integration;[1] concerning the special aspects of political integration and state-building I refer to Rudolf Smend's Integration Theory.[2] The German jurist Smend has elaborated stages of integration; he differentiates especially between personal and functional integration and considers functional integration to be the higher level.[3] In European history this process can be studied in monarchical state-building, which is reinforced by parliamentary 'games' of consent and conflict. The stabilising effects of these parliamentary 'games' presuppose sufficient homogeneity and communication among the ruling classes represented, so that the rules of parliamentary voting, with its possibility of defeat, will be tolerated and a sense of solidarity

1. T. Parsons, *The Social System*, New York and London, 1951; N. Luhmann, *The Differentiation of Society*, New York, 1982; by the same author: *Soziale Systeme. Grundriß einer allgemeinen Theorie*, Frankfurt, 1984.
2. R. Smend, *Verfassung und Verfassungsrecht*, Munich, 1928; cf. also the article 'Integrationslehre' in *Handwörterbuch der Sozialwissenschaften*, Stuttgart, Tübingen and Göttingen, 1956, vol. 5, by the same author, including review of critics.
3. The concept of 'functional integration' includes all forms of group action with integrative tendency up until the higher levels of decision-making by voting, acceptance of majority–minority rules, elections, representation.

within the country (the 'commonwealth') can develop. Otherwise there will be obstruction, segregation, separation and partition.

In pre-modern Europe these questions of political integration concerned only the nobility, the (noble) clergy and the urban patriciate. Taking a long-term view we can describe European social and cultural history as a process of increasing mobilisation, expanding literacy and the growing participation of all classes of the population, first as the result of religious movements, and then through 'enlightenment', which in turn was supported by transition from self-sufficient to exchange economies.[4] When these processes encouraged enlarging political participation, the question of political integration on the basis of sufficient homogeneity and communication arose at a new level. Western Europe produced the models of both the revolutionary and the evolutionary political integration of the nation, and, at the same time, it produced an appropriate theory.

The doctrine of the social contract referred in principle to the whole population of a given commonwealth; in further consequence it generated a concept of nation, on the basis of which nation-building could be defined as the result of the state population consenting actively or tacitly to a certain political order. The implicit prerequisite of this concept of nation was that communication was sufficient to produce that degree of homogeneity necessary for a successful process of political integration. Pre-eminently this is always a question of a common language (originally given or successfully introduced by cultural assimilation).[5] In the Western European states the establishment of a common language — at least for most of the country — had already been achieved when the extension of political participation was on the agenda; minority problems were of secondary importance only.

At the beginning of the nineteenth century this concept of a nation-state could hardly be transferred to Central and Eastern Europe because:

(1) dynastic state formation had diverged from ethnic foundations;

(2) monarchic absolutism had interrupted the beginnings of parliamentary integration either by depriving the estates of their power or

4. For the concept of modernisation cf. W. Zapf (ed.), *Theorien des sozialen Wandels*, Cologne and Berlin, 1969; especially K. W. Deutsch, 'Soziale Mobilisierung und politische Entwicklung', ibid., pp. 329–50 (first published in *Politische Vierteljahresschrift*, 2, 1961, also in English in *American Political Science Review*, 55, 1961, pp. 493–514).

5. The connections between communication processes and nation-building have been elaborated in particular by K. W. Deutsch, *Nationalism and Social Communication: An inquiry into the foundations of nationality*, New York and London, 1953. Cf. also K. W. Deutsch and W. J. Foltz (eds.), *Nation-Building*, New York, 1966; K. W. Deutsch, *Nationenbildung. Nationalstaat, Integration*, Düsseldorf, 1972.

by preventing the formation of *états généraux* in composite realms;

(3) absolutism had successfully established military and bureaucratic institutions to provide for peace, justice and welfare without the consent of the subjects;

(4) especially in Eastern and in East Central Europe there were no clear-cut ethnic and language units for several reasons: settlement was dispersed, social integration of the rural societies was low, because a backward self-contained economy prevailed; therefore the assimilatory power of leading languages was insufficient; and the low degree of political integration remained on the monarchical stage mentioned above.

The problems of political nation and nation-state are different in Central and Eastern Europe, but both spheres overlap; and this overlapping is very important to understand the entire complex.

In Germany, as in Italy, one ethnic nation was divided into a plurality of dynastic states as a result of late-medieval history. In the east we have three great realms covering a plurality of ethnic nations, namely Russia, the old and weak Ottoman Empire, and the Habsburg Empire; additionally there is a fourth state, Prussia, which is predominantly German, but which, by the inheritance of the Teutonic Knights and by the partitions of Poland, belongs to those multinational realms. So the most important German states included both, German and non-German territories.[6]

Interacting with these different structures of state-building and society, the modern processes of mobilisation, education and participation generated some different results by comparison with Western Europe. Inevitably the discrepancies between State and society or State and nation manifested themselves and became the key experience of all educated classes. In Germany, due to the situation of the country, a differentiation was made between what was called a political nation *(Staatsnation)* and what was called a cultural nation, and since the concept of the cultural nation was derived from original ethnic unity, it was considered to be the real nation.[7] Following the Romantic doctrine, nation-building was not the result of integration, much less of

6. Differentiation between the Western, Central and Eastern European type by T. Schieder, 'Typologie und Erscheinungsformen des Nationalstaates in Europa', *Historische Zeitschrift*, 202, 1966, pp. 58–81; T. Schieder, 'Der Nationalstaat in Europa als historisches Phänomen', in *Arbeitsgemeinschaft für Forschung des Landes Nordrhein-Westfalen, Geisteswissenschaften 19*, 1964, pp. 13–29.
7. E. Lemberg, *Nationalismus*, 2 vols., Hamburg, 1964; vol. 1, pp. 86–113, 129; short analysis also by M. Rainer Lepsius, 'Nation und Nationalismus in Deutschland', in H. A. Winkler (ed.), *Nationalismus in der Welt von heute*, Göttingen, 1982.

acts of volition or political processes, but it was the development of a
given nucleus or substance which was seen as an objective attribute of
every individual member.[8]

The history of the German national movement is well known and
need not be repeated here. Just a few catchwords: The feeling that the
ethno-cultural nation should rightfully claim political unification was
generated by the experience of Napoleonic occupation and patriotic
liberation and heightened by the memory of medieval political greatness.[9] As a matter of fact, the results of Napoleonic and post-
Napoleonic state-building meant consolidation, partial modernisation
and even semi-constitutional integration not of the nation, but of the
dynastic German states; these single states being allied only in the
German Confederation for the purpose of mutual defence.[10] Disappointment at these meager results of the great victory was localised
mainly in the national institution of the German universities; at first
the movement towards national unity was a matter of excitable students and professors, more Protestant than Catholic. It expanded to
become a credo of the German educated upper-middle classes, reinforced all the time by the beginnings of economic integration.[11] Their
political ideas can be described as an amalgam of western-modelled
liberal-constitutional goals and nationalism. By 1848 they split into a
broad moderate stream and a small radical or republican movement.[12]
There were similiar contemporary phenomena in Italy[13] and, on a

8. The Romantic concept of nation and its effects in Central and Eastern Europe are
sketched in E. Lemberg, *Nationalismus*, vol. 1, pp. 165–85.
9. Most significant: F. Meinecke, *Weltbürgertum und Nationalstaat*, Munich, 1962;
F. Valjavec, *Die Entstehung der politischen Strömungen in Deutschland 1770–1815*, Munich,
1951; W. Conze, 'Nation und Gesellschaft. Zwei Grundbergriffe der revolutionären
Epoche', *Historische Zeitschrift*, 198, 1964, pp. 1–16; R. Aris, *History of Political Thought in
Germany from 1789 to 1815*, 2nd edn., London, 1965.
10. Recent publications on modernisation and integration within the states of the
Rhenish Federation and Prussia: E. Weis (ed.), *Reformen im rheinbündischen Deutschland*,
Munich, 1984; B. Vogel (ed.), *Preußische Reformen 1807–1820*, Königstein, 1980. Concerning the constitutional system of the German Confederation see E. R. Huber, *Deutsche
Verfassungsgeschichte seit 1789*, vol. 1, 2nd edn., Stuttgart, 1975.
11. Short survey with references: W. Zorn, 'Sozialgeschichtliche Probleme der nationalen Bewegung in Deutschland', in T. Schieder (ed.), *Sozialstruktur und Organisation
europäischer Nationalbewegungen*, Munich and Vienna, 1971, p. 97–119; O. Dann, 'Nationalismus und sozialer Wandel in Deutschland 1806–1850', in idem. (ed.), *Nationalismus und
Sozialer Wandel*, Hamburg, 1978, pp. 77–128.
12. J. J. Sheehan, *German Liberalism in the Nineteenth Century*, Chicago and London,
1978; more specific by the same author, 'Liberalism and Society in Germany
1815–1848', *JMH*, 45, 1973, pp. 583–604; good survey over constitutional and national
goals of the different liberal and radical groups, in E. R. Huber, *Deutsche Verfassungsgeschichte seit 1789*, vol. 2, chapter 6.
13. H. Ullrich, 'Bürgertum und nationale Bewegung im Italien des Risorgimento', in
O. Dann (ed.), *Nationalismus und sozialer Wandel*, Hamburg, 1978, pp. 129–56.

different social basis, in Greece, Poland and Hungary.[14]

Something more needs to be said concerning the Habsburg realm, since it was the most prominent example of an East European multi-national empire, which was none the less deeply involved in the German world. Its complexity is caused by the fact that it was composed of both a plurality of historical states or countries and a plurality of ethnic nationalities, and that both factors overlapped only partially.[15] The major units were the so-called *Deutsche Erbländer* (German hereditary countries — roughly the present Republic of Austria and the southern Alpine parts, since lost); St Wencislaus's crown-lands (Bohemia, Moravia, Silesia); St Stephen's crown-lands (Hungary, Transylvania, Croatia, Slavonia, Dalmatia); the Polish possessions (Galicia); and the Italian crown-lands (Lombardy–Venetia). All these different countries were multinational in themselves, and the nationalities were very often arranged in a social stratification of dominance and subordination as a result of former conquest.[16] Thus the Polish nobility dominated Ruthenian peasantry in eastern Galicia, and a similar correlation existed between German or Germanised nobility and Czech or Slovenian peasantry, Hungarian nobility and Slovakian, Serbian or Romanian peasantry. Peasants' liberation had been postponed since the failure of Josephinian reforms.[17] Only the Germans, the Italians and, to a certain degree, the Czechs had developed urban middle classes; in the east, towns and boroughs were often dominated by German bourgeoisie; the same was true for Italian urbanisation in the Adriatic. Systematic colonisation by the Habsburgs had created German peasant settlements of considerable extent in the Hungarian south.

In history and sociology these stratifications have generated the distinction between so-called historical or political and so-called non-historical nationalities.[18] In this sense historical nations had possessed

14. K. G. Hausmann, 'Adelsgesellschaft und nationale Bewegung in Polen', in O. Dann (ed.), *Nationalismus*, pp. 23–47; N. P. Diamandouros et al. (eds.), *Hellenism and the First Greek War of Liberation (1821–1830): Continuity and Change*, Thessaloniki, 1976; for Hungary cf. note 25 below.

15. R. A. Kann, *Das Nationalitätenproblem der Habsburgermonarchie*, 2 vols., 2nd edn., Graz and Cologne, 1964, revised and enlarged edition of *The Multinational Empire*, 1st edn., New York, 1950. For differences between political and ethnic unities cf. vol. 1, chapter 1–2.

16. R. A. Kann, *Nationalitätenproblem*, vol. 1 *passim*. General views on ethnic differences combined with social stratification also F. Prinz, 'Die böhmischen Länder von 1848 bis 1914', in K. Bosl (ed.), *Handbuch der Geschichte der böhmischen Länder*, vol. 3, Stuttgart, 1963, pp. 80–102, 202–35. Authoritative work on social, cultural and legal questions of Habsburg nationalities: A. Wandruszka and P. Urbanitsch (eds.), *Die Habsburgermonarchie 1848–1918*, vol. 3, parts 1–2, 'Die Völker des Reiches', Vienna, 1980.

17. R. Rozdolski, *Die große Steuer- und Agrarreform Josefs II. Ein Kapitel zur österreichischen Wirtschaftsgeschichte*, Warsaw, 1961.

18. Short explanation in R. A. Kann, *Nationalitätenproblem*, vol. 1, pp. 50–6.

a ruling class (nobility) and had been able to form a political community (state), even if they had since declined. By that criterion the
small Slavic tribes and the Romanians were considered non-historical
nations. This distinction is useful for the understanding of feudal
crown-land patriotism, the ideology of historical crown-land federation, and the opposition to a federation on the basis of ethnic equality.
Political consciousness had frozen, so to speak, at earlier stages of
feudal integration.[19]

The whole ensemble was vaulted by the German dynasty and its
practical absolutism and backed by the essential instruments of the
army and the bureaucracy — both formed after German models and
held together by the German language. So the Germans felt themselves
to be more than a nationality, they were, if not the political nation in
the Western European sense of the word, so at least the decisive
backbone and governing body of the realm, being at the same time the
bureaucratic protectors of the peasant masses.[20] However, absolutism
ended at the borders of Hungary, after Joseph II had failed to abolish
the country's constitution.[21] Here the pre-absolutist rights of the land-
lord-dominated diet and local self-government still held sway.

As in other parts of Europe, intellectuals were the first to stir up
national feelings in the Habsburg countries. In practice they were
involved in elementary schooling and mass education. When the great
school reforms began in the age of Mary Theresa, the decision to
promote elementary education in the respective native languages was a
fundamental decision with far-reaching consequences.[22] Indeed a prac-
ticable alternative, to teach only in German, was not and could not be
considered. However, organisation and teaching in the native languages
involved first of all discovery and elaboration of those languages,
i.e. transformation of dialects into standardised grammar. The Slavic
and Romanian intellectuals, very often priests, who worked on this
subject, thus became interested in the folklore, mythology and cultural
history of their ancestors. So they discovered the 'history' of the

19. F. Prinz, in Bosl (ed.), *Handbuch*, vol. 3, p. 169, has demonstrated for the
Bohemian case, how the pre-modern originated idea of unity of the historical *Land* was
transmitted from one opinion-leading class to the other till the Czech Social-Democrats
like a 'Leitfossil' (leading fossil).
    20. Recent description of these specifically German bureaucratic-'liberal' ('Josephi-
nian') ideas and self-assurances by B. Sutter, in Wandruszka and Urbanitsch (eds.),
'Habsburgermonarchie', vol. 3, part 1, *Die Völker des Reiches*, pp. 154–81.
    21. E. C. Hellbling, *Österreichische Verfassungs- und Verwaltungsgeschichte*, 2nd edn.,
Vienna and New York, 1974, pp. 302–23 *passim*.
    22. E. Winter, *Barock, Absolutismus und Aufklärung in der Donaumonarchie*, Vienna, 1971.
Education and nationalities, ibid., pp. 202–46 *passim*.

so-called 'non-historical' ethnic groups, i.e. they established their identity in socio-cultural terms and this became a means for their cultural and political emancipation. In doing so they adopted the Romantic theory of the ethnic or cultural nation as the real nation. Herder's doctrine of *Volksgeist* proved to be the fitting ideology for those small nationalities which were deprived of political power and governmental authority.[23]

During the 1840s national feeling began to be linked with political ambitions, first of all within the historical nations. In Bohemia the traditional feudal opposition promoted efforts for Czech language and history and looked for political friends among the protagonists of Czech nationalism to win support for more Bohemian autonomy from bureaucratic centralism.[24]

In Hungary the 'liberal' faction of the magnates together with the nationalist gentry and intellectuals set up a parliamentary movement for autonomous political and economic development of the kingdom on the basis of national Magyar integration, proclaiming the Magyars as the only political nation of the realm.[25] Ideologically they took over the Western European model of nation-state and nation-building, which was directed against the non-Magyar inhabitants. Representing only 40 per cent of the population the Magyars of course stressed that model from the beginning, and this problem was to persist until the end of the realm in 1918. In 1844 they gained their first success by changing the language of parliamentary debate from Latin to Magyar, which led to heavy opposition from the other representatives; a prelude to 1848.

The other centres of prominent national movement, namely the Italian Risorgimento and the Polish insurrections, need only be mentioned here without giving further detail. What should be considered in the Polish case is the predominantly noble character of the rebellions (1830–1 against Russia, 1846 against Austria), and the Austrian government in 1846 was very successful in inciting Ruthenian riots against their Polish landlords, in this way checking them and suppressing the movement.[26]

Compared with the aspirations of the leading nationalities, the national movement of the non-historical nations of the monarchy

23. E. Winter, *Romantismus, Restauration und Frühliberalismus im österreichischen Vormärz*, Vienna, 1968, pp. 37–70 *passim*.

24. F. Prinz in Bosl (ed.), *Handbuch der Geschichte der Böhmischen Länder*, vol. 3, pp. 17–31; H. Schlitter, *Aus Österreichs Vormärz*, 4 vols., Zürich, 1920, vol. 2: *Böhmen*.

25. E. Andics, *Metternich und die Frage Ungarns*, Budapest, 1973; H. Schlitter, *Aus Österreichs Vormärz*, vol. 3: *Ungarn*.

26. H. Schlitter, *Aus Österreichs Vormärz*, vol. 1: *Galizien und Krakau*.

remained at a rather unpolitical level. But their leaders had already begun to preach resistance against domination, especially in the Hungarian case; they normally hoped for Habsburg protection against their immediate masters.[27] This aspect leads us to a special problem of integration in the Habsburg Monarchy: dynasty and bureaucracy developed at a very early stage the governmental technique of putting themselves into an arbitrational position through social protection of the lower classes and cultural protection of the small nations.[28] Of course we find such tendencies in all European monarchies, but in the Habsburg realm, where the disintegrating factors had a structurally greater meaning, this kind of absolutist-bureaucratic arbitration was appropriate to prevent higher forms of political integration in the long run.

If we regard the Revolutions of 1848 as a key event of the nineteenth century, then it must be in the sense that all the major political problems of Central Europe appeared on the agenda, but were not solved. The Revolutions were a kind of catalyst, which brought potential conflicts to the surface, changed the political consciousness of everyone involved and so created new conditions for the decisive political activities of the coming decades.

To analyse the national questions at stake I shall first choose the Frankfurt perspective and then turn over to the Viennese perspective, for here the same problems were debated in the greatest detail and at the same time, but with different intentions.

In Frankfurt, the seat of the German Diet, revolution was transformed very quickly into legal procedure, when the so-called 'Vorparlament', a spontaneous convention of liberal leaders with a strongly radical wing, decided not to proclaim itself as a constituent assembly, but to call for general elections, and when corresponding to that the old Diet of the German Confederation unanimously ordered such elections for a national constituent assembly to be held in every member state.[29]

Of course the complicated questions of German constitutional history cannot be discussed here. The most important implication of convoking a constituent assembly was the presumption that there

27. For the social aspects of Theresian and Josephinian reforms cf. e.g. R. A. Kann, *Geschichte des Habsburgerreiches 1526–1918*, 2nd edn., Vienna 1982, pp. 162–95. For the small Hungarian nationalities cf. Kann, *Nationalitätenproblem*, vol. 1, pp. 274–98, 309–21; Galicia, ibid., pp. 322–35.

28. For the 'Josephinian' tradition of the German modelled bureaucracy cf. Kann, *Nationalitätenproblem*, vol. 1, pp. 57–61 with references.

29. For constitutional and parliamentary questions cf. E. R. Huber, *Deutsche Verfassungsgeschichte* vol. 2, chapter 9; M. Botzenhart, *Deutscher Parlamentarismus in der Revolutionszeit 1848–1850*, Düsseldorf, 1977, chaps. 1–3.

existed a clearly defined German nation as basis of constituent power according to the doctrine of popular sovereignty. On the other hand, the single German states continued to exist undiminished, and the question of how to combine the constitution-making of the National Assembly with the principle of a constituent interstate convention was only postponed and remained on the agenda.[30]

In the Paulskirche, the radicals stood firm on the principle of popular sovereignty including its revolutionary consequences; while the overwhelming majority, the liberal right and left–centre, held the same beliefs in theory, but looked for practical co-operation with the monarchical state-governments without having any power to coerce dissident states.[31] What all the deputies regarded as the natural aim of their work was the transformation of the old Confederation into a real nation-state on a federal basis with a liberal constitution providing for civil rights of all Germans, central government and a central parliament furnished with sovereign competence in military and foreign affairs.[32] What they wanted was the formation of Germany as a new great power which could appear on the European stage with commanding force; and this would have meant an international revolution more complicated probably than most of them could imagine. This revolutionary aspect already arises with the question of what the extent of the German nation-state should be, and how the nation could be defined in territorial terms. In practice that question arose at the beginning, when the Frankfurt authorities had to decide who should be entitled to elect the national assembly. The first basic decision was that all territories belonging to the German Confederation should be included.[33] The boundaries of the Confederation were more or less identical with those of the Holy Roman Empire in 1789. Neither the one nor the other had followed the concept of nation-states. Non-German minorities were included in their boundaries in great numbers: Poles in Silesia; Czechs in Bohemia and Moravia; Slovenes in Styria, Carinthia, Carniola and the Littorale; Italians in Trieste, Gorizia and Trentino; and Dutch in Limburg.[34] On the other hand, coherent German settlement could be

30. E. R. Huber, *Deutsche Verfassungsgeschichte*, vol. 2, pp. 619–22, 791–820.
31. Ibid. pp. 792–820.
32. Ibid. pp. 773–842. A concise study in the Revolution of 1848 now G. Wollstein, *Deutsche Geschichte 1848/49. Gescheiterte Revolution in Mitteleuropa*, Stuttgart, 1986. Presentation of state of research and discussion in the recent volume of D. Langewiesche (ed.), *Die deutsche Revolution von 1848/49*, Darmstadt, 1983.
33. E. R. Huber, *Deutsche Verfassungsgeschichte*, pp. 606–10.
34. Statistics being uncertain the population of the provinces in question can roughly be specified (in millions): Prussian Silesia 3.2 Germans, 0.7 Poles; Bohemia–Moravia 4.4 Czechs, 2.5 Germans, 0.1 Poles; Styria 0.6 Germans; 0.4 Slovenes; Carinthia 0.2

found in countries outside the boundaries of the Confederation: so in Schleswig (two-thirds of the population) under Danish rule, in East and West Prussia and in Posen (Poznań) under Prussian government;[35] scattered German settlements existed within the entire Habsburg Monarchy outside the boundaries of the German Confederation, as well as in Russian Poland and in many parts of European Russia. The population of most parts of Switzerland was German speaking as it was in northern Lorraine and in the Alsace under French government.

The decision of the Frankfurt Diet to define Germany according to the boundaries of the Confederation meant that the Czechs, the Slovenes, some Poles, a lot of Italians and some Dutch were asked to elect deputies for Frankfurt. It followed that the Austrian government was called upon to organise elections in their 'German' countries, whereas Hungary, Galicia and Lombardy-Venetia were excluded.[36] So the existence and structure of the Habsburg Empire were implicitly questioned from the beginning. In contrast to the treatment of Austria, Frankfurt made an exception in the case of Prussia. Following a requirement of the Berlin government and in harmony with decisions of the provincial diets, the provinces of East and West Prussia were formally included into the German Confederation by a constitutional act of the German Diet, so that elections could be held.[37] A bit later the same was done with most parts of the Prussian province of Posen.[38] The second exception was made in the case of Danish governed Schleswig, the deputies of which were admitted to the national assembly.[39] Nobody in the sphere of political decision-making had the idea to admit representatives of Alsace-Lorraine.[40] The major prob-

Germans, 0.1 Slovenes; Carniola 0.4 Slovenes, 0.03 Germans; Littorale–Trieste 0.3 Slavs, 0.15 Italians, 0.008 Germans; Tyrol 0.5 Germans, 0.3 Italians; Limburg 0.25 Dutch.

35. In millions: Schleswig 0.2 Germans, 0.1 Danes; Eastern Prussia 1.2 Germans, 0.4 Poles, Lithuanians and others; Western Prussia 0.6 Germans, 0.5 Poles and others; Posen 0.8 Poles, 0.5 Germans and Jews. C. v. Czoernig, *Statistisches Handbüchlein für die Österreichische Monarchie*, 3rd edn., Vienna, 1861; C. F. W. Dieterici, *Handbuch der Statitistik des Preußischen Staates*, Berlin, 1861.

36. G. Wollstein, *Das Großdeutschland der Paulskirche. Nationale Ziele in der bürgerlichen Revolution 1848/49*, Düsseldorf, 1977, pp. 267–70. For the reservations of the Viennese government against supremacy of Frankfurt decisions cf. Wollstein, p. 268, and E. Prinz, *Prag und Wien 1848*, Munich, 1968, pp. 31–3.

37. E. R. Huber, *Deutsche Verfassungsgeschichte*, vol. 2, pp. 639–41. Act of 11 April, 1848.

38. Ibid. pp. 639–43; cf. notes 49–60 below.

39. The formal incorporation of Schleswig into the German Confederation was, however, postponed for fear of international complications. For the whole complex cf. Ibid. pp. 666–73.

40. R. Buchner, *Die deutsch-französische Tragödie 1848–1864*, Würzburg, 1965, pp. 19–36, 50–8.

lems which are connected with the boundary questions now should be discussed. They will guide us to the problem of a German nation-state in Europe in general.

Concerning Alsace-Lorraine a short explanation can be given. There was no *irredenta* in that country, so that there existed no challenge to Frankfurt coming out of the local situation to deal with the question. Moreover, German activities of course would have touched the integrity of French territory, and this not only would have been dangerous but also contrary to the general line of German liberal foreign policy. In ideological terms the great enemy of European liberty was despotic Russia; and if a general war should come out of the Revolutions, it should be a western crusade against Russia, provoked at best by the Polish question. These ideologic preferences had been common since the 1830, and also in 1848 the perspective of an alliance with progressive France played its role in Frankfurt and Berlin.[41] Nevertheless Pan-German nationalists in the Paulskirche like Ernst Moritz Arndt repeatedly claimed Alsace for Germany in a vague sense for the future.[42]

Compared to this the Schleswig case generated actual problems which proved to be one of the crucial points of Frankfurt foreign policy. In terms of constitutional and international law the situation of Schleswig was rather complicated. The Danish King governed both Schleswig and Holstein as duke; this meant by personal union only. Holstein was a member-state of the German Confederation, Schleswig was not; on the other hand both duchies were linked together by an old and rather obsolete medieval treaty of union concluded by the respective provincial estates.[43] Contrary to the German national ambitions the Danish nationalists in Copenhagen had for a long time been urging the King to unify Schleswig with Denmark, and in 1848 he gave way and declared the incorporation of this northern duchy.[44] Thus, provoking resistance of the German national party, a provisional government of Schleswig-Holstein was established in Kiel, which asked for German help. The German Confederation declared war on Denmark to protect German interests and charged Prussia with military execution. The Prussian occupation caused Russian and British diplomatic intervention. Facing these dangers Berlin arranged an armistice without

41. Cf. notes 51 and 54, below.
42. G. Wollstein, *Das Großdeutschland*, pp. 248, 296.
43. Constitutional situation and events until the armistice (August/September, 1848), cf. E. R. Huber, *Deutsche Verfassungsgeschichte*, vol. 2, pp. 660–81.
44. Ibid. pp. 666–7.

seriously consulting Frankfurt and postponed the Schleswig-Holstein question to a future treaty.[45] These stories are well known; here we have to consider the principal position of the national assembly in that national question. Formally the German representatives elected in Schleswig under the provisional government were acknowledged and received as ordinary members in the Paulskirche, the question of constitutional incorporation of that territory was postponed for the time being.[46] Unfortunately some of the most important and most influential liberal-conservative members of the national assembly, those famous political professors and historians, were the most prominent protagonists of the national case in the duchies.[47] They argued in favour of the historical boundaries of Schleswig, thus approving of the incorporation of a considerable Danish minority (about one-third of the population), and influenced the assembly not to comply with propositions of partition on ethnic lines, which would have been relatively clear cut. Here the historic argument was used aggressively following the motto *in dubio pro Germania*.[48]

The same motto, but with the opposite argument, can be found in the Polish case. The incorporation of East and West Prussia was never questioned by the assembly. A discussion of their German character was never considered necessary, although there were considerable Slavic minorities.[49] Much more complicated and disputed was the Posen problem, because here both the whole Polish question and major questions of Germany's new position and orientation in Europe were at stake. Under the fourth partition of Poland in 1815, i.e. the partition of the Grand Duchy of Warsaw, both Russia and Prussia had promised to preserve Polish nationality, but as an answer to the rebellion of 1830–1 Russification and Germanisation were initiated.[50] Since that rebellion enthusiasm for the Polish cause was common to European liberalism in general including the German, especially on the

45. Ibid., pp. 671–81.

46. Cf. footnote no. 39; G. Wollstein, *Großdeutschland*, pp. 41–2.

47. Most prominent among the historians are F. C. Dahlmann, G. Waitz, J. G. Droysen, all of them protagonists of Prussian leadership and the *kleindeutsch* solution; then the brothers K. G. C. and W. H. Beseler, both jurists — the first as Professor of Civil Law, the second, chief of provisional Schleswig–Holstein Government, later guardian of the University of Bonn; the historian and Germanist A. L. J. Michelsen; and the Germanist Jacob Grimm.

48. So the suggestion of Palmerston for the partition of Schleswig according to ethnic lines was refused both by Copenhagen and the Provisional Government in Kiel respectively. For the whole debate cf. G. Wollstein, *Großdeutschland*, pp. 23–97.

49. Incorporation had been effected legally already on 11 April 1848 by the Federal Diet; cf. footnote no. 37; for ethnic composition cf. notes 34 and 35.

50. M. Broszat, *Zweihundert Jahre deutsche Polenpolitik*, 2nd edn. Frankfurt, 1972, pp. 66–109.

radical left and the left-centre.[51] So the Frankfurt Vorparlament regarded it an honorary obligation to proclaim the restitution of Poland as one of the great revolutionary goals imposed by historical justice and expiation.[52] In Berlin the Prussian King, under advice from his new liberal ministry, announced a programme of national reorganisation of the Grand Duchy of Posen. A reorganisation board including Polish representatives was established in Posen, imprisoned rebels were amnestied and at once began to form local national committees and to organise national arming.[53] In liberal perspective Posen should become the nucleus of a new Poland, its reorganisation would stimulate movements in Russian Poland, Russia would not remain quiet, and by these provocations the formation of liberal Europe against despotism could be strengthened, perhaps even by war, and the great eastern autocratic alliance of the three black eagles would be destroyed forever.[54] Now the Prussian King was not the man to risk such a *bouleversement des alliances* so unfamiliar to Prussian political traditions.

Actually the Posen reorganisation caused domestic Polish–German disturbances, provoked armed conflicts and led the German minority to apply for protection in Berlin and Frankfurt.[55] On the proposal of the Prussian government the province was divided; the parts including a German majority were formally incorporated into the German Confederation by an act of the Frankfurt Diet. Then the Prussian military made itself heard and demanded the city and fortress of Posen for Germany. So in a second formal act not only the fortress, but also the relevant lines of communication were incorporated into Germany, thus including areas with great Polish majorities. So just a small portion remained for national reorganisation, and this, too, for the time being under Prussian military control.[56] Politically Polish reorganisation was already dead, when the German parliament assembled. But here the question of recognition of the Posen mandates gave occasion to a great debate on Poland, which proved to be one of the most interesting

51. E. Kolb, 'Polenbild und Polenfreundschaft der deutschen Frühliberalen, Zu Motivation und Funktion außenpolitischer Parteinahme im Vormärz', *Saeculum*, 26, 1975, pp. 111–27.
52. G. Wollstein, *Großdeutschland*, pp. 109–14.
53. Ibid., pp. 98–109.
54. This new line of Prussian foreign policy was pursued by the Prussian March-Minister of Foreign Affairs, Heinrich A. Baron v. Arnim-Suckow, who hoped for a liberal war of national unification against despotic Russia in the course of an all-western alliance. Ibid. p. 102; E. R. Huber, *Deutsche Verfassungsgeschichte*, vol. 2, pp. 576–8, 639–40.
55. G. Wollstein, *Großdeutschland*, pp. 114–23, with reference to the extensive older literature.
56. Ibid., pp. 118–35; E. R. Huber, *Deutsche Verfassungsgeschichte*, vol. 2, pp. 641–2.

debates held in the Paulskirche. It was a rear-guard fight, in which the
left defended an active pro-Polish policy, for the opportunities of which
Posen should remain an unpartitioned nucleus, even if German
minorities were excluded from Germany. But the vast majority was
quite content with the fact of partition and accepted it.[57] What was
remarkable was the opportunistic change of arguments, being in favour
of historic unities against ethnic division in the Schleswig case, whereas
now unity was rejected for the benefit of the German minority. Even
more important was the burgeoning change from liberal ideology to
so-called *realpolitik*. Enthusiasm for Poland now was discredited as
sentimental or mawkish, politically wrong because the existence of
Poland was against Germany's vital interests because the Poles would
request a return to the boundaries of 1772.[58]

Above all this 'healthy' political egoism was combined with doc-
trines of historical progress derived from the Hegelian school and with
theories of race superiority. In this sense the partitions of Poland were
not the result of cruel power-politics, but the burial of a political
corpse, murdered by the Polish nobility. The nobles, who alone formed
the nation, had proved to be inept both politically and economically;
they had suppressed the peasantry without ever developing the country.
So, according to the laws of history Poland was occupied by the higher
developed people, whose administration and colonists could do more
for the country and especially for the Polish peasantry than the Polish
elite.[59] Germany's civilising mission in the east was the enticing perspective, which opened up in the Paulskirche not only with respect to
the Polish question, but still more in the case of Austria now to be dealt
with.

The most prominent question of national minorities within the

57. For the whole debate cf. Wollstein, *Großdeutschland*, pp. 135–72. Minutes of the
debates and votes, 24–8 July 1848 in F. Wigard (ed.), *Stenographischer Bericht über die
Verhandlungen der deutschen constituierenden Nationalversammlung zu Frankfurt am Main*, 8 vols.
and register, Frankfurt 1848, vol. 2, p. 1121–248. Final votes: motion for postponement
and further inquiry: 333 against, 139 in favour; motion for declaration it be an honorary
obligation of the German people to restore Poland: against 331, in favour 101, absten-
tions 26; motion of the reporting committee on questions of international law to
acknowledge the partition of Posen effected by the Federal Diet and to recognise the
Posen deputies: in favour 342, against 31, the left protesting by absence. *Stenographischer
Bericht*, vol. 2, 1228–33, 1240–8, 1233–9.

58. Prominent is the famous speech of Wilhelm Jordan, Prussian writer and originally
affiliated to the left (Deutscher Hof) in *Stenographischer Bericht*, vol. 2, pp. 1143–51. Best
summary of the debate with critical judgement by G. Wollstein, *Großdeutschland*,
pp. 135–8.

59. Jordan, ibid. For the importance of history and philosophy of history in political
reasoning during the Revolution cf. K. G. Faber, 'Nationalität und Geschichte in der
Frankfurter Nationalversammlung', in *Ideen und Strukturen der deutschen Revolution 1848*,
Frankfurt 1974, pp. 103–22, especially pp. 110–14.

German Confederation was the Bohemian case. Following its fundamental decision to include Bohemia, the Vorparlament invited Frantisek
Palacky, the recognised leader of the Czech national movement, to join
their company when preparing for the national assembly. This gave
Palacky the occasion to formulate his famous letter of rejection, in
which he stated that Bohemia was part of Austria but not of Germany;
the links to Germany were only based in feudal dependency of medieval origin and had no constitutional meaning. Never could the
Czechs take part in a German nation-state.[60]

Meanwhile patriotic movements had begun in Bohemia against
Viennese autocratic and bureaucratic centralism. In the first phase the
three important groups, namely the Bohemian nobility and their
conservative Czech allies, the more radical Czech lower-middle classes
and students, and the German bourgeoisie of the capital and the cities,
co-operated in a common national committee and sent appeals to
Vienna for more autonomous self-government for Bohemia, being
prepared to acknowledge the equal status of both nationalities.[61] But
nationalist conflicts began very soon, occasioned by incidents in the
streets of Prague and then decisively roused by the Frankfurt question,
which operated as a catalyst. The Czech leaders unanimously refused
Bohemia's participation in the elections for the Frankfurt Assembly,
whereas the Germans wanted to secure Bohemia's inclusion by all
means. So the Germans left the national committee in Prague.[62] The
Czech radicals began to speak about the Czechs being the original
inhabitants of the country and the Germans being only late immigrants
and guests; the Sudeten-Germans founded an 'Association for the
protection of German rights in Bohemia', which became a strong lobby
in Vienna and Frankfurt and organised fraternisation meetings with
Saxons at the borders.[63] The Viennese government issued the writs of
election also in Bohemia as required, but did not enforce participation.

60. Vorparlament and Bohemian case: cf. E. R. huber, *Deutsche Verfassungsgeschichte*,
vol. 2, p. 601, 643; Jiři Kořalka, 'Prag-Frankfurt im Frühjahr 1848: Österreich zwischen
Großdeutschtum und Austroslawismus', in H. Lutz and H. Rumpler (eds.), *Österreich
und die deutsche Frage im 19. und 20. Jahrhundert*, Munich, 1982, pp. 117–39; F. Prinz,
Handbuch, vol. 3, pp. 41–3. For Palacky now F. Prinz, 'František Palacký und das
deutsch-tschechische Verhältnis aus der Sicht der tschechischen Geschichtswissenschaft
unseres Jahrhunderts', *Bohemia*, 18, 1977, pp. 129–43; G. Wollstein, *Großdeutschland*,
pp. 195–202.
61. S. Z. Pech, *The Czech Revolution of 1848*, Chapel Hill, 1969; P. Burian, *Die
Nationalitäten in "Cisleithanien" und das Wahlrecht der Märzrevolution 1848/9* Graz and
Cologne, 1962, pp. 52–9; F. Prinz, in *Handbuch*, vol. 3, part A. Cf. below note 98.
62. S. Z. Pech, *Czech Revolution*; G. Wollstein, *Großdeutschland*, pp. 189–202; P. Burian,
Nationalitäten, p. 64.
63. G. Wollstein, *Großdeutschland*, p. 195 with references: F. Prinz in *Handbuch*, vol. 3,
pp. 43–7; P. Burian, *Nationalitäten*, pp. 74–80.

So the Czech boycott had the result that 13 constituencies voted regularly, in 7 only a minority did, and 46 constituencies did not vote at all.[64] Among the German–Bohemian representatives for Frankfurt there were some extreme nationalists making gloomy speeches about the Slavic flood and about wars of races for survival as a law of history; but more of them spoke for national agreement and peaceful settlement.[65] It was a Bohemian who introduced the later article 188 of the civil rights catalogue, by which minority rights in language and cultural development were granted.[66] Some deputies demanded that Frankfurt should take measures to enforce elections without saying how, but this was rejected.[67] In principle the Paulskirche was convinced that Bohemia, situated in the centre, was and should remain a part of Germany. New excitements arose in Frankfurt, when at Whitsun a Pan-Slav congress was assembled in Prague. Organised by the Czech groups this congress in fact united mainly Austrian Slavs, namely speakers for the Czechs, Poles, Ruthenians, Croats and Serbs. Bakunin was the lone but famous speaker for Russia.

The congress fulfilled its purpose as a platform for anti-Frankfurt manifestations, some of them quite outspoken. Frankfurt was denied any jurisdiction over the Bohemian countries. Likewise anti-Magyar speeches were made. In contrast to this, the congress hailed the existence of a federated Austria which was expected to become Slavic-orientated by the natural consequence of democratic majorities.[68]

Close connections between the Slavic deputies and the Czech radicals, especially the students in Prague, added fuel to the general excitement, and following mutual provocations between them and the military, riots erupted at Whitsun, barricades were erected, and fighting began.[69] In Frankfurt the national assembly had answered the convocation of the Slavic congress by constituing a committee for Slavic matters, in which sharp anti-Slavic opinions prevailed, and which,

64. F. Prinz, *Prag und Wien 1848*, pp. 36–41; Burian, *Nationalitäten*, p. 73.
65. F. Prinz, 'Die Sudetendeutschen im Frankfurter Parlament', in *Zwischen Frankfurt und Prag*, Munich, 1963, pp. 103–32.
66. Titus Mareck from Graz (but of Bohemian origin), deputy for Styria, took the Bohemian case for his demand of 27 May 1848, that the National Assembly should make a solemn statement in favour of minority rights, which was supported by the German–Bohemian group and voted almost unanimously on 31 May. G. Wollstein, *Großdeutschland*, pp. 205–8. For Art. 188 cf. below footnote 83. For Mareck cf. F. Prinz, 'Die Sudetendeutschen', p. 118.
67. G. Wollstein, *Großdeutschland*, pp. 207–10. Sharp nationalistic tendencies against the Czechs in the speech of Ernst Moritz Arndt.
68. L. D. Orton, *The Prague Slav Congress of 1848*, New York, 1978.
69. For history of events see R. Kiszling, *Die Revolution im Kaisertum Österreich 1848–1849*, 2 vols., Vienna 1948; vol. 1, pp. 149–56.

when news about the Whitsun riots reached Frankfurt, moved for military intervention in Bohemia by non-Austrian German troops to secure German interests. But the debate on that motion showed very soon that the moderate majority hesitated to follow such a decisive and revolutionary national policy and to interfere with the complicated Austrian situation. So the conservative friends of Austria could carry an address which expressed the expectation that the Austrian authorities would restore order.[70] The Viennese government of course wanted to keep Frankfurt out of the whole affair and tried to settle the Prague conflicts by sending a committee[71] But in fact the Austrian military did not pay much attention to its government. The Prince of Windischgraetz, an ultra-conservative noble and commander of the completely intact northern army, took the opportunity to inflict the first considerable defeat on the Revolution by reconquering Prague, suppressing the congress and subjecting all of Bohemia to a state of siege.[72] Many Frankfurt deputies and a lot of newspapers now hailed Windischgraetz as the protector of the Germans, and only a few left-wing members observed the turn of the political tide.[73]

In Bohemia political life was now suppressed, whereas in Frankfurt the whole question was postponed until the great debate on Austria's position in the German Constitution.

Compared with the Bohemian problem the national disputes in the south-east Slovenian areas were much less spectacular. The Slovenes did not vote for Frankfurt, but they also did not organise protest activities. The few activists concentrated their demands on constitutional change in the mixed provinces to gain more equality.[74] In the Italian city of Trieste there was a considerable movement sympathising with the Lombardy–Venetian rebellion and hoping to be conquered. But these radical sentiments were not shared by the leading Italian merchants who knew very well that their prosperity depended exclusively on the city's incorporation into Austria.[75] In the Frankfurt As-

70. The reaction of the National Assembly on the Bohemian case from 7 June to 1 July is characterised by G. Wollstein, *Großdeutschland*, pp. 210–19. Despite sharp nationalistic tendencies of a minority the differences compared to the Posnanian case are remarkable. The soft declaration promoted mainly by the Reichs-Minister of the Interior, Schmerling (a prominent Austrian), and the moderate Austrian deputies was voted 'by a majority', *Stenographischer Bericht*, vol. 1, p. 676, 1. 7. 1848, without figures. At the time of voting the Assembly was already familiar with Windischgraetz's victory.
71. F. Prinz, *Prag und Wien 1848*, pp. 68–79.
72. Ibid. pp. 80–95. For history of events cf. R. Kiszling, *Die Revolution im Kaisertum Österreich*, vol. 1, pp. 49–56; P. Müller, *Feldmarschall Fürst Windischgrätz. Revolution und Gegenrevolution*, Vienna, 1934, chap. 3.
73. G. Wollstein, *Großdeutschland*, p. 218; F. Prinz, 'Die Sudetendeutschen', p. 120.
74. For the local activities cf. Burian, *Nationalitäten*, pp. 118–51. Cf. note 104 below.
75. Ibid. pp. 151–6.

sembly there was no doubt that Trieste had to be maintained as a German port, to secure a stronghold for an active Mediterranean policy. Some deputies even required the extension of the German territory to the entire peninsula of Istria to gain suitable naval bases.[76] More dispute arose in the case of Trentino. The Italians of South Tyrol had elected representatives for Frankfurt for the sole purpose of urging the exclusion of their districts from the German Confederation. Only a leftist minority supported this motion for the sake of Italy; the vast majority followed the historical and military arguments of the professors and German Tyrolese that Trentino had to remain within German boundaries.[77] Here again we find the opportunistic instrumentalisation of history. One of the parliamentary experts for Italian questions was the historian Friedrich von Raumer, specialist in Hohenstaufen history and of the great times of medieval Imperial domination of Italy. He favoured the concept that the new Germany should have commanding influence in northern Italy, and this meant that Austria should keep hold of its Italian possessions.[78] A considerable majority of the national assembly followed him in this view. Certainly there was, as in the Polish case, radical-liberal support of the Lombardy–Venetian rebellion and of Italian national unification, but these factions in Frankfurt were too weak to carry parliamentary declarations of sympathy for the Italian cause.[79] All such tendencies were completely swept away, when Radetzky's victories were hailed in August 1848. Now the Paulskirche voted a declaration which recommended to the Italians the formation of an Italian confederacy of which the Habsburgs should be members as kings of Lombardy–Venetia.[80]

Looking at the panorama of nationality problems from Schleswig to Trentino we realise that most of them concerned Austrian territories.

76. G. Wollstein, *Großdeutschland*, pp. 235–7.

77. As in the Schleswig, the Posen, and the Bohemian cases, the deputies of the region played a decisive role as opinion leaders in the question of Trentino, too. Against the liberal Italian representatives stood the conservative German-Tyrolese deputies, backed by the Assembly's committee on questions of international law against any separation of territory belonging to the German Confederation. The German left's support of the Italian Tyrolese was rather weak and favoured autonomy more than separation. However, the main debate took place (12 August 1848), when Radetzky's army had reoccupied Lombardy, and the Italian national movement was beaten for the time being (cf. *Stenographischer Bericht*, vol. 2, p. 1559 — only 'majority' against separation is recorded without figures). For the whole debate see G. Wollstein, *Großdeutschland*, pp. 223–35; for the situation in the Tyrol cf. Burian, *Nationalitäten*, pp. 161–74; for the function of 'historical' arguments cf. Faber, 'Nationalität und Geschichte', pp. 114–16.

78. T. Schieder, 'Das Italienbild der deutschen Einheitsbewegung', in T. S., *Begegnungen mit der Geschichte*, Göttingen, 1962, pp. 210–35 (first published in *Studi Italiani*, 3, 1959), for Raumer and the Paulskirche, ibid. pp. 215–21.

79. G. Wollstein, *Großdeutschland*, pp. 225–9, 237–42.

80. Ibid. pp. 240–1.

So dealing with them was always overshadowed by the general question of what the future of the entire Habsburg Monarchy should be. In the Paulskirche this serious problem remained in the background for a long time after having been postponed until the general debate on the charter of the Constitution. The solution offered by the constitution committee was implied in the first three articles of their draft. According to these articles the German Reich consisted of the territory of the hitherto existing German Confederation. In the case that a German and a non-German land had the same monarch, these states had to be separated in terms of political law and a purely personal union established; the indigenous status of all officials and the authority of Reich legislation had to be guaranteed.[81] For Austria this meant that Frankfurt was not prepared to include the entire Habsburg Monarchy (i.e. including Hungary, Galicia, Lombardy–Venetia, Dalmatia) into the German nation-state, because this obviously would have been incompatible with the essence of a nation-state. But Frankfurt was prepared and determined to include the non-Germans within those boundaries, as all the debates hitherto examined had already suggested. Of course this, too, was a violation of national ideas, but in Frankfurt it was justified by historical, geographical, and military arguments.[82] All complications deriving from those little shortcomings were expected to be met by the constitutional provision granting minority rights.[83] Dissolving Austria as a unified state meant that there was to be no special Austrian status by reference to its non-German territories, but that Austria should clearly be subject to the central government of the Reich. Foreign policy had to be made in Frankfurt, not partially in Vienna. So far the Constitution wanted to provide for a clear-cut

81. Debates in the draft committee, wording of the draft (with minority votes) and reasons: J. G. Droysen (ed.), *Die Verhandlungen des Verfassungsausschusses der deutschen Nationalversammlung*, Leipzig, 1849, pp. 314–42, 414–16, 422–31. Debate in assembly, 19–27 October 1848, in *Stenographischer Bericht*, vol. 4, pp. 2717, 2722–7, 2770–937.

82. The famous 'Frage an Österreich' (question towards Austria) has always been one of the central objects of historiography on 1848. For our purposes best recent treatment in G. Wollstein, *Großdeutschland*, pp. 266–306.

83. By Article 47 of the *Grundrechte* national development was granted to the non-German speaking tribes of Germany, namely equal rights of their languages within their respective areas in Church, education, inner administration, and judicature. Deliberately the draft committee had followed the same definition already chosen by the Mareck declaration of 31 May, 1848 cf. note 66 above. The debate (15 February 1849, *Stenographischer Bericht*, vol. 7, p. 5207–10) showed unanimous awareness of the importance of minority rights for the construction of the new Reich. Drafts, motives and important debates of the basic rights discussion in Frankfurt printed and commented in H. Scholler, *Die Grundrechtsdiskussion in der Paulskirche. Eine Dokumentation*, 2nd edn., Darmstadt, 1982. An earlier view with reference to Paulskirche, Ludwig Bergstraesser, 'Ursprung des Minderheitenrechts in Deutschland', in *Außenpolitische Studien: Festgabe für Otto Köbner*, ed. W. Arntz, Stuttgart, 1930.

decision for the benefit of a nationally integrated German state with a Great-Power status. But that did not mean that German influence upon the non-German Habsburg possessions should be diminished. This became very clear during the four days' debate on the initial articles of the draft.

The Austrian and the other German conservatives opposed the dissolution of the Habsburg Monarchy, because they were interested in the maintenance of the monarchic sovereignty of the individual German states at the cost of central and constitutional authority. They argued that securing the integrity of Austria as a whole would serve German interests best, because the German character of Austrian government would provide for a maximum of German superiority in the entire realm, which, at the same time, would serve as the most solid basis for further expansion of German influence in South East Europe.[84] But the majority of the house and especially the leading liberal-conservative professorial notables were not prepared to disclaim a strong national government.[85] So in the right-centre factions the possibility was discussed to found the German Reich without Austria, and a special plan was developed to link this smaller Reich with the entire Austrian Monarchy in a wider confederacy, bound together by a constitutional treaty providing for common institutions.[86] But this suggestion, too, only won a minority. The great majority of the national assembly, including the majority of the Austrian representatives, neither renounced strong national government nor renounced inclusion of German Austria into the coming Reich. So the propositions of the initial draft articles were carried by a vast majority in October 1848.[87] But neither did this majority, generally speaking, want to separate the New Germany from the non-German parts of the Habsburg Monarchy completely. The constitutional dissolution of that monarchy could politically be better described as a loosening and a transition to new forms of indirect rule, which was to be secured by means of monarchic personal union.[88] The speeches from the different sides of the house

84. Recapitulation of the great debate in G. Wollstein, *Großdeutschland*, pp. 266–91; the conservative arguments, ibid., pp. 269–73, 281–3.
85. Ibid., pp. 278–81, 283.
86. The famous Gagern plan was first presented in open court in the debate of October, but politically pursued only from December 1848 on, when the Austrian government after reconsolidation had refused dissolution and Gagern thereupon had followed Schmerling as Minister-President in Frankfurt. Cf. E. R. Huber, *Deutsche Verfassungsgeschichte*, vol. 2, pp. 796–807; G. Wollstein, *Großdeutschland*, pp. 280, 291–306.
87. Final vote 27 October: §2 of the draft 340 in favour, against 76; §3 of the draft 316 in favour, against 90 (Austrian deputies: 115 in favour, against 41). E. R. Huber, *Deutsche Verfassungsgeschichte*, p. 798.
88. G. Wollstein, *Großdeutschland*, pp. 283–91. Even in 1849, when the conflict be-

showed a broad accord in favour of the penetration of German civilisation, commerce and political influence throughout the entire South East and the Adriatic; to a lesser degree northern Italy was also mentioned. German settlement along the Danube should be enforced on the lines already initiated by Mary Theresa; many deputies regretted the German mass emigration to the United States and wanted to divert those streams to Hungary.[89] The Frankfurt Assembly conceived of the future structure of Europe as a nucleus–satellite model, in which Germany should dominate the smaller nationalities, especially in the South East. The Paulskirche was convinced that the work to be done was establishing the German Reich not only as a European Great Power, but as a hegemonial empire, containing Russia in its present boundaries in the east and leaving France and Great Britain as maritime powers in the west, but gathering in all the rest, especially in the centre and central east.[90] There were, too, fanciful ultra-nationalist professors like Arndt and Grimm who proclaimed the future restoration of Switzerland, Alsace-Lorraine and both Netherlands to the German Empire and adumbrated an all-Germanic continental alliance including the Scandinavian states and the Baltic.[91] These voices were not representative, but there was general consent concerning the special German role in East-Central Europe, and thinking and speaking in terms of Great-Power conceptions was widespread.

So we can say that the conception of a German nation-state was from the very beginning combined with supra-national imperialistic perspectives. In my eyes the preponderant explanation of this entanglement lies in the historical development of the east German states, especially of the Habsburg Monarchy, and in the lack of clear-cut ethnic units. The difficulties in defining the German boundaries, to say what the German nation was, and to determine a legitimate frame of national integration tempted most of the deputies to seek refuge in attack and to look for a solution by ambitious interpretation of national

---

tween Frankfurt and Vienna escalated and the Prussian King was elected Emperor, the *kleindeutsch* solution was considered by its protagonists as a provisional stage for the time being towards a larger central European organisation in the future. Ibid. pp. 291–306 *passim*.

89. Ibid., pp. 287–8.

90. A nucleus–satellite model supported by a great majority covering all factions: this is the central result of Wollstein's book. Renewed presentation of these perspectives in concise form: G. Wollstein, 'Mitteleuropa und Großdeutschland. Visionen der Revolution 1848/49', in D. Langewiesche (ed.), *Die deutsche Revolution 1848/49*, Darmstadt, 1983, pp. 237–57.

91. G. Wollstein, *Großdeutschland*, pp. 32–3, 47, 56, 127–8, 209–10, 248–9, 296, 316.

interests and of German 'mission'. The general West–East descent of
modernisation, civilisation and integration as well as the emerging
power vacuum in South East Europe psychologically favoured such
tendencies. A supplementary explanation should be found in the
character of the Frankfurt experiment. The slogan of the 'professors'
parliament' is of course very familiar and might be unjust on the whole;
but with reference to international relations and foreign policy there
were men at work who did not have the experience of a well-trained
governing class making political decisions within a given institutional
framework. These theorists scarcely perceived the real consequences of
their suggestions for the structure of European power distribution.
Compared with these goals and claims, the Bismarckian foundation of
the Hohenzollern-Reich was intentionally a limited operation. However, the far-reaching consequences of this act led to a vigorous revival
of those hegemonial dreams of the Paulskirche in the twentieth century,
which Germany then tried to put into political practice.[92]

The crucial point of the German aspirations in 1848 was the Austrian question. The Paulskirche viewed Austria from the standpoint of
German hegemony, whether it be that the realm should be dissolved,
or that it should be a German dominated unit. This was also no doubt
the perspective of the Austrian deputies. The question to be put now is
whether there was a chance for a concept to maintain the Habsburg
Empire on a specifically Austrian basis, i.e. its reconstruction as a
commonwealth *sui generis* by acknowledging its multinationality. To
follow this question let us now take up the Viennese perspective.

First some remarks on the complicated revolutionary situation. After
the fall of Metternich some moderate old bureaucrats considered as
'liberal' were called into government and promised a constitution.[93] At
the same time the court gave way to a Magyar parliamentary revolution and conceded the establishment of a separate Hungarian Ministry,
responsible to the Hungarian Reichstag in Pest. So dualism was
deepened and the way opened to a separate Hungarian state, linked
with Austria only by personal union.[94] By constitutional reforms the
Magyar political classes at once began to transform the kingdom into a

92. For *Mitteleuropa* cf. H. C. Meyer, *Mitteleuropa in German Thought and Action 1815–1945*,
The Hague, 1955; for continuity problems A. Hillgruber, *Deutsche Großmacht- und Weltpolitik im 19. und 20. Jahrhundert*, Düsseldorf, 1977.
93. F. Walter, *Die Österreichische Zentralverwaltung (ÖZV)*, part 3: *Von der Märzrevolution
1848 bis zur Dezemberverfassung 1867*, vol. 1: *Die Geschichte der Ministerien Kolowrat . . .*,
Vienna, 1964, pp. 2–18; E. C. Hellbling, *Österreichische Verfassungs- und Verwaltungsgeschichte*, 2nd edn., Vienna and New York, 1974, pp. 346–8.
94. Text of Fundamental Laws of April: E. Bernatzik, *Die österreichischen Verfassungsgesetze mit Erläuterungen*, 2nd edn., Vienna, 1911, p. 78–100.

constitutional nation-state with eligibility bound to the knowledge of Magyar. This led to opposition of Croats, Serbs, and Romanians and subsequently to a Hungarian civil war, which, in the autumn of 1848, gave to Court and military the chance to intervene and to reconquer Hungary.[95]

In Lombardy-Venetia national rebellion and the intervention of the King of Sardinia led to the retreat of the Austrian army; the Viennese government began to negotiate about the cession of Lombardy, but the generals made their own policy, and after having gained the necessary reinforcements, reconquered the territory in August, imposing a state of siege upon the Italian provinces.[96] In Galicia there was some temptation for the Polish nobles, but in remembering 1846 all remained calm, especially after the governor had immediately promised peasant liberation to the Ruthenians at the cost of the state.[97]

In Bohemia, the nobility and the Czech party required the same status Hungary had gained, namely inner autonomy, parliament and government for the united historical crown-lands of St Wencislaus. Being in straitened circumstances, Vienna made appropriate promises in the first days of April, but unlike Hungary a saving clause was made that these be compatible with the future Austrian constitution.[98] In the next weeks the conservative Bohemian nobility tried to establish a provisional government in Prague in coalition with the Czechs;[99] but then the nationality conflicts escalated to the Pentecost rebellion and to military suppression (as already mentioned above), putting an end to all policy-making under the stage of siege.

In Vienna itself the weak bureaucratic central government was pressed by several lower-class and student riots, made concessions to all sides and strove to keep a minimum of authority. It was placed in a very difficult position when the Emperor and the Court fled to Innsbruck, later to the fortress of Olmütz, and began to follow an informal separate policy together with the military. In terms of power-politics the most important fact within this entire development was, that — except for Hungary — the Imperial Army in the north and the south, although multinationally composed, remained an intact instrument in

95. History of events: R. Kiszling, *Revolution*, vol. 1, pp. 67–86, 161–174, 217–236; vol. 2, pp. 1–119, 161–302. For the problems concerning the application of the national state model to the kingdom of Hungaria cf. L. Gogolák, 'Ungarns Nationalitätengesetze und das Problem des magyarischen National- und Zentralstaates', in Wandruszka and Urbanitsch, *Die Habsburgermonarchie*, vol. 3, part 2, pp. 1207–303.
96. R. Kiszling, *Revolution*, vol. 1, pp. 86–122, 174–201.
97. Ibid., vol. 1, pp. 66–7.
98. F. Prinz, *Prag und Wien 1848*, Munich, 1968, pp. 16–30.
99. Ibid. pp. 31–67; P. Burian, *Nationalitäten*, pp. 52–75.

the hands of the staff.[100]

Nevertheless the government did its best to maintain the integrity of the Cisleithanian Habsburg state and to fulfil its promise for a central constitution. In relation to Frankfurt, the order to issue elections for the Paulskirche was obeyed, but from the beginning and repeatedly thereafter Vienna formally stated that all Frankfurt decisions and legislation had to be approved by the government if they were to be valid in Austria.[101] That meant that the constituent power of the National Assembly, according to the doctrine of people's sovereignty, was denied. Against Frankfurt, Vienna drew up its own policy of constitutional integration; firstly by convoking the existing provincial diets, which were to elaborate drafts modernising the provincial constitutions, and secondly by providing for a representative system in the centre.[102] We have to set aside here the work of the provincial diets, although it would be very interesting to examine how they faced up to the inner-provincial nationality problems.[103] In the centre, the government was anxious to produce a *fait accompli* by quick action: already at the end of April a constitution for the Austrian Empire except Hungary and Lombardy–Venetia was imposed by decree. This charter followed the classic scheme of constitutional monarchy by establishing distribution of the functions of power and a two chamber representation on a census basis of members. Reading it you would not get the idea that the state was multinational in composition. It implied the fiction that there was an Austrian political nation only divided into social classes according to the Western constitutional model.[104]

The decree did not fulfil its purpose of stabilising the political situation; intimidated by riots by the radical Viennese students, the government cancelled the charter and issued writs of election for an Austrian constituent assembly based on a broad franchise.[105] In these elections all the Cisleithanian nationalities took part, and the Czechs in particular, after their previous frustrations, came around to acknowl-

---

100. The fact that only the army had saved the continuance of the Habsburg realm was one of the basic experiences for the formation of the coming neo-absolutist policy and for the specific self-consciousness of the military. Antonio Schmidt-Brentano, *Die Armee in Österreich. Militär, Staat und Gesellschaft 1848–1867*, Boppard, 1975.

101. F. Prinz, *Prag und Wien*, p. 33; R. Kiszling, *Revolution*, vol. 1, pp. 123–4.

102. P. Burian, *Nationalitäten*, pp. 27–8; K. Hugelmann, 'Der ständische Zentralausschuß in Österreich im April 1848', in *Jahrbuch für Landeskunde von Niederösterreich*, 12, 1913, Vienna, 1914, pp. 170–260.

103. This is the main object of Burian's book, *Nationalitäten*, chap. 3.

104. Hellbling, *Verfassungs- und Verwaltungsgeschichte*, pp. 348–9; P. Burian, *Nationalitäten*, pp. 28–34; Bernatzik, *Österreichische Verfassungsgesetze*, pp. 101–10.

105. For events R. Kiszling, *Revolution*, vol. 1, pp. 128–60. Problems of franchise: P. Burian, *Nationalitäten*, pp. 34–40.

edge central representative institutions.[106] In Austrian history this was a very important moment; it was the first and was to be the last constituent assembly the realm ever had. In contrast with the German assembly in Frankfurt, its convocation implied the assumption that the inhabitants of the Austrian countries could act as a political nation, i.e. as a competent sovereign.[107] The Frankfurt Assembly and the Viennese Assembly were of course incompatible in terms of the theory of constituent power.

In the eyes of the rural constituencies the abolition of the manorial system was the main task of the coming assembly. To this end they elected peasant deputies, many of whom had low educational standards.[108] When this truly democratic parliament was opened in July it turned out that about a quarter of the deputies did not understand German. Nobody had paid attention to that possibility before, and consequently conflicting debates marked the opening session. But the representatives in general were very interested in successful proceedings and constructive results, partly for the social legislation just mentioned, partly for stabilising the realm on a federated basis. So a pragmatic and improvised solution of the language question was found, which, however, in historical perspective was in fact detrimental to the classic concept of integrated parliamentary decision-making by debate.[109] Under what circumstances multilingual parliamentarism can work is a principal question of political theory, which I can only mention in passing here. The first great task the Reichstag had to cope with was the abolition of the manorial system. In September the assembly could finish legislation on this subject successfully in co-operation with the government.[110] Then the entire political life of the capital was disrupted by the radical Viennese October riots. When the Reichstag was convoked again in the small town of Kremsier, the political scene had changed completely. Revolution was under military control, and a new power-conscious government was in office, which was determined only to grant a certain

106. One of the Czech leaders later confessed, that the Czechs would not have come if they had succeeded to establish the all-Bohemian diet and government, P. Burian, ibid. p. 75, note 134.
107. H.-H. Brandt, 'Parlamentarismus als staatliches Integrationsproblem: Die Habsburger-Monarchie', in A. M. Birke and K. Kluxen (eds.), *Deutscher und Britischer Parlamentarismus/British and German Parlamentarism*, Munich, 1985, pp. 69–105, here pp. 76–7.
108. R. Rozdolsky, *Die Bauernabgeordneten im Konstituierenden Österreichischen Reichstag 1848/49*, Vienna, 1976.
109. Vivid description in P. Burian, *Nationalitäten*, pp. 40–7.
110. Course of legislation in F. Prinz, *Hans Kudlich 1823–1917*, Munich, 1962, pp. 88–107.

breathing space to the assembly.[111] Under these circumstances all factions were interested in a parliamentary success by elaborating a respectable draft of a constitution. The result of the draft committee's work, the famous *Kremsierer Verfassungsentwurf*,[12] for the first time tried to solve the Austrian federation problem on the basis of equal rights for the nationalities. Two concepts of federation, namely federation of the historic countries or federation of ethnic units, were in competition. The Czech and German conservatives preferred the historic principle, the non-political nations and the Sudeten-Germans demanded ethnic criteria. But the committee found a compromise:[113] the historic *Länder* were maintained and even strengthened by making the governors and their councillors responsible to the provincial diets in all matters concerning provincial legislation. This would have meant partial dis-solution of the traditional central bureaucratic regime.[114] On the other hand the power of the *Länder* was defined by dividing them into units formed as far as possible in conformity with ethnic settlement and provided with extensive self-government especially in all matters of education, school, language and encouragement of national culture.[115] Backing this system, the catalogue of civil rights granted equal rights to all languages and nationalities.[116] We can see that in Kremsier the nationality problem was conceived as a problem of regionalism. On the higher levels of representation, *Landtage* and central Reichstag, the existence of nationalities was ignored and the fiction of the one political nation was maintained. This was not adequate to the situation of multinationality. Some Czechs required that the parliaments be par-titioned into national divisions for certain types of decision, but this was refused by the majority as incompatible with the principle of parliamentary decision-making.[117]

111. F. Walter, *Österreichische Zentralverwaltung*, vol. 3, part 1, pp. 223–43.
112. Text in Bernatzik, *Österreichische Verfassungsgesetze*, pp. 115–45. Debates in A. Springer (ed.), *Protokolle des Verfassungs-Ausschusses im Österreichischen Reichstage 1848–1949*, Leipzig, 1885.
113. Analysis of debates by J. Redlich, *Das Österreichische Staats- und Reichsproblem. Geschichtliche Darstellung der inneren Politik der habsburgischen Monarchie von 1848 bis zum Untergang des Reiches*, 2 vols., Leipzig, 1920, 1926, vol. 1, pp. 221–323; P. Burian, *Nationalitäten*, pp. 175–214; R. A. Kann, *Nationalitätenproblem*, vol. 2, pp. 29–45.
114. Kremsier draft, articles 102–9; Bernatzik, *Österreichische Verfassungsgesetze*, pp. 123–4; Hellbling, *Verfassungs- und Verwaltungsgeschichte*, pp. 349–50; W. Brauneder and F. Lachmeyer, *Österreichische Verfassungsgeschichte*, 2nd edn., Vienna, 1980, pp. 119–22.
115. Kremsier draft, articles 123–9 in connection with art. 3 and art. 112; Bernatzik, *Österreichische Verfassungsgesetze*, pp. 116, 125, 127.
116. Draft of basic rights, art. 21 in connection with art. 139 constitution draft (supreme court). Ibid, pp. 129, 142; G. Stourzh, *Die Gleichberechtigung der Volksstämme als Verfassungsprinzip 1848–1918*, in A. Wandruszka and P. Urbanitsch (eds.), *Habsburger-monarchie*, vol. 3, part 3, pp. 975–1206, here pp. 975–86.
117. P. Burian, *Nationalitäten*, pp. 188–90, 196–7.

And yet these Czechs had discovered a useful theoretical device. Parliamentary integration as a more intense level of integration produces, so to say, a certain burden of integration, consisting in the principle of majority and its toleration. The main precondition of such a toleration is homogeneity; what is not homogeneous cannot produce proper majorities. All parliamentary systems have produced mechanisms to protect essential matters, in which group inequalities are rooted, from the application of the majority principle; be it the division of estates into houses, the *itio in partes* of the old German Diet in all matters concerning denomination status, or a catalogue of basic rights (e.g. property rights) not subject to vote.[118] The crucial point of granting equal rights to nationalities in a multinational state is not to apply the majority principle to questions of nationality. This means that the classic parliamentary system is inapplicable to such a situation. To save parliamentarism the constitutional system has to provide for instruments of a national *itio in partes* and for specific voting modalities concerning certain clearly defined matters. The Kremsier draft was far from such a solution: the Habsburg Monarchy never could solve this problem, and one may question where in the world such a task has ever been tackled successfully.[119] Nevertheless the mere fact that in Kremsier the representatives of the nations were able at all to find a constitutional compromise was such a valuable political achievement that the government would have done well to seek agreement with the constituent assembly. However, constitution- making in Kremsier did not include Hungary and Lombardy-Venetia, and the deputies only expressed their hope and expectation that a constitutional agreement covering all parts of the realm could be attained by their accession to it.[120] Of course this would have meant a new and even more complicated transaction, especially with the Magyars. But in March 1849 the Imperial government gave up the attempt to create a constitution by agreement and returned to military conquest and autocratic rule. After a period of transition monarchic absolutism was

118. Cf. H.-H. Brandt, 'Parlamentarismus', pp. 77–80; U. Scheuner, 'Konsens und Pluralismus als verfassungsrechtliches Problem', in G. Jakobs (ed.), *Rechtsgeltung und Konsens*, 1976, pp. 33–68.
119. Later attempts, especially the introduction of curias in the diets of Moravia 1905, Bukowina 1908–10, Galicia 1914: G. Stourzh in A. Wandruszka and P. Urbanitsch, *Habsburgermonarchie*, vol. 3, part 2, pp. 1158–60, 1167–86. Description and analysis of the various reform ideas is the main object of R. A. Kann, *Nationalitätenproblem*, vol. 2.
120. Kremsier draft, article 6; Bernatzik, *Österreichische Verfassungsgesetze*, p. 116. For respective aspirations cf. R. Wierer, *Der Föderalismus im Donauraum*, Graz and Cologne, 1960, p. 47.

restored formally as well.[121]

This may lead us to some conclusions about the failure of the Central European Revolution in 1849. Regarding this failure in terms of integration processes, the causes prove to be different in the German and in the Austrian case. In Frankfurt the task was not reforming the constitution of an existing state, but state formation itself. Now, modern European history seems to me to show in general that the normal path of political integration is secondary parliamentarisation of an already established monarchic unit or collective separation from a primary established monarchic unit. There is no example of parliamentary state-building in a void and at the cost of existing sovereign states, and Germany is no exception to that principle. Actually German as well as Italian national unification resulted from conquest or domination by the most powerful state. In Austria, on the other hand, there was a monarchically preformed unit which had not sufficient socio-political homogeneity to enforce parliamentarisation upon the monarch. Between the heterogeneous nationalities there were fields of conflict as well as fields of consent, but the balance between them was so precarious, that active obstetrics practised by a sympathetic dynasty would have been necessary to promote government by consent. The political and mental tradition of the House of Habsburg of course displayed different values, and especially in 1848 and 1849 fears of revolutionary deprivation of the dynasty prevailed. So the realm fell back to the *niveau* of absolutism. Earlier in this paper I made use of the idea that there is a specific burden vested in parliamentary integration. Sometimes and under certain circumstances dictatorship may provide alleviating functions for conflicting parties unable to tolerate that burden of integration.

121. Comprehensive descriptions in Walter, *Österreichische Zentralverwaltung*, vol. 3, part 1, pp. 284–579.

MICHAEL STÜRMER

France and German Unification

It was after the trials and tribulations of 1848 that Alexis de Tocqueville, statesman and historian, summed up past experiences and future anxieties and advocated a fundamental change in France *vis-à-vis* 'les Allemagnes'. Tocqueville wrote in his 'Memoires':

> It is an ancient tradition of our diplomacy that one has to see that Germany remains divided between a great number of independent powers; and that was evident in fact when behind Germany nothing existed except Poland and a half-barbarian Russia; but is this still the case in our day? The answer which one has to give to this question depends on the answer which one has to give to another one: which is in our day what danger does Russia imply for the independence of Europe? I happen to think that our occident is threatened to fall, sooner or later, under the yoke or at least under the direct and irresistible influence of the tsars, and I believe that our first interest is to favour the union of all the Germanic races in order to oppose this menace. The state of the world is new; we have yet to change our old principles and not to fear to fortify our neighbours so that they are in a position to push back one day, together with us, the common enemy.

At the same time, however, the grandson of Malesherbes sadly recorded a conversation that had taken place between the French chargé d'affaires at the Court of St Petersburg and the Tsar. Nicholas I presented an alternative scenario of Germany's future, and his was the one to prevail over Tocqueville:

1. A. de Tocqueville, *Souvenirs*, Paris, 1964.

If the unity of Germany, which you don't desire any more than we do, will come about, it will need a man to handle it, even better than Napoleon did, and if this man should falter, this mass in arms would become threatening, and this would be your affair and ours.

It is worth remembering that, for the French, the German Question is much older than for the British. French Foreign Minister Robert Schuman gave expression to a trauma, when, in 1950, he remarked: 'Dès que l'Allemagne a fait son entrée dans l'histoire, il y avait une Question Allemande'.

It tends to be ignored by most Germans, and even more by most of their neighbours, that the Thirty Years War of the seventeenth century was the great seminal catastrophe of German history. What had begun as a noble uprising against the house of Habsburg soon turned into a battle for the ancient German constitution and the equilibrium of Catholics and Protestants, and thus almost inevitably into a European war. Germany was made Europe's battlefield, with more than half of the population paying the price of life, liberty, and estate. This was the time when France asserted herself as a great power, while French jurists advised the Cardinal de Richelieu that the French King could rather part with a fat province than with the right of German princes to form alliances with foreign powers against the Empire and the Emperor. In 1648, the peace treaty of Westphalia ratified a European regime over the heart of Europe, with the French King more powerful than the Emperor and the Swedes firmly established in North Germany — until 1815. The last assault of the Ottoman Empire against the heartland of Europe in 1683 was carefully co-ordinated with the final French assault on Strasburg and the Landgraviate of Alsatia. At the peace conference of Utrecht in 1713 the *iustum potentiae equilibrium* was established by Britain, and the silent assumption was that the weakness and passivity of Germany allowed the West European powers to divide the world between them. The eighteenth century added two important elements: Firstly the dualism between Habsburg and Prussia that became a side-show to the world conflict between France and Britain over India, the St Lawrence in Canada, and the Caribbean. Secondly, after twenty-five years of the Silesian Wars Russia rose to be the master of the Central European situation, only to be pushed back, in her turn, by Napoleon, Bismarck, Ludendorff, the Western powers in 1919 and 1920, and — transcending every limit of tradition and reason — Hitler. ·

The Vienna Congress, while not resurrecting the Holy Roman

Empire, reconstituted its ancient European role: that of chessboard of the world powers. The German equilibrium was restored in order to neutralise the German potential through both the German constitution and the European regime which held it in place. 1848 was the Revolution that failed: that is the accepted wisdom throughout the historical profession. In reality, throughout Europe the hopes and the frustrations of 1848 revived all the old problems, and added a new one: that of mass-democracy and its most formidable expression, modern nationalism. After 1848, Prussia's semi-absolutist ruling class was faced with the unpleasant choice of growing simply obsolete and fading out of history, or of forging an alliance with the mass age, through revolution from above. For Imperial France this was bound to put the inevitable question on the agenda, not only of French hegemony in Europe, but also of the French Emperor's ability to maintain it. Soon after 1848, all those questions were focused in one overriding one: was war inevitable between Imperial France and post-revolutionary Prussia?[2]

The European Power Projection

The question as to the inevitability of war between Bismarck's Prussia and Napoleon's France has to be seen in both a wider perspective and in a narrow one. It concerns the meaning of war within the European system of the nineteenth century and the link between war and the political legitimacy of states and regimes; and it concerns, more narrowly, the chain of events, both military and political between the Franco-Austrian War of 1859 and the Franco-Prussian War. It is along these lines that the courses and motives have to be sought that underlay the war of 1870; a war which, for Germans and Frenchmen alike, was to be a source of political identity as well as the most important historical watershed between the fall of Napoleon and the end of Hitler. The war was formative for France's Third Republic as much as for the German nation-state. What I propose to do here is to concentrate on the framework of international relations down to the

---

2. Cf. H. Nicolson, *The Congress of Vienna. A Study in Allied Unity: 1812–1822*, London, 1946: H. A. Kissinger, *A World Restored*, Boston, 1957; E. Fehrenbach, 'Preußen-Deutschland als Faktor der französischen Außenpolitik in der Reichsgründungszeit', in E. Kolb (ed.), *Europa und die Reichsgründung: Preußen-Deutschland in der Sicht der großen europäischen Mächte 1860–1880*, Munich, 1980 (*Historische Zeitschrift, Beiheft*, 6), pp. 109–37; W. D. Gruner, *Die deutsche Frage. Ein Problem der europäischen Geschichte seit 1800*, Munich, 1985.

Peace of Prague, 1866 and on the role of Prussia in Germany and the precarious alliance of Prussian *raison d'état* and German nationalism; that is of revolution from above and revolution from below, resulting in what Disraeli in 1871 was to call 'the German revolution' — in fact a rebellion against the old established control of the Great Powers over the heartland of Europe.

The point of departure is the question whether within the European system, as it had emerged at Vienna, the formation of a national power-centre in the heart of Europe was feasible without war. The history of the smaller states in Europe reminds us that the Kingdom of Belgium could be created and insulated from diplomatic rivalry when it suited the Great Powers in 1830. History also underlines, however, that in March 1848 even the rather humane thought of the first post-revolutionary Prussian Government to grant autonomy to the Poles in the Province of Posen and to allow them to raise a small army, provoked the threat of all-out Russian attack on Berlin. Within two years two more threats of war were to follow from the same quarter. The Tsar claimed a veto over German affairs and was able to enforce it. And there was indeed little doubt that the comfort and the power projection of all the continental powers were bound to suffer if one day Prussia would unify Germany from the Danube to Denmark under her leadership.[3]

The Vacuum in Central Europe after 1848

But had the old rules, created at Vienna, survived 1848? The Crimean War and the War of Italian Unification had invalidated the code of behaviour between the anti-revolutionary powers as-sembled at Vienna. Defeat in the Crimea turned Russia's face to the East, for twenty years to come, and forced the unwieldy Empire into domestic reforms that handicapped Russian foreign policy and under-lined the value of an ally in Berlin, while hitherto Prussia had been worthy only of contempt. Without Prussia's support Russia had no prospect of throwing off the clauses of the Paris Peace Treaty of 1856 that demilitarised the Black Sea, or of keeping the Austrians in check.

The Franco-Austrian War of Italian Unification in 1859 whetted the appetite of nationalists all over Europe, above all the German liberals.

---

3. M. Stürmer, '1848 in der deutschen Geschichte', in *Dissonanzen des Fortschritts: Essays über Geschichte und Politik in Deutschland*, Munich, 1986, pp. 89–108.

The lessons were simple to learn: a great power could be defeated, the map of Europe could be changed in the name of nationalism, annexations like those of Nice and Savoy were possible and acceptable, without compensation for onlookers, and with some waving to the democratic gallery in form of a plebiscite. Two years later the American Civil War (1861–5) did not only distract the attention of the Foreign Office in London, it also provoked French intervention in Mexico and, once the Union had conquered the Confederacy, forced the French Emperor into a hasty retreat and into a domestic crisis of formidable dimensions. This crisis largely coincided with the war of 1866 and its aftermath.

The Vienna system had inspired counter-revolution in 1849. Five years later, however, it had gone out of fashion, and ten years later it had ceased to function. What remained was a system of uneasy balance in which Central Europe, for the first time after two and a half centuries, was free, or nearly free, of the combined pressure brought to bear by the European powers. Ludwig Dehio, in his *Gleichgewicht oder Hegemonie* (1948) described this new state of affairs as a 'trough of European power politics'.[4] Indeed the Russian giant, having vetoed all Prussian ambitions through the use of force, in 1848 and 1849, had been beaten by the Western powers and needed the Prussian alliance. Austria was demoralised by the war of 1859, its finances in chaos, its capacity to survive in question, and its role in Germany fundamentally weakened. For Palmerston's England every non-revolutionary answer to the German Question, as long as it was confined to a Central European re-arrangement and did not threaten British markets, seemed to be acceptable.[5] It was France, and France alone, where it was determined that the continuing control of Germany was the guarantee of her security. In Paris traditional French power projection since Richelieu united with the needs of the government of Napoleon III to sail before the wind of public opinion and to give a new gilding to Caesar's laurel crown.

Prussia: Hammer or Anvil of German Unity?

But it was not only in France but also in Prussia that the

4. L. Dehio, *Gleichgewicht oder Hegemonie. Betrachtungen über ein Grundproblem der neueren Staatengeschichte*, Krefeld, 1948.
5. Cf. K. Hildebrand, 'Großbritannien und die deutsche Reichsgründung', in E. Kolb (ed.), *Europa und die Reichsgründung*, pp. 9–62.

question of German leadership was seen as the real test of viability and strength of the monarchy. The Prussian *ancien régime* had not been subjected to the standards of mass democracy; but without the political consensus of the middle classes it could no longer be managed. Counter-revolution had won in 1848, but only half way. In the European context the Vienna system had not survived its last triumph, and within Prussia the foundations of State and monarchy had been shattered profoundly; the social equilibrium had changed in favour of the liberal bourgeoisie. The revolution that failed resulted, nevertheless, in a constitution and the rise of political parties. The government did not need the confidence of parliament, but ministers could not manage without resort to parliamentary majorities. In fact, the 1848 Revolution had not failed, and it had not succeeded. Nationalists were frustrated, the promoters of constitutionalism had been politicised, the battallions of social revolution had been defeated but were still, through the industrial revolution, rising fast. Thus, victory and defeat are, if one considers the balance-sheet of 1848, illusory and meaningless categories.

Above all, the 'mad year' had brought home the lesson that Prussia could no longer be the model state of enlightened absolutism that it had been for the best part of the past century. It would have to be national leadership that promised new legitimacy, wherever national leadership was to be found: in the Paulskirche in Frankfurt, in the parliaments of the German states, with the industrial bourgeoisie, with the working-class movement, in the Zollverein — and at long last in Schleswig–Holstein, in Vienna and in Paris.

The rise of Bismarck provides a case-study of how Prussian *raison d'état* changed, against the professed beliefs of the old power elite: Bismarck entered politics in 1847, almost by accident, and he rose to speak for noble hunting privileges — 'I am a Junker and I want to have the advantages of it', he said in parliament.[6] In 1848 he gained a high profile as an ultra-conservative, agitating for counter-revolution. He won a reputation as a rabid reactionary. 'Only to be used if the bayonet reigns supreme', his monarch remarked. In the aftermath of 1848, with an illusive return to the Vienna system and the conservative millennium in sight, Bismarck continued to defend counter-revolution, the Vienna system and Prussian *raison d'état*: 'It is not worthy of a great state, to fight for an issue which is not part of its own vital interest. I see

6. Cf. L. Gall, *Bismarck. Der weiße Revolutionär*, Frankfurt on Main, Berlin and Vienna 1980, pp. 63–124; E. Engelberg, *Bismarck, Urpreuße und Reichsgründer*, Berlin, 1985, pp. 207–362.

Prussian honour in Prussia's refusal to enter into any shameful connection with democracy, and it is Prussia's interest that nothing should happen in Germany without our consent'. Thus he pronounced his contempt of democracy and his belief in Prussian egotism, and by doing so he graduated from backbencher to diplomat. He was appointed Prussian representative at the Bundestag at Frankfurt, and soon he developed second thoughts, reflecting on legitimacy and the virtues of Bonapartism. He arrived at the surprising conclusion, written in a letter to his old mentor Leopold von Gerlach in 1857: 'Situated in the centre of Europe we cannot afford that kind of passive incompetence which is happy to be left in peace. It will endanger us tomorrow as it did in 1805, and we shall be the anvil if we do nothing to be the hammer'.[7]

Bismarck: Conservatism and the Winds of Public Opinion

Bismarck was the first Prussian conservative to understand that Prussia's survival as a great power depended on the alliance being forged between the old elites and the national movement.[8] It was Bismarck, again, who understood that French vital interests, whoever was in power at the Seine, were linked to the prevention of German unity. In the early part of his career he did not oppose Prussia's hegemony over Germany — on the contrary, he believed it was necessary and natural. He opposed the national movement because it was democratic and liberal and because it was foolish enough to take on two of the three great continental powers at the same time — Russia and Austria — 'while the third one, greedy for booty, arms heavily at our border and knows very well that it is in the cathedral at Cologne that the jewel can be found which would help to close the French revolution and to stabilise the forces in power'.

Beyond Clausewitz: War Unlimited

After 1848 the Germans and French saw the German Question rise to be the measure of their power and identity. That

7. O. v. Bismarck, *Die gesammelten Werke*, vol. 14, Berlin 1933, p. 47 (May 30, 1857).
8. H. A. Kissinger, 'The White Revolutionary: Reflections on Bismarck', in *Daedalus, Journal of the American Academy of Arts and Sciences*, 97 (1968), pp. 888–924.

should have been a warning signal. For not only was the political framework challenged — constitutionalism in Prussia and Bonapartism in France — there was also the question where the war, once it had started, could and would end: nowhere else than in the destruction of the defeated political and constitutional system. There was no compromise feasible. The cabinets in Paris and Berlin could still prevent war, but, once it occurred, sooner or later it was bound to turn into a popular war, in fact a crusade.

In his magisterial study *Vom Kriege* Carl von Clausewitz, the Prussian General, had warned statesmen of the nineteenth century that war must never be allowed to transcend the limits of reason and politics.[9] But Clausewitz must have known that his caveat, while it disciplined the old sport of kings, would fail to prevent the struggles that were to be fought for the identity of nations and the preservation of a given power structure. As far as the long crisis and finally the war between Berlin and Paris is concerned, the warning of the Prussian general-philosopher was lost, although both sides combined their preparations for war with genuine willingness to keep the peaceful option open almost down to the last moment. On both sides of the Rhine a feeling prevailed that once popular war were unleashed, it would be difficult and perhaps impossible for governments to regain control. To put it in the words of Gerhard Ritter, the German historian: in the mass age war would turn into a crusade, and it was the dynamism of war that was bound to triumph over the reason of statecraft ('Kriegshandwerk' over 'Staatskunst').[10]

Clausewitz had lived through the age of revolutionary war, when the cabinet wars of the eighteenth century had been superseded by the crusaders of revolution and counter-revolution, and when absolutist manoeuvre strategy had been replaced by the battle of annihilation. He resigned himself to the fact that war had always been a formative element of human history, and probably would always be the father of all things, the law of states and the measure of their legitimacy. The Vienna system mustered enough collective wisdom to fence in the war through the solidarity of the monarchs against social revolution. A system of legitimacy was created which determined the status quo to be just and durable if for no other reason than that it existed.

Clausewitz had done his best to subject the craft of war to the art of politics and never to allow war to reign supreme. This amounted to

9. R. Aron, *Penser la guerre — Clausewitz*, Paris, 1976, pp. 139–48.
10. Cf. G. Ritter, *Staatskunst und Kriegshandwerk. Das Problem des Militarismus in Deutschland*, 4 vols., Munich, 1954–68.

philosophical containment of the revolutionary age; it was an argument against all the national take-offs of the nineteenth century and it was fundamentally an attempt at saving the nineteenth century from itself. 'Die fortgesetzte Staatspolitik mit anderen Mitteln': war was to be not the end, but the continued effort of politics by other means; never the *raison d'être* of states, never their beginning, and never their end. But Clausewitz had failed to give a recipe of how to keep the lid on Pandora's box.

The Schleswig–Holstein War, provoked by the Kingdom of Denmark and conducted by the two German powers in 1864, began as a duel and ended as a military walk-over: the democratic and national undertones of the students' and professors' uprising of 1848 were played down by Prussian and Austrian victors. The plebiscite, following the French model applied in Savoy and Nice, was buried in the peace treaty and never took place. Then the war of 1866 followed, the war of Prussia and Italy together, carefully prepared, against Austria and Austria's unfortunate German allies. It was one of those rare instances where war was carefully initiated, in political and financial terms as much as in military terms, and then enacted like a surgical operation. The two wars of 1864 and 1866 were in fact Clausewitzian wars: limited objectives, limited means, more a duel than a crusade, and brought to a halt before the revolutionary potential of either side had ever been touched.[11]

If, however, the military cards at the battle of Königgrätz in summer 1866 had fallen the other way, it remains an open question as to how the war would have been contained, once it went beyond cold-blooded cabinet war. Bismarck had put some explosive charges under the Danube monarchy. Above all he was prepared to renew the Hungarian Revolution, put down in 1848, and to support the Hungarians through Prussian money and, if necessary, Prussian guns. The temptation to side with social and political revolution was not alien to him. Quite often he had threatened it, and it is to be remembered that German unification began as a revolution from above, and ended the same way. At the same time he did everything in his power to limit the dynamism of revolution, to discipline German nationalism through the *étatisme* of Prussia, and to subject the nation-state to Prussian *raison d'état*. This was a policy of contradictions: it was the policy of a White revolutionary, as Henry Kissinger put it so paradoxically. Thus, the German

11. Cf. G. A. Craig, *Germany 1866–1945*, Oxford, 1978; M. Howard, *The Franco-Prussian War. The German Invasion of France 1870–1871*, Princeton, N. J., 1979.

War of 1866 remained an isolated duel: none of the onlookers, neither France, nor Russia, drew its pistol. But after 1866 the whole of Europe awaited the next war: Prussian financial circles, German liberals, the 'Third Germany' in the South, all with many mixed feelings conspicuously displayed. Everywhere the expectation was that the great crisis was still to come. And as everybody believed a war would come, this belief turned into a self-fulfilling prophecy. On the one hand the power-projection of France and the prestige of the French Emperor were involved. On the other hand Prussia's hegemony over North Germany, the Zollverein and the newly formed military alliances between Prussia and the South were at stake.

Was War Inevitable?

Still, in the aftermath of Austria's defeat and Prussia's triumph war was not inevitable. But when it came, a few years later, the motives were not only to be found in the structure of continental power-politics or in the action of the governing elites. In the last analysis they were to be found in what many million human beings on both sides of the Rhine hoped or feared. The previous wars had been, through careful planning and by accident, Clausewitzian wars. The war between France and Prussia, once it broke out, was bound to escalate into a national war, whether the leaders wanted this or not. So another Clausewitzian war was not on the cards.

What would French war aims be? To defend the Vienna system was absurd for Napoleon III who, since his early days, had done much to annul it.[12] To prevent the formation of a nation-state in Central Europe was contradictory for a monarch who pretended to be the protector of nations, who utilised the democratic principle whenever it suited him and who derived legitimacy not from the supranational concepts of the European order, but from the national egotism of France. Cartesian *clarté* is a principle for philosophy seminars, it was not the principle guiding Napoleon's policy. France could have no other objectives than to prevent by diplomatic means or military pressure, or a combination of both, Prussian hegemony over Germany. But what would be the outcome, if, nevertheless, war simply occurred or, worse still, if the Prussian rulers took the initiative? Where would such a war end? What

---

12. Cf. E. Fehrenbach, 'Preußen-Deutschland als Faktor de französischen Außen-politik'.

objectives would it have? What limits would it find? The frontier of the Rhine, so often referred to in France as God's gift to the French nation could never be the end, it could only be the beginning of more wars to come. The *layout* of French politics after 1866 did not only contain contradictions, it also contained the very reason of French defeat.[13]

Since the Crimean War Russia's place in the European Concert had been suspended. The Tsar still needed Prussia to throw off the clauses that had demilitarised the Black Sea since 1856. In addition, apropos the Polish uprising of 1863, the Russians received assurances that under Prussian leadership German nationalism was not for export, and certainly not to Poland. England's attention was concentrated on the Eastern Mediterranean where the Suez Canal was being built; the rest of British attention was divided between the United States, Canada and Ireland. The era of Gladstone was absorbed by domestic reform.

Austria in her turn looked to the south east, a new balance with the Hungarians had to be struck, and it was no longer Prussia that counted as the number one enemy, but Russia, the 'Third Rome' that wanted to inherit the Ottoman Empire and drive the Cossack's horses to the Mediterranean.[14] It was this nightmare that in the summer of 1870, when the Austrians were contemplating military intervention while expecting a long war, rendered Austria neutral. There had been a temptation to pay back the Prussians for the defeat of 1866. But it turned out that the war of 1866 had turned Austria's face in an eastward direction.

In this situation it was France, and France alone, that stepped between Bismarck's Prussia and German nationalism and their common objective, the nation-state from the Alps to the North Sea. Was war inevitable? In July 1866 Bismarck had feared that France would intervene if the war against Austria lasted any longer. Napoleon and his government were taken by surprise by the speed first of Prussian action and then of Prussian peace diplomacy. In addition the French military *preparedness* was seriously weakened by the consequences of the Mexican expedition. But the new Central European order of 1866 implied two uncertainties: would Prussia take the fate of South Germany into her own hands, notwithstanding mounting popular resentment? And could all this take place without a major European war?

13. A. J. P. Taylor, *The Struggle for Mastery in Europe 1848–1918*, London, 1971, pp. 171–227.

14. Cf. H. Lutz, *Österreich-Ungarn und die Gründung des Deutschen Reiches. Europäische Entscheidungen 1967–1871*, Frankfurt on Main, 1979.

In 1866, at the negotiating table first at Nikolsburg and then at Prague, a third party had been present, though invisible: Napoleon III. Bismarck did everything in his power to make the armistice identical with the final peace treaty, in order to put a stamp on the reshaping of central Europe. King William I had wanted gains from Austria, the military demigods had insisted on a triumphal march into Vienna. Bismarck restricted the gains to extensive annexations in North Germany and threatened, if the peace were endangered through the 'maison militaire', to throw himself out of the window of his hotel. He reminded the triumphant generals, as he reported to his wife, 'that we do not live alone in Europe, but with three powers who hate us and who envy us'.[15]

With the sad exception of 1870, when Bismarck let the annexation of Alsace and a part of Lorraine go ahead, he understood that the German Question could only be defined and answered within the given European framework. He was, as George F. Kennan has underlined, the last of the European statesmen of the nineteenth century to have an overall vision of the European system.[16] That is why he did everything to formulate the Prussian answer to the German Question in isolation, step by step, in order to prevent the veto which a European alliance would cast, through its very existence. Looking back at the end of his life, he reminded the Germans that their unity had been won 'so to speak under the threatening guns of the rest of Europe'.

Throughout his life he had lived under the trauma of 1756; the Kaunitz Coalition of Austria, France, Russia and Sweden — with the Swedes suitably replaced by Great Britain in the course of the nineteenth century. He reflected on the 'cauchemar des coalitions', and he meant both the threat to Germany from foreign powers, and the threat to foreign powers from a powerful Germany.[17] Thus he practised the art, so rare at any time, of preserving some restraint even in triumph.

In 1866, the speed of war was due to Moltke, the speed of peace to Bismarck. He had three objectives:

(1) to contain the popular enthusiasm and to control the military establishment and, once victory had been won, to secure the stability of the Habsburg monarchy;

(2) to save Austria's face and pre-empt any sort of *revanche*; ever since

15. O. v. Bismarck, *Die gesammelten Werke*, p. 717 (July 9, 1866).
16. Cf. G. F. Kennan, *The Decline of Bismarck's European Order. Franco-Russian Relations 1875–1890*, Princeton, N.J., 1979.
17. *Die große Politik der europäischen Kabinette*, vol. 2, no. 294, pp. 153–4 (Diktat des Reichskanzlers Fürst von Bismarck, z. Z. in Kissingen).

1866 Bismarck tried to revive something of the old Reich's solidarity by tying Austria to the new Germany of Prussia's creation;

(3) to prevent the French Emperor from intervening by offering the world a peace treaty that looked like a French success. In fact the Prague Peace Treaty of 1866 took due note of French interests, it preserved the 'Third Germany' as a subject of international law while rendering economic and military integration of the South under the hegemony of the North irreversible.

Moltke, the architect of victory in 1866, remarked soon after the Prague Peace Treaty that it was time to consolidate the North of Germany in order to resist future pressure from West *and* East with sufficient power. He expected a challenge to the new order in Germany from France. Such a test of strength would 'either destroy the new formation or give it a permanent and unchallenged existence'. The success, in fact the future of Germany, Moltke said, depended on how far Prussia succeeds, within the short period granted by fate, to gain not only moral, but also material leadership in Germany.

After 1866 war with France was not inevitable. But a situation had arisen which was ambiguous, and fraught with promises as much as with threats. In Berlin the situation was not accepted as a lasting answer to the German Question, not by the liberal enthusiasts of *kleindeutsche Einheit*, and not by Bismarck. Forcefully he intervened against the liberal proposal integrating Baden into the North German Federation, arguing that to do so would endanger Prussia's taking control of the whole of South Germany.

In Paris the future control of France over 'les allemagnes' was presented, by the left-wing opposition, as a question of to be or not to be. 'Revanche pour Sadova' became a battle-cry in domestic politics, directed more against the Emperor and his weakness than against Prussia and her strength. Napoleon III was accused of 'lâcheté', of an insufficient identification with French concerns and a sell-out of French security interests. On both sides of the Rhine governments were in power who tended to look at the new state of things as neither durable nor desirable and who were pressed, by strong elements in the public arena, to revise the status quo by diplomatic means or, if necessary, by the use of force.

In addition, in Prussia the political conflict with the liberals over the army's role had been postponed by constitutional compromise, but had

18. E. Fehrenbach, 'Preußen-Deutschland als Faktor der französischen Außenpolitik' pp. 130–7.

not been solved. The military had received assurances that, for the time being, the budget would be paid per head of nominal strength, and no questions asked. But after four years, in 1871, a new conflict over the military budget and thus over the fundamental constitutional issues was on the agenda. How should it be contained? Any major conflict with the Liberals over the army budget threatened not only Prussian military hegemony over Germany, but it was bound to ruin every chance of winning over the South to the nation-state under Bismarckian auspices. There was no answer to this dilemma, except the final defeat of Bismarckian conservatism, or its triumph in war.

If there is a recipe in politics to make a precarious situation even more precarious, it was inherent in the situation which had arisen between Prussia and France after 1866: a peace that commanded no confidence, and the prospect of a war that would put the legitimacy and the strength of the two sides to a severe test and which would, once started, whip up the passions of the masses and be driven from cabinet war to national war. Would this war ever occur? After 1866 it needed only a further decline of government power, and a good enough reason. The real origins of the 1870 war, however, were to be found in the history and geography of Europe.

KLAUS ZERNACK

Germans and Poles: Two Cases of Nation-Building

Nation-Building and European History

In modern medieval studies — in Germany and in Poland — there is a strong tendency to see the unity of European history in the Middle Ages and in the Modern period in the perspective of the emergence and the continuing influence of the European nations. This approach was anticipated fifty years ago by Hermann Heimpel who said that historically what is 'European' about Europe is that its history is the history of nations.[1] Since then this view has been corroborated; the results of research over the decades have amply substantiated this approach. Out of the wealth of details, significant lines of periodisation and regionalisation have become visible.[2] The benefits for our discussion today are evident: on the one hand, the danger which rested in the ideological abuse of all older 'nation' phenomena by nationalistic historiography has been banned; on the other hand, the drifting away of the historical problem 'nation' into a 'timeless category of world history which cannot explain anything'[3] has also been pre-

1. See H. Heimpel, *Der Mensch in seiner Gegenwart*, 2nd edn., Göttingen, 1957, p. 68: 'Europa und der Nationalstaat, diese Gegensätze sind aufeinander bezogen. Die Idee der Nation ist selbst ein europäische Idee, mit Europa ist seine nationale Zotrennung, aber mit den Nationen ist Europa gegeben'.
2. See mainly the Marburg series, *Nationes*, vols. I–V, H. Beumann and W. Schröder (eds.), Sigmaringen, 1978–85, E. Müller–Mertens, *Regnum Teutonicum. Aufkommen und Verbreitung der deutschen Reichs- und Königsauffassung im frühen Mittelalter*, Berlin, 1970, B. Zientara, *Świt narodów europejskich* (*The Dawn of European Nations*), Warsaw, 1985.
3. R. Jaworski, 'Zur Frage vormoderner Nationalismen in Ostmitteleuropa', *Geschichte*

vented. Lines of continuity become visible, not in the sense of organic growth from the beginning, but as a functional connection of problems. This leads us to an understanding of 'nation' as a structural element of European history.

Empirically we can observe several thrusts in two periods of nation-building: the first period lasted from the ninth to the eighteenth centuries and the second occurred during the nineteenth and twentieth centuries. Both periods are, of course, distinct in that they belong to different ages — to Old Europe and the Modern World, to feudalism and capitalism. But as a constitutive force of European history as such they belong together. Herein lies the specific role of 'the Europe of nations' as a model in world history: thus we can observe the so-called Third World being moved by a nation-building thrust that seems to be a powerful echo of the first stage of European nation-building.[4]

Before the ninth/tenth century, before the beginning of the first stage, things were different. The shaping of the medieval *gentes* in the period of the great migrations of the barbarian tribes is not the same process as the formation of the European nations in the High Middle Ages. The most rigorous in conceptual differentiation in this respect is Helmut Beumann. He concludes that: 'The nations appear as a new formation in European history as the result of a process of integration which corresponds to the disintegration of the Franconian Empire'. The Great Empire, in which the long period of Frankish rule culminated, played an integrative role with regard to all the *gentes* of the *Völkerwanderung* period. (It is not purely accidental that the name of the Emperor — King Charles — came to mean 'the crowned king' in Slavonic languages.) The Carolingian Empire, therefore, stands like a great mediatory system between the two levels — the *gentes* of the Early Middles Ages and the *nationes* of the High Middle Ages. In other words, the disintegration of the Franconian Empire did not mean a relapse into the status quo of the *gentes*; it led to something new.[5]

In this interpretation the Franconian Empire appears as the vehicle of transition in world history, and in this process notice must be taken of continuity and change alike. The cultural shift from the South–North axis of the Old World to the West–East axis in European

und Gesellschaft, 5, 1981, p. 404.
   4. B. Zientara, 'Nationale Strukturen des Mittelalters', *Saeculum*, 32, 1981, p. 301–16.
   5. H. Beumann, 'Die Bedeutung des Kaisertums für die Entstechung der deutschen Nation im Speigel der Bezeichnung vom Reich und Herrscher', in *Nationes*, vol. I, 1978, pp. 317f.

history is without doubt the most important consequence of the transformative force of the Carolingian Empire. However, in the mediation between the levels of the *gentes* and the *nationes*, there are also factors which furthered continuity, in both a functional and an intentional sense.

These insights into the development from the *gentes* of the Early Middle Ages — the Franks, the Alemanni, the Jutes and the Anglo-Saxons — to the *nationes* of the High Middle Ages — the French, the Germans, the Danes and the English — totally reverse the direct wording of the sources. The sources, if they have any terminological references at all, rather express a succession from *natio* to *gens*.[6] Thus, the dominating vocabulary of the sources, which of course can never replace the scholarly elaboration of concepts, could confirm the naïve viewer in his doubts as to whether one can speak of nationhood at all in the Middle Ages. This scepticism — based on an uncritical reading of the sources — was, and still is,[7] often joined by an unthinking assertion namely: that the nation is a strictly modern phenomenon, a product of the bourgeoisie. The consistency with which this claim is being made among certain types of historians means, in my opinion, giving up interest in universal history in a diachronic sense. As a result, the unity of history as an object of historical study is uncritically sacrificed. František Graus, in a thought-provoking and outspoken article, recently criticised historical writing in the Federal Republic of Germany for this very reason.[8]

Thus, the concept 'nation' is used in modern medieval studies not as something emerging from the sources, but as a historiographic term. We must always create artificially a category of terms in order to study historical problems. In German we have accepted terms such as *Stadt*, *Staat*, *Gesellschaft*, *Adel* and *Herrschaft* in our historiographic vocabulary for a long time. The historian often creates these terms in the process of criticising older historical traditions while examining historical

6. For example, in the oldest Polish chronicle *Galli Anomymi cronicae et gesta ducum sive principum Polonorum*. See the edition of C. Maleczyński in the series *Monumenta Poloniae Historica*, Nova series, II, Cracow, 1952; B. Zientara, 'Populus – gens – natio. Z zagadnień wczesnosredniowiecznej terminologii etnicznej' ('On the Problem of Ethnic Terminology of the Early Middle Ages') in: *Cultus et cognitio. Studia z dziejów średniowiecznej kultury (Gieysztor-Festschrift)*, Warsaw, 1976, pp. 673–82; H.-D. Kahl, 'Einige Beobachtungen zum Sprachgebrauch von natio im mittelalterlichen Latein mit Ausblicken auf das neuhochdeutsche Fremdwort "Nation"', *Nationes*, vol. I, pp. 63–108.
7. W. Schlesinger presents as impressive list of examples in 'Die Entstehung der Nationen. Gedanken zu einem Forschungsprogramm', in *Nationes*, vol. I, pp. 16f.
8. F. Graus, 'Die Einheit der Geschichte', *Historische Zeitschrift*, 231, 1980, pp. 631–49.

phenomena.[9] They become his historical questions and always represent an attempt to reconstruct history.

In my contribution to our discussion I have the same intention. In concentrating on the German and the Polish examples I want, on the one hand, to demonstrate — in the face of widespread doubts — the historical existence of the problem of nation in the pre-modern period and, on the other hand, to make evident that even with respect to modern nation-building the French Revolution is only relatively speaking a turning-point in the history of Central Europe.

The Germans and the Poles in European History

In this connection the Polish and German examples are characteristic: the Poles created their modern nation without a bourgeois revolution. They found their way from 'Old' European liberty to liberal constitutionalism. Its fulfilment, however, in the form of an independent Polish state was prevented by the partitions. So the 'Polish Question' did not find its solution. In contrast to Poland, modern nation-building in Germany was delayed for a long time internally due to the stubborn traditions of dynastic states under the *ancien régime*. What was finally achieved in 1871, the foundation of a national realm, was by no means a solution to the 'German Question'.

So we could say that the *external* partitions with respect to the Poles and the historical tradition of Germany's *internal* division were the basic conditions under which the modern nation-building of these neighbours in Central Europe should be considered. The state of Prussia embodies this German–Polish nexus — the specific connection of the German and the Polish question — in a very illustrative way. I will return to this point at the end of my paper.

First of all, I would like to treat the problem in four stages. Before talking about our actual subject — the Modern period — I would like to deal with three striking comparative aspects of German–Polish developments from the Middle Ages to the Modern period, in order to illustrate briefly the thrusts of nation-building in Old Europe. First, I will discuss the formation of national structures in Central Europe in the Early Middle Ages; secondly, the land colonisation of the High

9. For this — the method of 'Begriffsgeschichte' — see the introduction to the first volume of O. Brunner, W. Conze, R. Koselleck (eds.) *Geschichtliche Grundbegriffe. Historisches Lexikon zur politisch-sozialen Sprache in Deutschland*, Stuttgart, 1972, pp. XXIIf.

Middle Ages as feudal modernisation, thus concluding the first phase of the nation-building process; and thirdly, the republican models of the Early Modern period as the foundation for the political nations of Central Europe. After that, I will analyse in more detail the effects of absolutism, power-politics and revolution on the two nations concerned.

Modern research on *nationes* has traced the first impulses for the emergence of the German and Polish nations (that is to say, the beginnings of German and Polish history) back to the process of the disintegration of the Carolingian Empire.[10] In this respect it is rewarding to study carefully the broad field of the *Ostpolitik* of the Franconian Empire. Since the divisions of the Empire in the ninth century, this was primarily the task of the East Franconian realm. In contrast to the conditions in the West, the universal Christian powers, the Emperor and the Pope, had but a diffuse influence on the long eastern land border of this realm in Central Europe. The stronger the tensions between the secular and the Church powers in the course of the tenth and eleventh centuries became, the more likely it was that a need for 'national' policy would result. In Central Europe, on both sides of the Carolingian eastern border (in other words: where the worlds of the Christians and the barbarians collided) this must have been a strongly felt need.[11]

The situation here during the tenth century is determined, furthermore, by the effects of the establishment of autochthonous dynasties to the east of the old cultural border. The Poles, the Bohemians and the Hungarians quickly established powerful princedoms by conquering older tribal lands. Outside the limits of old Roman–Franconian culture, 'pioneer' societies, as I would like to call them, were in the making. Despite their rapid Christianisation they were structurally very different from the area to the west of this border.[12]

To the west of this line, an imperial kingdom (the *regnum teutonicorum*) rose as a superstructure above the powerful tribal duchies of the former *Ostreich*. They were already *regna*, nearly kingdoms of their own. The greater kingdom of the Ottonians needed stabilisation in face of the duchies as well as the emerging Hungarian state with its expansionist

10. *Nationes*, vol. I, vol. III; Zientara, *Świt narodów europejskich* (cf. above, Footnote 2).
11. K. Zernack, 'Die deutsche Nation zwischen Ost und West', in *Nationalgeschichte als Problem der deutschen und der polnischen Geschichtsschreibung*, Brunswick, 1983, pp. 69ff.
12. The best study on this subject now is F. Graus, *Die Nationenbildung der Westslaven im Mittelalter* (= *Nationes*, vol. III), Sigmaringen, 1980.

tendencies towards Central Europe. To increase its prestige, the new
kingdom laid claim to the imperial traditions of the Franconian monarchy. In this process it also had to build up its own position in Central
Europe in competition with the young emerging Christian powers on
its eastern border, particularly with Poland. The renewal of the title of
Kaiser by Otto I in 962 also served this purpose.[13]

Furthermore, the Church of Rome intervened in these developments and, by creating national archdioceses, encouraged the nation-
building of the peoples of peripheral regions in the East and soon
thereafter also in the North. As Helmut Beumann put it: 'Here it was
easier to establish the concordance of the political and the religious
institutions than in the former realm of the Franks or in Germany. The
idea of nation could echo back from the East and support the development of national consciousness in the area from which its elements
originated'. At the peak of the conflict between the universal powers —
the Emperor and the Pope — in the course of the Investiture Crisis, the
concept of nation was even used in open controversy against the
Empire.[14]

After the Investiture Crisis, the question of state sovereignty became
very important for the nation-building process. But this question
remained disputed in Christianity for a long time, and the longer this
was the case, the more the distinction between the formative processes
of state on the one hand and nation on the other became apparent.

It was in East Central Europe, as František Graus has shown, that
the building of a political nation first reached its completion.[15] Thus,
the consciousness of Polonia — as a political union of its leading groups
— was able to survive the periods of a weak state. Graus finds domestic
developments responsible for this increased consistency. Walter Schlesinger speaks of the structural consolidation of the *Großvölker*.[16] It is

13. H. Beumann, 'Das Kaisertum Ottos des Großen. Ein Rückblick nach tausend
Jahren', *Historische Zeitschrift*, 195, 1962, pp. 529–73; idem, 'Laurentius und Mauritius.
Zu den missionspolitischen Folgen des Ungarnsieges Ottos des Großen', in *Festschrift für
Walter Schlesinger*, vol. II, H. Beumann (ed.), Cologne and Vienna, 1974, pp. 238–75;
H. Ludat, 'Böhmen und die Anfänge Ottos I', in *Politik, Gesellschaft, Geschichtsschreibung.
Gießener Festgabe für F. Graus zum 60. Geburtstag*, Cologne and Vienna, 1982, pp. 131–64;
idem, *An Elbe und Oder um das Jahr 1000. Skizzen zur Politik des Ottonenreichs und der slavischen
Mächte in Mitteleuropa*, Cologne and Vienna, 1971, pp. 9ff.
14. H. Beumann, *Die Bedeutung des Kaisertums*, p. 362.
15. F. Graus, *Die Nationenbildung der Westslaven*, pp. 85ff.
16. W. Schlesinger, *Die Entstehung der europäischen Nationen. Protokolle der Arbeitstagungen
des Konstanzer Arbeitskreises für mittelalterliche Geschichte*, March/October 1965, no. 127, p.
14; no. 132, pp. 132f.

at this point, as a result of the protracted consolidation of the viable elements of a nation — such as the dynasty, the concept of land, the holy patrons of the nation — that a national consciousness could be articulated by the ruling elites. These outbursts of national consciousness are generally highlighted in research, so that the impression has arisen that the emergence of nations during the Middle Ages is merely a matter of the development of consciousness. But this is primarily a problem of tradition. Since the political elites articulate and represent this consciousness, it is most easily traceable in the sources. It was, however, always the reflection of something inherent in the structure of the society. But as an expression of the superiority of the larger group to which one belongs, this concept of nation is by no means the most important value in the world of the Middle Ages. There was Christendom, there was the *res publica nationum*, for example, and a ruler such as the German King could be the king of many peoples.

However, the social expansion in the course of the colonisation during the High Middle Ages and the ethnic mix resulting from the settlement processes in the princedoms of East Central Europe led to a more general use of national slogans. Emotional outbursts and thus the first expressions of a medieval concept of nationalism resulted. Especially in the cities, where people lived very close to one another, these emotional feelings became virulent. For this reason Graus has said that the completion of the first nation-building process is unthinkable without the emergence and development of the medieval bourgeoisie in connection with the founding of cities from the thirteenth century onwards. One could go even further and say that the mature, feudalistic development of society in the High Middle Ages is in itself the reason for the stabilisation of the European world as a community of nations after the disintegration of the Carolingian Empire — a stabilisation as social entities constituted with an articulated group consciousness of their ruling elites, that is to say, as political nations. This was particularly the case in East Central Europe (in Poland, Bohemia and Hungary, which we must consider as the most characteristic examples for the High Medieval upswing).[17]

This is all embedded in a structural difference between East and West which is based on the problem of imperial succession and the formation of states in the tenth century: apparently the nations emerging from the former Franconian Empire had to go through more complicated nation-building processes under the influence of the

17. K. Zernack, *Osteuropa. Eine Einführung in seine Geschichte*, Munich, 1977, p. 35.

Roman–Frankish traditions and their transformation. In the case of the Germans, the French and the Italians these processes in the pre-modern period are never so final as in the case of the nations without an imperial tradition, the Poles, the Bohemians and the Hungarians. As for the latter, it is far easier to discern the impulses leading to the foundation of a nation, and the formation of the medieval nation is completed here more quickly. And since they lack an old imperial allegiance, they also have a special need to develop their own imperial tradition out of the national consciousness of the ruling elites. This is apparent in the *Corona-Regni* concept of the estate republics of the Late Middle Ages.[18] Thus two centres of European nation-building processes came into being during the Middle Ages — one on each side of the old Franconian *Ostgrenze*. Germany and Poland are so to speak the prototypes. Northern Europe tended more to the East Central European type, the Apennine Peninsula to the Western type. The two special cases are Russia and England on the fringes in East and West.

Although the observation is correct that nation-building and the establishment of states are not identical processes, it is just as important for the study of nations to observe the correlation between the two processes. One should remember that in respect to the influence of 'state' on national societies, there are different levels and areas of intensity. With the 'Ideal Type' of political feudalism, as developed by Otto Hintze, one can also discover important 'constitutional' connotations in the history of state and nation. For Hintze this feudalism was realised where a knighthood emerges as an estate, attains local and regional prominence on account of its standing as landlord, and finally shares power in the monarchy by developing estate institutions.[19]

The political nations in Germany and Poland in the Early Modern period are the expression of such a mature feudalism. Constitutionally, their development involved the interpenetration and homogenisation of

18. The older concepts: M. Hellmann (ed.), *Corona Regni. Studien über die Krone als Symbol des Staates im späten Mittelalter*, Wege der Forschung III, Darmstadt, 1961; J. M. Bak, *Königtum und Stände in Ungarn im 14.-16. Jahrhundert*, Wiesbaden, 1973; K. Górski, *Communitas, princeps, Corona Regni. Studia selecta*, Warsaw, Poznań and Toruń, 1976; F. Graus, *Die Nationsbildung der Westslaven*, pp. 89ff.; W. H. Fritze, 'Corona regni Bohemiae. Die Entstehung des böhmischen Königtums im 12. Jahrhundert im Widerspiel von Kaiser, Fürst und Adel', in W. H. Fritze, *Frühzeit zwischen Ostsee und Donau. Ausgewählte Beiträge zum geschichtlichen Werden im ostlichen Mitteleuropa , vom 6. bis zum 13. Jahrhundert*, L. Kuchenbuch and W. Schich (eds.), Berlin, 1982, pp. 209–96, here pp. 291ff.

19. O. Hintze, 'Wesen und Verbreitung des Feudalismus', cited here according to the reprint in the volume edited by G. Oestreich: O. Hintze, *Feudalismus – Kapitalismus*, Göttingen, 1970, pp. 12–47, here pp. 17ff.

the 'republic' of the estates (*Ständerepublik*). This state form is represented in its ultimate perfection by the Commonwealth of the Polish Nobles brought about by their supra-ethnic assimilative power and their highly developed political culture. To be sure, this political freedom grew at the expense of social equality.[20]

Despite fundamental differences with respect to the constitutional role of the aristocracy (namely the princes of the Reich), the Holy Roman Empire of the Early Modern period is structurally quite similar to Poland. Focusing on the differences first, one notices the following: in Poland the initial, regional particularism of the High Middle Ages was overcome quickly, the balance of power among the nobles permitted the integration of the old *provinciae*, which had caused previous fragmentation, into the state. The republic of 1569 in the so-called Union of Lublin is, at the same time, a federal, united state.[21] In Germany, by contrast, the sovereign princes of the territories attained complete independence, which furthered the development of regional consciousness, one could say of territorial patriotism. In the Reich the free cities, the clergy and the imperial knighthood were the bearers of unity; they articulated German national consciousness in its most striking form, which showed increasingly humanistic and less and less constitutional traits.[22]

With what right can we, nevertheless, speak of a basic constitutional analogy between Germany and Poland in this period? Both Reichs were able to survive the ordeal of the Reformation and the accompanying confessional conflict because the republican Reich-structures could be applied in a stabilising manner, albeit for different reasons and with varying strength. In Poland the danger of a political split along confessional lines was historically avoided from the outset. The Reformation was not needed to achieve the political rights of the nobles, and

20. Polish historians have always paid great attention to the problems of political culture of the nobles' republic. For recent works see J. Tazbir, 'Recherches sur la conscience nationale en Pologne aux XVIe et XVIIe siecles', *Acta Poloniae Historica*, 14, 1966, pp. 5–22; J. A. Gierowski (ed.), *Dzieje kultury politycznej w Polsce (The History of Political Culture in Poland)* Warsaw, 1977; J. Tazbir, *Kultura szlachecka w Polsce. Rozkwit — upadek — relikty* (The Szlachta-Culture in Poland. The Blossoming — the Decline — the Remnants), Warsaw, 1978; Z. Kowalewski, *Rzeczpospolita nie doceniona. Kultura naukowa i polityczna Polski przedrozbiorowej (The Unappreciated Republic. The Scholarly and Political Culture of Poland Before the Partitions)*, Warsaw, 1982.

21. 'St. Russocki, Zwischen Monarchie, Aristokratie und Adelsdemokratie', in *Das spätmittelalterliche Königtum im europäischen Vergleich*, Sigmaringen, 1987, pp. 385–404.

22. Most recently H. Lutz, 'Die deutsche Nation zu Beginn der Neuzeit. Fragen nach dem Gelingen und Scheitern deutscher Einheit im 16. Jahrhundert', *Historische Zeitschrift*, 234, 1982, pp. 529–99; idem, *Das Ringen um deutsche Einheit und kirchliche Erneuerung. Von Maximilian I. bis zum Westfälischen Frieden, 1490 bis 1649*, Berlin, 1983.

the Reformation in Poland was primarily a problem of belief.[23] (Admittedly, Orthodoxy in connection with the Cossack question confronted the republic with a task which, as the seventeenth century came to show, could not be mastered with the commonwealth concept.)

The Holy Roman Empire, however, was hardly able to make use of the opportunity of the confessional armistice (in the so-called 'Augsburg Interim' of 1548) to prevent its disintegration into a Protestant and a Catholic nation. In the consciousness of the Germans little was left of the compromise of 1548–55. Nevertheless, it was possible to hold together the two confessional bodies in one nation of Germans. And, not least, this was due to the stabilisation of the Empire as a 'republic' — as a constitutional body protecting German liberties — by foreign intervention during the Thirty Years War. The prevention of Habsburg hegemony by means of constitutional politics from outside,[24] that is, in the context of a European peace settlement, saved the 'empire with two nations' which yet was to keep its fragile identity as one Germany. In that sense the Holy Roman Empire is comparable in a very revealing way to the *Rzeczpospolita obojga narodów*.

In attempting to integrate the history of Poland into the history of European nations, the outstanding Polish historian of nation-building, the late Benedykt Zientara, came to the conclusion that the political nation — restricted to one single estate, the *Szlachta* — was bound to lead the state into catastrophe.[25] I find this judgement somewhat exaggerated and would like to pose the question regarding the downfall of both old republics — Poland and the Holy Roman Empire — in Central Europe differently. That brings me to the main part of my paper.

The destruction of the Holy Roman Empire as a viable form for the political existence of the German nation commenced with the struggle against the system of 1648. The Peace of Westphalia was soon considered an instrument of French hegemony, and so, since the 1680s there had been an effort to contain 'the exorbitant court' of France.[26] But some of the protagonists of this new balance of power against

---

23. G. Schramm, *Der polnische Adel und die Reformation*, Wiesbaden, 1965.
24. The stabilisation of Central Europe by international security policies was the concept of the Swedish *Reichskanzler* Axel Oxenstierna, see G. Barudio, *Gustav Adolf der Große*, Frankfurt, 1982, pp. 492ff.
25. B. Zientara, 'Nationale Strukturen' (cf. above, Footnote 4), p. 308.
26. Ranke shows this in his famous essay 'Die Großen Mächte', *Historisch-Politische Zeitschrift*, 2, 1833, pp. 1–51.

France disapproved also of the old republican principle in Europe. That applies to the new Great Power Russia with respect to Poland and Sweden, to the rising power Prussia with respect to Poland and Germany, and to Austria with respect to the many lands under its rule, especially Hungary. Nevertheless; these new powers in the East soon recognised the value of the bankrupt, old systems in establishing their spheres of influence here. Russia and Prussia played a key role in manipulating them, to conserve 'anarchy'.[27] The undermining of the political viability of the Holy Roman Empire and the Polish Republic by a joint policy of the two upstarts accounted for the fact that in the course of the eighteenth century, at least in Germany, the national orientation towards the Empire slowly disappeared. Other loyalties became more important for the political elites and the absolutist bureaucracies of the Early Modern states in Germany. In the last period of the Empire, at the turn of the eighteenth century, it was thus possible to imagine that an Austrian, a Prussian or a Bavarian nation could be a political reality, whereas the German national consciousness won a new, so to speak a philosophical base; it was the consciousness of a nation of the educated, of the intellectuals. As Werner Conze put it: 'the "German nation" became an often used, emotional concept of values', which was mainly, but 'not totally separated from a political understanding of nation'. This was the later so-called 'Kulturnation'.[28]

The specific German–Polish connection with respect to nation-building in this period is entirely influenced by this new system of Great Powers into which Austria and Prussia let themselves be drawn. Leopold von Ranke has shown — and his explanation is still valid — how the new system of the eighteenth century pushed France into revolution. How the same powers managed to draw 'the overwhelming power and ambition of Russia' into Central Europe by way of partitioning Poland, this apparently was not recognised by the famous Prussian historian. Today we must say that the simultaneous occurrence of the upheavals in France and the partitions of Poland, that is, of the revolutionary liquidation and the annexationist conservation of the *ancien règime*, is of immense importance for the history of nations in

27. K. Zernack, 'Negative Polenpolitik als Grundlage deutschrussischer Diplomatie in der Mächtepolitik des 18. Jahrhunderts', in *Deutschland und Rußland. Festschrift für G. von Rauch*, Stuttgart, 1974, pp. 144–59; idem, 'Das preußische Königtum und die polnische Republik im europäischen Mächtesystem des 18. Jahrhunderts (1701–1763)', in *Jahrbuch für die Geschichte Mittel- und Ostdeutschlands*, 30, 1981, pp. 1–20.
28. W. Conze, '"Deutschland" und "deutsche Nation" als historische Begriffe', in O. Büsch and J. J. Sheehan (eds.), *Die Rolle der Nation in der deutschen Geschichte und Gegenwart*, Berlin, 1985, p. 30.

transition to the Modern period.[29]

Just as in the Middle Ages we also have in the Modern period two Europes, two historical aspects of the European nation. The border runs now along the line determined by the French Revolution. In the West the future belonged to the socially emancipated and politically more and more active nations; contrasting with the East where conservative empires persisted. The nations there still had to attain their emancipation in bitter struggles, in delayed revolutions which never completely reached their goals — revolutions which were tamed by the imperial hegemonial system. After the dissolution of the old Empire, the German nation was caught between these two fronts and was politically crushed between the two 'half'-German Great Powers in the East, Prussia and Austria, and the third Germany in the West. Thus, also in modern times one can perceive a clear structural difference between the German and the Polish nation, analogous to the situation in the Middle Ages. Although there are external similarities in the process of dissolution of both republican systems[30] at the turn of the nineteenth century, I would like to stress that the consequences were totally different.

After the fall of the Empire, 'Germany' was no longer able to adopt a political concept of nation. At the close of the Old European age, we are confronted with the most profound breach in the history of the German nation. Henceforth and without the Holy Roman Empire, nation-building in Germany had to start from totally different premises. The claim often made by Marxist as well as by conservative historians, that absolutism facilitated the transition to the modern age in Central Europe as a kind of revolution from above, is valid only in a very narrow sense. The effects of absolutism in Germany and of the Revolution in France were similar only *ex negativo*: the old European nations of the Germans and the French were a thing of the past.

Poland, on the other hand, which never experienced genuine absolutism, kept alive the political concept of nation of the old *Rzeczpospolita* and modernised it in the course of the constitutional debates of the famous Four Years' Parliament from 1788 to 1791. Not even the removal or alienation of the State could invalidate the ability of this political concept of nation to mobilise the people. Even after 1793, the year the May Constitution was suspended, this concept remained an integrative factor, independent of the existence of a state. In this

29. For a new interpretation see M. G. Müller, *Die Teilungen Polens 1772, 1793, 1795*, Munich, 1984.
30. K. v. Raumer and N. Botzenhart, *Deutschland um 1800*, Wiesbaden, 1980, p. 179.

respect, what Rousseau said in his *Considérations* (in the year of the first partition of Poland) was confirmed: Poland was now, since the destruction of the Swedish Republic by the absolutist coup of Gustav III, the last haven of political culture of Old Europe, the last rock of political openness in the surf of universal tyranny.[31] This was no rhetoric. This thinker on the threshold of a new era did not, of course, overlook the *barbarie féodale* which burdened Poland. The debates of this 'Long Parliament' had been concerned with the possibilities and ways of overcoming Poland's social deformities.

Without doubt the Constitution of May, 1791, the product of these debates, broke with the social tradition of the feudal nation of the nobles. In this question one should trust the judgement of contemporaries such as Joachim Christoph Schulz, August Ludwig Schlözer and Edmund Burke, and pay no heed to later doubts, which are still to be heard today. A generation later Joachim Lelewel, in particular, interpreted in very clear terms the transformation of the political nation from an association of privileged groups into a stratum of citizens.[32] In the new political system there was now a place for other groups of the old 'estate' society, which had not felt themselves represented until then.

Thus, by way of 'modernisation', an old European nation was saved. This has to be seen in the wider context of the general reform efforts in the period. It was also in this connection that the Early Modern states Prussia and Austria saw opportunities for their own nation-building. But these prospects were frustrated by the effects of the French Revolution as manifested by Napoleon. It is true that the German national consciousness of the bourgeois and intellectual elites was articulated during the wars of liberation more clearly and more politically than it had been in the circles of the Enlightenment and the educational reform.[33] But at the same time this consciousness had a tense relationship with the claims of the monarchies in Germany and their stubbornly conservative aristocracies and bureaucracies. Thus, one can say that, in principle, the Polish May Constitution and the French Revolution had the same meaning for the question of nationhood in Central

31. J.-J. Rousseau, *Oeuvres complètes*, vol. III, Paris, 1964, p. 976.
32. 'Trzy konstytucje polskie 1791, 1807, 1815 porównal i róznice ich rozwazyl Joachim Lelewel w roku 1831' ('Three Polish Constitutions 1791, 1807, 1815 compared and analysed for differences by J. Lelewel in 1831'), in *Dziela* VIII, 1961, pp. 467–544. For a modern interpretation of the May Constitution see E. Rostworowski, *Ostatni król Rzeczypospolitej. Geneza i upadek konstytucji 3 Maja (The Last King of the Republic. The Genesis and the Fall of the Constitution of 3 May)*, Warsaw, 1966.
33. H. Schulze, *Der Weg zum Nationalstaat. Die deutsche Nationalbewegung vom 18. Jahrhundert bis zur Reichsgründung*, Munich, 1985, pp. 63ff.

Europe, but their effects in Poland and Germany, both with very different traditions, led to totally contrary paths.

Poland's path through the Reform Era of Stanislaw August and the May Constitution was a successful attempt at constitutional reform with the assistance of an intact and functioning political public opinion (*politische Öffentlichkeit*). The political foundations of the old nation of nobles, that is its freedom in the republic, its will and its ability to reform, remained in force also for the modern nation of citizens during the period of partition. Precisely because of the partitions, the new emancipatory concept of nation was linked with the tradition of the state of the old republic. This can be easily illustrated by early Polish Romanticism in its interpretation of national history as the foundation stone of nationhood.[34] It is significant for our German–Polish comparison that in Germany before 1848 the interpretation of national history never served in a similar way as a godfather for an emancipatory concept of nationhood. It was only by creating the idea of *Volksgeschichte* (the history of the 'folk') that the traditional weakness of the political nation in Germany could be compensated for historiographically.[35] As James J. Sheehan put it: 'The national interpretation of German history was formed during a series of bitter struggles over Germany's future between the liberals and their enemies'. Ultimately, the historiographical myth of the 'German mission of Prussia' emerged as the victor.[36]

It is evident that the validity of such a development of nation-building as I am presenting in this paper cannot be grasped within the framework of a universal theory of a bourgeois society. For such a theory the basic problem would only be the degree of backwardness of a nation such as the Poles, whose spokesmen remained for generations the nobles and the intellectuals. But it is precisely this political spectrum and the orientation of these groups which are the object of penetrating modern historical research in the field of modern nation-building in Poland.[37] It becomes apparent that the spokesmen are only seldom aristocrats, who inclined more and more to a conservative co-existence with the powers of partition (Prussia and Austria at least).

34. M. Wawrykowa, *"Für Eure und unsere Freiheit"*. *Studentenschaft und junge Intelligenz in Ost- und Mitteleuropa in der ersten Hälfte des 19. Jahrhunderts*, Wiesbaden, 1985, pp. 52ff.

35. K. v. See, *Die Ideen von 1789 und die Ideen von 1914*, Frankfurt, 1975.

36. J. J. Sheehan, 'The Problem of Nation in Germany History', in Büsch and Sheehan, *Die Rolle der Nation*, Berlin, 1985, p. 10.

37. T. Łepkowski, *Polska — narodziny nowoczesnego narodu 1764–1870* (Poland, the Birth of a Modern Nation, 1764–1870), Warsaw, 1967; Z. Stefanowska (ed.), *Tradycje szlacheckié w kulturze polskiej* (Gentry Traditions in Polish Culture), Warsaw, 1976; J. Jedlicki, *Klejnot a bariery społeczne* (Coats of Arms and Social Barriers), Warsaw, 1968.

Instead of the aristocrats, the strong group of the 'middle nobility', together with the artist-intellectuals rose to the leading position in the national movement. The Polish sociologist Wladyslaw Markiewicz has analysed this group with respect to its nation-building effect:

> There are only a few nations in the world in which writers and artists play such a great role in shaping public opinion and society as was the case in Poland. The price for this was the continuously diminishing importance of political and economic functions in attempting to preserve the nation. That was understandable during the period of partition and in the first years of independence, but in time it led to a mystification of the social position of the so-called creators of the national culture. . . . It is certainly still controversial, whether the Poles would have faired better if enterprising businessmen, instead of writers and clever organizers of economic life, had formed the national physiognomy, as was the case in most bourgeois democracies.[38]

From what has been said so far, it should have become clear what is to be understood by the political culture and mentality of a modern nation. They are the forces which sustained the nations of the nineteenth century in their conflicts with the existing states of Central Europe. In the period of the revolutions from 1830 until 1848 those Polish–German differences which our comparative reflections have already discerned for the eighteenth century become clearly evident. In the year 1848 the Polish concept of nation was integrated into the general demand for freedom and independence ('for your and our freedom') in contrast to the dichotomous liberalism of Germany, fractionised from the very beginning into a radical democratic (republican) and a moderate constitutional but 'imperial' (monarchist) wing.[39] It is true that the feeling of solidarity among the Germans was strong enough to prevent a Prussian, an Austrian or a Bavarian nation, but it was unable to develop, beyond the Deutsche Bund, a modern concept of a state for the Germans in Central Europe. This modern nation-state would have necessitated an unbroken liberal concept of the nation — and secondly more favourable circumstances in European policy. Under the conditions of 1848, however, the radical-liberal vision of a Europe of separate and equal nations had no prospect of success.[40] But also all the other attempts at a solution of the German Question —

---

38. W. Markiewicz, 'Die Bildung der modernen polnischen Nation', in *Nationalgeschichte*, Brunswick, 1983, p. 50.

39. See M. G. Müller, 'Deutsche und polnische Nation im Vormärz.' in *Polen und die polnische Frage in der Geschichte der Hohenzollernmonarchie*, Berlin, 1982, pp. 85ff.; *Die deutschpolnischen Beziehungen 1831–1848: Vormärz und Völkerfrühling*, Brunswick, 1979.

40. G. Wollstein, *Das Großdeutschland der Paulskirche*, Düsseldorf, 1977.

whether the starting points were Old Austrian, Pan-Germanic or Prussian — 'lesser' German — *sooner or later*, as is well known, failed. Since 1848 German history has presented itself as the dilemma of the German concept of nation in contrast to Poland's consciousness of national identity. This is a problem of German–Polish relations which has left its mark on the history of Central Europe until today.

The Problem of 'Beziehungsgeschichte'

In deliberating on the problem of relations I would like now, in conclusion, to draw your attention to a rather neglected aspect of nation-building which I have treated in detail elsewhere. A constitutive factor of the history of European nations is that they have relations with each other, primarily as Christian nations (though not only as such). This factor is already apparent in the process of becoming a nation, in the Christianisation from above. That is to say, in that European history became a history of peoples and states around the year 1000, these early Christian nations already have relations with one another, in fact, they attain their specific national individuality as an effect of their relations to other nations. Thus, nation as a constitutive factor of European history is unthinkable without the interrelatedness of the national histories of Europe.[41]

But the relations between the nations can be of varying intensity. That depends on the geographic as well as the political factors. Of course, bordering nations always have more relevance for historical relations than those at a greater distance. But the importance of geographical proximity can be neutralised by political connections. Here one need think only of the relationship between France and Poland in the Early Modern period or of the problem of modern British–Russian relations. On the other hand, as times change factors which were once relevant for relationships can become less important and can take on a new aspect. This is illustrated quite well, for example, by the relations between Sweden and Russia in the course of history.

Without doubt Prussia especially has contributed to the peculiar intensity of German-Polish relations. Starting with the first steps in

---

41. For a more detailed study see K. Zernack, 'Das Jahrtausend der deutsch-polnischen Beziehungsgeschichte als Problemfeld und Forschungsaufgabe', in *Grundfragen der Beziehungen zwischen Deutschen, Polaben und Polen*, Berlin, 1976.

state formation associated with the name of Prussia until the threshold of its downfall — in other words, from the period of the State of the Teutonic Order in Prussia until the dissolution of the Hohenzollern monarchy — Prussia was a state between the nations of the Germans and the Poles, and as such it had a profound effect on the historical nature of German–Polish relations.[42]

This special influence of Prussia between the two nations acquired a new quality when Prussia made itself the pace-setter for German unity and opted for the integrative nation-state. The Prussian 'small German' solution to the German Question was based territorially after 1848 on an undivided Prussia, and that conditioned the non-solution of the Polish question. This meant the perpetuation of the partition of Poland. The young Theodor Fontane complained bitterly at the time about Prussia's traditional inability to practise constitutionalism.[43] This shortcoming was peculiar to Prussian Germany. In that respect the Hohenzollern monarchy contrasted sharply with Austria, the other 'semi-German' power: Prussia programmatically renounced federal principles in settling its nationality problems. Since 1871 it stood between the nations of the Germans and the Poles no longer as a more or less just authority as was the case before the founding of the Reich; it was now the instrument of an imperial and integrative German nationalism. The Poles could only counter with their own nationalism, which was increasingly uncompromising and took hold of ever broader sections of the population. In other words, the Poles opposed the Prussians by showing their will to fight for the rebirth of their national independence, based geographically on the republic which had been divided at the end of the eighteenth century.

Under these circumstances, historical research and thinking in Poland developed an understanding of Polish history which regarded the effects of Prussian policy increasingly as a danger to their existence. Soon two antagonistic concepts, Prussia's German mission and the Polish view of a century-old, deadly German threat to Poland, opposed each other. This confrontation became increasingly irreconcilable the graver the national conflict of the Germans and the Poles became in the age of the World Wars.[44]

Much of this is still effective today. In Poland it has a powerful effect — more so than in Germany — upon interpretations of the current

---

42. K. Zernack, 'Die Geschichte Preußens und das Problem der deutsch–polnischen Beziehungen', in *Jahrbücher für Geschichte Osteuropas N.F.*, 31 (1831), pp. 28ff.
43. Letter to Bernhard von Lepel, Berlin, 12 October 1848.
44. A. Lawaty, *Das Ende des Staates Preußen in polnischer Sicht*, Berlin, 1986.

situation in Central Europe. The German public and most of the German historians — one can even venture to say in both German states — tend to become irritated with the radicalism of this historical thinking of their Polish neighbours. On the other hand, it is true that the contact between the German and Polish historians is more intensive and unprejudiced than ever before, and without doubt both sides agree on the interpretation of many crucial questions which were controversial in the past. But it will take some time before there is a broad effect, which could bring about a profound change in the attitudes and mentalities so deeply rooted in both nations.

GÜNTHER HEYDEMANN

The 'Crazy Year' 1848: The Revolution in Germany and Palmerston's Policy.

The word 'Vormärz' occurs frequently in academic as well as more popular historical writing. As a result, what it stands for — the definitive end of the 1815 Restoration marked by the outbreak of the European Revolution of 1848 — has, perhaps, been stripped of some of the immediacy and perplexity with which contemporaries experienced that period of history. For within a few weeks an upheaval took place from Palermo to Kiel and from Paris to Budapest which seemed boundless in its dynamism.

The 'Wiener Ordnung', 'the repose of Europe' (Castlereagh), established by the European powers in 1815 to replace the old European order that the events of 1789 and Napoleon had destroyed, was, of course, constantly disturbed from the outset. Certainly there was no shortage of revolts and revolutions between 1820 and 1847. But since

Author's Note: This essay attempts to outline the essential features of Lord Palmerston's policy towards the Frankfurt National Assembly and its efforts to bring about a unification of Germany. Due to the limited space available, it is restricted to the British foreign policy actually pursued during this phase. Queen Victoria's and Prince Albert's criticism of it, and that of the Tory opposition, is dealt with only peripherally. Criticism by the Court, whose *spiritus rector* was undoubtedly the Consort, is discussed in detail in: H. R. Fischer-Aue, *Die Deutschlandpolitik des Prinzgemahls Albert von England 1848–52*, Coburg and Hanover, 1953; F. Eyck, *The Prince Consort. A Political Biography*, London, 1959; and B. Connell (ed.), *Regina v. Palmerston. The Correspondence between Queen Victoria and her Foreign and Prime Ministers, 1837–1865*, London, 1962, esp. pp. 106ff. Benjamin Disraeli's speech to the Commons on 19 April 1848 was the classic expression of Tory opposition to Palmerston's policy towards Germany; cf. *Hansard*, Third Series, Vol. XCVIII, pp. 509–24. See also F. G. Weber, 'Palmerston and Prussian Liberalism, 1848', *The Journal of Modern History*, 35, 1963, pp. 125–36, and W. J. Orr, 'British Diplomacy and the German Problem 1848–1850', *Albion*, vol. 10, 1978, pp. 209–36.

the first sparks in Palermo in January 1848, which were fanned into flames in Paris just a few weeks later and quickly became an all-consuming European conflagration, events had taken on extraordinary and unprecedented dimensions.

Only Great Britain and Russia, the two powers on Europe's flanks, and at the same time the dominant states of the period, had remained untouched.[1] London and St Petersburg were suddenly confronted by a completely new situation and could no longer act, but merely *react*, since the revolutionary flood had swept away monarchs and ministers with whom they had been in close contact but a few days earlier. The conventional centres of power, Paris, Vienna, Berlin, not to mention the smaller courts, had disappeared and left a power vacuum in the continent of Europe. The fall of Metternich had become the symbol of the victorious revolution. This was the very man whose name was identified with the political watchwords of the time: Restoration and Reaction.

Professional observers had, of course, been predicting a full-scale revolutionary upheaval for years. In England in particular, the increasing political instability especially in Germany and Italy had been noted with growing concern. But now the crisis of political legitimacy that had been smouldering on the continent for decades had, by the immediate juxtaposition of an 'old-style economic crisis since 1846 and a crisis of modern industrial growth 1847/48',[2] led to social tensions which needed immediate political and socio-economic solutions and were far worse than the most pessimistic predictions.

Crisis management was called for. But British policy towards Germany and the German states during the Revolution, far from existing in a vacuum, was a continuation of principles and perceptions moulded by the developments since 1815.

England's role in the creation of a post-Napoleonic peace settlement was as great as her contribution to the suppression of French continen-

1. On the reasons why no revolution occurred in Britain, despite decades of crisis in home policy, cf. A. M. Birke, 'Die Revolution von 1848 und England', in K. Kluxen and A. M. Birke (eds.), *Viktorianisches England aus deutscher Perspektive*, Prinz-Albert-Studien, vol. 1, Munich, New York, London and Paris, 1983, pp. 49–60. For Russia in this connection cf. E. Oberländer, 'Das politische System Nikolaus' I. (1825–1855)', in T. Schieder (ed.), *Handbuch der Europäischen Geschichte*, vol. 5, Stuttgart, 1981, pp. 648–53.
2. M. Stürmer, 'Nationalstaat und Massendemokratie im Mächtesystem 1848 oder die Geburt eines Dilemmas', in J. Becker and A. Hillgruber (eds.), *Die Deutsche Frage im 19. und 20. Jahrhundert*, Schriften der Philosophischen Fakultäten der Universität Augsburg, vol. 24, Munich, 1983, pp. 37–50, p. 47.

tal expansion. Under her massive political influence a European order had been created based on the principles of balance and a levelling of interests. To the British, the stabilisation of the central European area by a kind of regional balancing system was of particular importance; and the creation of the Deutscher Bund as a Confederation of states assured the safety of Central Europe, the main theatre of war at the time of the great enemy Napoleon. The conglomerate of German states, along with the great German powers of Prussia and Austria to the north and south, made an attack from outside — here the British were thinking primarily of France or Russia — into an incalculable risk, while at the same time the German states themselves were too weak to undertake any military initiatives of their own. This, at least as far as Central Europe was concerned, was the principle upon which the 'Wiener Ordnung' was based.

In fact, the establishment of a stable peace was the main political aim of British policy. The British were quite aware, however, that only the bare essentials of security policy had been achieved.[3]

It was almost equally important to them to channel firmly the emergent political dynamism of liberalism and nationalism which had been greatly stimulated by the battles with and against Napoleon. All the more so since the 'Wiener Ordnung' basically tended to suppress such inclinations. However, fundamental disagreement soon developed between Great Britain and the continental Great Powers as regards the political handling of this difficult matter. England's membership of the Holy Alliance was little more than a formality, and when, after 1815, Russia, Austria and Prussia gradually tried to create the right for the alliance to political and military intervention in the event of an uprising in one of its member states, England retreated. As long as a revolution did not spread beyond national boundaries, incapacitate the newly-established European balance or interfere with British security interests, they saw no reason to intervene.[4]

3. See the overview by K. Bourne, *The Foreign Policy of Victorian England, 1830–1902,* Oxford, 1970, with its invaluable source edition; see also, with a critical assessment of the latest research literature, A. Sked (ed.), *Europe's Balance of Power,* London and Basingstoke, 1979 and F. R. Bridge and R. Bullen, *The Great Powers and the European System 1815–1914,* London and New York, 1980. In recent years W. D. Gruner has compiled new material on Britain's policy towards Germany before and after 1815, cf. idem, *Die Deutsche Frage. Ein Problem der europäischen Geschichte seit 1800,* Munich, 1985, with extensive bibliographical details. On the older view of German historiography, since rejected by researchers, that Britain opposed all attempts at German unification from the start, cf. K. Hildebrand, 'Die deutsche Reichsgründung im Urteil der britischen Politik', *Francia,* 5 (1977), pp. 399–424 with details of earlier literature.
4. Cf. for example, Castlereagh's circular note to the British representatives at foreign courts of 19 January 1821, extracts of which are reprinted in G. Schönbrunn (ed.),

This conflict, however, was not merely political but ideological too. As a constitutional monarchy with a long parliamentary tradition Great Britain felt superior to the autocratic monarchies on the Continent. The First Reform Act of 1832 had done much to prove that reforms and political compromises were perfectly appropriate means of dealing with socio-political pressure at home. For this reason, particularly in the 1830s and 1840s, Britain was constantly suggesting that the Central and Southern European states, riddled as they were with crises and uprisings, should introduce constitutions. This earned her the reputation of being a supporter of liberal constitutional and nationalist movements, but was at the same time the main politico-ideological line pursued by Britain right up to the outbreak of the Revolution, the only variations being with regard to points of emphasis, which changed with alternating Whig and Tory governments.

In addition, there was an economic factor that was becoming increasingly important. The states of the German Confederation constituted England's most important continental market. As the first country to experience the Industrial Revolution it was essential for Britain to be able to export her products, especially since the British economy had suffered so greatly as a result of the Continental Blockade and the transfer from a war economy to a peacetime one. The Zollverein, founded by Prussia in 1834, whose protectionist customs duties made it much more difficult to import British goods, was thus an obstacle to British economic policy, even though in the long run it might become an even larger export market.[5]

Thus, as regards Germany between 1815 and 1848, British security, ideological and economic interests were not always at one. Lord Palmerston, who became Foreign Secretary again in Lord John Russell's Cabinet in July 1846, made this quite clear in a memorandum written six months before the outbreak of revolution in Germany.[6] The British were fundamentally opposed to any disruption of the system of collective security created at Vienna and therefore supported liberal–

Geschichte in Quellen. Das bürgerliche Zeitalter 1815–1914, Munich, 1980, p. 32. On the question of 'British interests', about which no definitive conclusion has yet been reached, cf. K. Hildebrand, '"British Interests" und "Pax Britannica". Grundfragen englischer Außenpolitik im 19. und 20. Jahrhundert', *HZ*, 221 (1975), pp. 623–39 and W. Gruner, '"British Interest" und Friedenssicherung. Zur Interaktion von britischer Innen- und Außenpolitik', *HZ*, 224 (1977), pp. 92–104.

5. The thesis that British recognised early on the Zollverein's function as a forerunner of German unification, as presented in the work by M. Vogt, *Das vormärzliche Deutschland im Urteil englischer Schriften, Zeitschriften und Bücher 1830–1947*, (Mach. Diss.), Göttingen, 1962, must be treated with some caution, although the work is otherwise rich in material.

6. Quoted again in Bourne, *The Foreign Policy*, pp. 277–80.

constitutional movements in the German states. But at the same time the Zollverein was regarded as an obstacle to British economic and trade policy.

Shortly before the outbreak of revolution in Germany, Palmerston followed the same course as he had done in Italy, where the uprisings in Milan and Palermo just two months earlier had initiated the year of revolution. In the autumn of 1847 Palmerston had sent Lord Minto on a special mission to the Italian courts to get reliable information about the tense political situation and to advocate political reform. Now, in February 1848, he ordered Sir Stratford Canning, one of his most able diplomats and British Ambassador to the Ottoman Empire to go overland to Constantinople so that he could call in *en route* at Hanover, Dresden, Berlin, Vienna and Munich and get first-hand information from the German courts.

But by the time Canning reached Berlin the situation had changed radically. Just before he arrived the Revolution had broken out, shattering the traditional pillars of the Prussian state. The King was discredited by his over-hasty support for the revolutionary movement, the confidence of the Officer Corps and the bureaucracy was shaken and the army was demoralised by street fighting. What was even more disquieting, however, was the radical about-turn in foreign policy taken by the new liberal Camphausen–Hansemann Cabinet which had just taken office. This was heading for a full-scale European conflict over the Polish question without taking any possible consequence into account. Prussian Foreign Minister Heinrich von Arnim Suchow intended to grant a constitution to those Poles living in the Grand Duchy of Posen (Poznań). In Canning's view this would inevitably lead to an intensification of the conflict with Russia — and thus to war in Europe — since it struck the very Achilles' heel of Russian security policy. Canning was astonished at the naïvety of the new Prussian government which seemed to assume that French and English support for its pro-Polish policy — a policy antagonistic to Russia — would be forthcoming. But he was just as amazed by the stupidity of this policy itself: East and West Prussia were excluded from the debate on Poland, as if the Polish question were restricted to the Grand Duchy of Posen.

> Baron d'Armin and his colleagues appear to overlook every consideration but that of favouring the Poles of the Grand Duchy in their enterprise for the rescue of Poland from the dominion of Russia. They are ready to incur a war

with Russia for the object. They hope eventually to obtain the countenance and support of England, they reckon with confidence upon having that of France.[7]

Canning was also disturbed by the Polish policy of the Vorparlament in Frankfurt. This favoured the establishment of a new Polish empire as recompense for the division of Poland. But at the same time it wanted to include West and East Prussia in the German Confederation as part both territorial and as regards international law, of a German nation-state. What this policy did not take into account, however, was the considerable number of Poles living in these areas. Was this the work of enthusiastic, but politically naïve, amateurs?

Of course, the Polish policy of both Berlin and Frankfurt was so unbalanced that it was bound to misfire. Liberals in Germany immediately lost all sympathy with Poland when continued attacks by the militia of the newly-founded Polish National Committee in Posen on Germans resident there led to Prussian troops being called in.[8] Palmerston, who was receiving constant reports from Canning, must have felt justified in his wait-and-see attitude towards the developments in Germany. He was in complete agreement with Canning's final report:

> Necessity or fortune may possibly suggest due seasons the means of stemming this torrent and guiding its turbulent waters into a safer channel. But for the present at least there would seem to be little beyond an outward abatement of violence to encourage hope — and much in that growing disregard of settled principles to warrant a painful feeling of anxiety for the future destinies of Prussia, and, by a natural consequence, of Germany and Europe.[9]

But even before the crisis over the Polish question had been diffused another one had emerged: the Schleswig-Holstein question. This too was on the periphery of the new nation-state (about whose boundaries many liberals had greatly exaggerated conceptions); again the problem of ethnic minorities was involved, and again the conflict immediately assumed European proportions. What is more, the political consequences of the permanent influence of this conflict on the question of

7. Quoted from Stürmer, 'Nationalstaat und Massendemokratie', p. 40 (Canning to Palmerston, 3 April 1848).
8. Cf. E. Kolb, 'Polenbild und Polenfreundschaft der deutschen Frühliberalen. Zu Motivation und Funktion außenpolitischer Parteinahme im Vormärz', *Saeculum*, 26 (1975), pp. 111–27 which illustrates the rift between Poland and Germany caused by the Polish policy of the German liberals during the Revolution of 1848–9.
9. Quoted from Stürner, 'Nationalstaat und Massendemokratie', p. 43 (Canning to Palmerston, 3 April 1848).

the constitution, which still had to be settled by the Frankfurt National Assembly, were immense. For the attempts at the social and constitutional reform by the liberal bourgeoise, who formed a majority in the Assembly, were counteracted by the serious conflict in foreign policy and largely discredited. No attempt will be made here to reiterate the extremely complicated national and constitutional problems involved in the Schleswig-Holstein question.[10] The complexity of the matter is perhaps summed up by Palmerston's comment that there were only three people who could get to grips with it: himself, Prince Albert and a German professor of history who had since died. What it came down to, in a nutshell, was that Danish and German liberal nationalists were at loggerheads. Each wanted to incorporate the Duchy of Schleswig into their own state, in an attempt to exploit politically the national majority or minority living there.

In the chronology of events it was particularly unfortunate that the death of King Christian VIII (20 January 1848) greatly intensified Danish constitutional problems, increased the political tension and enforced the claims of the liberal revolutionary movements in the two states.[11] The Danish revolutionary movement adopted the policy of the new King Friedrich VII. Its aim was to break the link between the two duchies that had existed since 1460, based on the principle of 'up ewig ungedeelt', and to attempt, by force of arms, to incorporate Schleswig into the Kingdom of Denmark. At the zenith of the revolutionary wave in Germany this led to the establishment of a provisional government in Kiel (24 March 1848), which sought military assistance from the German Confederation, which the revolution had not affected, in suppressing the Danish troops in Schleswig.

Danish belligerence caused a huge outcry amongst the German public, which was in any case politically aroused. In the light of the nationalist fervour that was an essential component of the Revolution in virtually all European countries in 1848, the battle for Schleswig-Holstein became a symbol of the battle for German unity itself. On 12 April the Bundestag decided to send Federal troops into Schleswig —

10. Cf. the comprehensive work on this complex of problems by K. A. P. Sandiford, *Great Britain and the Schleswig–Holstein Question 1848–64: A study in British Diplomacy, Politics and Public Opinion*, Toronto and Buffalo, 1975, esp. pp. 19–33. On the foreign policy of the Paulskirche see G. Wollstein, *Das "Großdeutschland" der Paulskirche. Nationale Ziele in der bürgerlichen Revolution 1848–49*, Düsseldorf, 1977.

11. H. Lutz, *Zwischen Habsburg und Preußen. Deutschland 1816–1866*, Die Deutschen und ihre Nation, vol. 2, Berlin, 1985, p. 251. The behaviour of the German Liberals in the Schleswig–Holstein question is dismissed in A. J. P. Taylor, *The Struggle for Mastery in Europe*, 4th edn., Oxford and New York 1983, p. 13, with the sentence: 'It was almost as though Italian nationalists had regarded Malta as their first essential aim'.

an act that contravened international law since Schleswig, unlike Holstein, was not part of the German Confederation. The arrival of Federal troops and the Prussian militia soon afterwards escalated the conflict into a European affair, since now, in addition to the problems of national and international law, the balance of Europe was at stake. Admittedly, the significance of the Baltic Sea as a route for international trade and transport had diminished in the course of the nineteenth century. But Britain was as concerned as ever that Denmark should continue to defend the northern Bosporus, thereby denying Russia the opportunity to gain control of the gateway to the North Sea. The close dynastic links between Russia and the Danish royal family were regarded as potentially dangerous in this totally uncertain political situation. Thus, a mere four weeks after the outbreak of revolution in Germany, England's lengthy, and not always successful involvement in the German–Danish conflict began. At the same time the National Assembly at the Paulskirche in Frankfurt inherited from the German Confederation an 'almost inextricable tangle of pressing constitutional and international problems'.[12] The political maturity of the Parliament created by the revolution would be put to the test, in the eyes of the European powers, by its political handling of these problems.

There is no doubt that the situation in Northern Germany which had emerged within a month was not in England's interests. Shortly before the outbreak of revolution Palmerston had underlined once again to Fox-Strangways, British Ambassador to the German Confederation in Frankfurt, the British attitude to the unpredictable state of affairs in Germany: England had but limited interest in German unification since the balance created by the Congress of Vienna was still considered adequate and the British government had no desire to commit itself to a definite plan to unify Germany. Moreover, Palmerston preferred an agreement reached by the individual German states on the future composition of Germany to a unification process 'produced by a revolutionary movement and a National Assembly convened for this purpose'.[13] Palmerston approved completely of the attempts by the Paulskirche at constitutional and social reform. But he still had his reservations, as evidenced by Britain's refusal, on formal grounds, to give official recognition to the Frankfurt National Assembly:

12. Lutz, *Zwischen Habsburg und Preußen*, p. 251.
13. Cf. G. Gillessen, *Lord Palmerston und die Einigung Deutschlands. Die englische Politik von der Paulskirche bis zu den Dresdener Konferenzen (1848–1851)*, Lübeck and Hamburg, 1961, p. 26. Gillessen's work, and that of W. E. Mosse, *The European Powers and the German Question 1848–71 with special reference to England and Russia*, Cambridge, 1958, are the leading works on the subject to date and have greatly influenced the present essay.

The Diet which was constituted in accordance with the provision of the Treaty of Vienna, and to which a British Minister has hitherto been accredited, has dissolved itself, and although that Diet by its last act devolved upon the Arch Duke John as *Reichsverweser* the functions with which the Diet itself had been invested, yet the Arch Duke John has been invested by the German Parliament at Frankfurt with only a temporary and provisional character and that Parliament has not as yet determined what is to be the final and permanent arrangement for the Supreme Authority of United Germany.[14]

For this reason he sent an observer rather than an accredited ambassador to Frankfurt. On Palmerston's behalf, Lord Cowley, Wellington's nephew, one of the best German experts among British diplomats and superbly equipped to fulfil his function in Frankfurt, was to represent British interests. As his first task Cowley had to proclaim British economic interests — in the event of a unified Germany —, in which customs barriers should be lower than those of the Zollverein.[15]

The focus of Britain's interest in Germany remained, however, on the Schleswig-Holstein question. And yet it was the intransigent policy of the Paulskirche in this very matter that was to cost it its political reputation as far as Palmerston was concerned.

A more deep-rooted reason for this was undoubtedly the completely different perspectives of the two sides. The overwhelming majority of the representatives, from far left to centre right, with broad support from the populace, regarded the incorporation of Schleswig-Holstein as a *conditio sine qua non* of the future German nation-state. The British — and indeed the Russians — on the other hand could not see 'why a reorganization of Germany should necessarily involve the destruction of the Danish monarchy'.[16]

This far-reaching divergence of opinion was soon to lead to considerable frustrations on both sides. In response to Disraeli's famous speech on Schleswig-Holstein on 19 April 1848, Palmerston gave a speech in the House of Commons in which he demanded that Prussia, the decisive military power in the German–Danish conflict, should withdraw her troops from Schleswig.[17] He also offered his services as an intermediary, thereby putting Prussia under indirect pressure. As a result, an order was sent from Berlin at the end of May to the Prussian General Wrangel to withdraw behind the Eider Line. A solution to the

---

14. Quoted from Mosse, *The European Powers*, p. 23.
15. Cf. ibid.
16. Ibid., p. 20.
17. *Hansard*, Third Series, vol. XCVIII, pp. 524–6.

problem seemed to be in sight. Hopes of a settlement were dashed, however, by the decision of the Paulskirche of 9 May when its representatives in the National Assembly declared the Schleswig-Holstein question to be a matter for the nation, at the same time denying Prussia the right to negotiate single-handed with Denmark. This also put an end to Palmerston's aim as intermediary, namely to call a cease-fire as a basis from which the dispute could be settled. And then even Prussia went off the rails and indulged in the inconsistency so symptomatic of Friedrich Wilhelm IV and his policy, by opening new negotiations with Denmark from which England was excluded.

When a cease-fire was eventually brought about Prussia wanted to sign the treaty jointly with Frankfurt so that responsibility would be shared; for the pressure of public opinion was felt as strongly in Berlin as it was in Frankfurt. But the representatives in the Paulskirche opposed this suggestion for two reasons: firstly because they had always rejected Prussian leadership in the negotiations and secondly because they considered the compromise that had been negotiated to be too disadvantageous to Germany. Thus both sides tried to palm off responsibility without being able to find any solution to the conflict. Being aware of all this, Lord Cowley had the embarrassing task of conveying to Palmerston the lack of political perception amongst the ministers and representatives in Frankfurt:

> I really have scruples in committing to a despatch all that is to be said upon the state of affairs here, and upon the character of men, who have undertaken to conduct them. The affairs themselves seem to be getting into greater confusion every day — and as to the Ministers, a more useless inefficient body of men were never brought together.[18]

The cease-fire eventually agreed between Prussia and Denmark in Malmö on 26 August 1848 had been achieved with great difficulty and only under pressure from England and Russia. Its rejection by the representatives in the Paulskirche was the final straw as far as Palmerston was concerned — their political reputation in his eyes was ruined. Cowley was instructed to ask those representatives whom he knew 'whether they are mad and really intend to disavow the Prusso-Danish armistice. If they are deliberately determined to rush into conflict with Europe, including as it seems, Prussia, well and good, let them take the consequences. *Quos Deus vult perdere dementat prius*'.[19]

18. Quoted from Mosse, *The European Powers*, p. 24.
19. Ibid.

On 16 September 1848 the cease-fire was finally agreed to after all, by a majority of one. But it was too late to change Palmerston's unfavourable impression. He had long since been aware that Frankfurt's suicidal destruction of its own political authority would inevitably shift the balance of political power back to Berlin and Vienna.

While Palmerston was outraged by the German liberals' failure to grasp the reality of the situation, the Germans themselves were becoming increasingly critical of Britain's attitude. Six months after the outbreak of revolution the majority of representatives at the Paulskirche had doubts as to whether British policy really favoured a unification of Germany.[20] German liberalism had a strong nationalistic streak, most clearly evident in the north as representing the German 'Irridenta'.[21] This opposed the view that England was, as ever, basically in favour of German unification, but was prevented from supporting the Germans over the Schleswig-Holstein question by her own interests in the balance and security of Europe.[22]

A series of factors finally brought the men of Frankfurt to their senses: the September uprising; the obvious re-emergence of the old powers and elites; temporary respite from the politically difficult problem of Schleswig–Holstein; growing awareness amongst the moderate liberals of their own powerlessness; and the fact that work on the Constitution, postponed for so long, was at last started. The majority of the representatives reluctantly accepted that Prussia would have to play a leading role in solving the question of German unity. Similarly, they also came to the conclusion that if any part of Austria at all could belong to a future united German state, it was her German territories, but nothing more.

In the mean time, Cowley's precise reports had earned him Palmerston's growing confidence. In the late autumn of 1848 he became the main advocate of the idea that German unification should be arranged between Frankfurt and Berlin. On 8 October he was the first to inform the Foreign Secretary of Gagern's plan to constitute a smaller German Confederation for the unification of Germany. This smaller German Confederation should exclude Austria, but should maintain a constant alliance with the Habsburg Monarchy — Gagern's idea of 'engerer und

20. Gillessen, *Lord Palmerston*, p. 152.
21. H. Schulze, *Der Weg zum Nationalstaat. Die deutsche Nationalbewegung vom 18. Jahrhundert bis zur Reichsgründung*, Munich, 1985, p. 90.
22. Cf. Gillessen, *Lord Palmerston*, p. 152.

weiterer Bund'.[23] On 27 October, however, the vote on Articles 2 and 3 of the Constitution showed that the majority of Representatives favoured a solution whereby the German areas of Austria were included in a greater Germany (*großdeutsche Lösung*). The resignation of the Schmerling government, brought about by Schwarzenberg's rejection of any firm commitment, dealt a severe blow to plans for a greater Germany. But even then Gagern — who succeeded Schmerling as prime minister — was unable to gain the majority needed to execute his plan. Palmerston was so irritated by the lack of decision in Frankfurt that he had remained silent on the subject of Germany since the end of September. But now he indicated to Cowley, his observer in Frankfurt, that he considered Gagern's plan to be reasonably realistic.[24] Otherwise, he still felt justified in his wait-and-see attitude towards the uncertain political developments in Germany, following the principle *in dubiis siste*.[25] However, there was still no progress towards the realisation of Gagern's plan which required at least minimal co-operation between Frankfurt and Berlin. A series of events then occurred which must have seemed to the representatives of the Paulskirche like one piece of bad news after the other: the transfer of the Prussian National Assembly from Berlin to Brandenburg in order to separate it from its political basis; the reinforcement of the army in Berlin; the formation of citizens' defence units to protect against supporters of the radical democrats (which meant a further split in the revolutionary movement); and the formation of a conservative government which, on 5 December, dissolved the Prussian National Assembly and proclaimed a new constitution. For the most difficult political problems still had to be tackled; final agreement had not been reached on the constitution, nor was it clear what role Prussia or the Prussian King would play in any future unified Germany.

On 28 January 1849 Prussia boosted the chances of a *kleindeutsche Lösung* by issuing a circular note suggesting in a deliberate affront to Austria a union based on the existing German Confederation, thereby indirectly staking a claim to leadership of this purely German organisation. In essence, this was Gagern's plan, even though the Prussian King did not approve of the preliminary decisions on the Constitution formulated in Frankfurt. With Palmerston's tacit consent Cowley redoubled his efforts to increase co-operation between Berlin and Frankfurt.[26]

23. Cf. ibid., p. 50, note 146 (Public Record Office, F.O. 30/111).
24. Cf. ibid., p. 57, note 170 and 171 (PRO, F.O. 208/36).
25. Cf. ibid., p. 70, note 213 (Palmerston in a letter to Prince Albert, 8 May 1849).

On 4 March 1849, however, the political picture changed again when Schwarzenberg proclaimed the new Austrian Constitution, the Reichstag at Krems having been dissolved by form of a *coup d'état* so to speak. Austria's German territories were no longer permitted to join a future unified German state. Just five days later Schwarzenberg sent a note to the central government in Frankfurt with the suggestion that all the Austrian states, including the non-German ones, should join, thereby staking Austria's claim to leadership of this major Central European state with its 70 million inhabitants.

This had the effect of a catalyst. In the Paulskirche an unexpected coalition was formed between the moderate liberals and the left-wing. As a result of Gagern's 'clever move' (Gagern's 'kühner Griff') the left now conceded to the liberals the election of the Prussian King as German Emperor, while the liberal centre withdrew their reservations about universal suffrage. On 28 March Cowley informed Palmerston that Friedrich Wilhelm IV had been elected German Emperor by the Paulskirche.[27]

Cowley was greatly concerned by the liberal/left-wing alliance. This was an indicator to him that a degree of constitutional freedom had been reached beyond what could be expected of a people inexperienced in parliamentary or democratic procedures. He felt that acceptance of universal suffrage was recognition of the sovereignty of the people.[28] On 28 April, however, Friedrich Wilhelm IV turned down the imperial crown and at the same time rejected the Frankfurt Constitution. The die was cast against German unification, the fate of the first German parliament as representative of the whole German nation was sealed. There was a brief epilogue in Stuttgart where a rump parliament saw the final resurgence of radical democratic forces in south-western Germany. But, as in Austria, they were too weak to defeat Prussia's renewed political and military might.

When the curtain finally fell on the political stage in Frankfurt, power of decision over future developments in Germany returned unchallenged to Berlin and Vienna, even though the flames of the Revolution had not yet been fully extinguished. In German matters the dominant role fell to Berlin, since the government in Vienna was still preoccupied

26. Cf. ibid., p. 61.
27. Cf. ibid., p. 63, note 191 (PRO F.O. 30/124).
28. Cf. ibid., p. 65, note 198 (PRO F.O. 30/125).

with the suppression of Hungary. On 7 July 1849 Palmerston therefore sent lengthy and detailed instructions to Westmoreland, his ambassador in Berlin, as to how Britain's policy was to be represented after the experiences of the Revolution in Germany.[29]

This communication is of particular importance in that it summarises the British assessment of the political developments in Germany since the outbreak of the Revolution. It also outlines the specific options available to Britain in the future with regard to a possible unification of Germany. Still working on the principle that Britain should not interfere in Germany's affairs, Palmerston basically favoured a unification of Germany under Prussia: 'It would no doubt be advantageous to the German People, with reference both to their internal interests, and to their foreign relations, and it would consequently on that account be advantageous to Europe at large'. The Foreign Secretary considered Prussia to be best suited to the role of leadership because she alone, of all the German states, fulfilled two essential criteria: 'A substantial powerful state' and at the same time 'heart and soul German'. The central German states of Hanover, Saxony, Württemberg and Bavaria had insufficient power to qualify for the role. And Austria, constantly beset by the problems inherent in her various nationalities, was also unsuited to the task. Palmerston was quite aware, however, that Prussia could not expect immediate wholehearted support in this task, but would have to work cautiously towards it: 'It is most desirable for the working out of such a scheme, that Prussia should disarm the jealousies and allay the fears of the smaller sovereignties by respecting their political existence, and by not expecting from them any sacrifices which would be incompatible therewith'. A consolidation, as regards security, of the Central European area, with its proven potential to disrupt the balance of Europe, would push even British commercial interests into second place.

It would be both precipitous and unhistorical, however, to see this important document on British policy towards Germany in the nineteenth century as a prophecy of the unification of Germany under Bismarck's Prussia a good twenty years later. Not only would this contradict the process of 'trial and error' that was to characterise the next two decades; it would also take no account of the fact that at this stage the *kleindeutsche Lösung* had no claim to priority.[30] The decisions

29. Cf. V. Valentin, *Bismarcks Reichsgründung im Urteil englischer Diplomaten*, Amsterdam 1937, p. 500. The following quotations from this letter.

30. Cf. the presentation of the various models for unification in Schulze, *Der Weg zum Nationalstaat*, p. 110.

reached by the National Assembly in the spring of the 1849 had not dealt such a severe blow to the supporters of the *großdeutsche Lösung* under Austria that such a solution had passed into the realms of fantasy. Not did Prussia yet enjoy the whole-hearted support necessary for her to assume this unifying role. On the contrary, the zigzag course of Prussian policy under Friedrich Wilhelm IV, which was to lead to the diplomatic defeat of Olmütz two years later, meant that at first Prussia completely lost her footing as the pacemaker of German unification. Indeed, many contemporaries formed the impression that she was unsuited to the role.

None the less, from Palmerston's point of view, the *kleindeutsche Lösung* under Prussia had at least one thing in its favour: most of the multi-national complications arising from the various aspiring nationalisms of the day could be avoided. It would not have been in Britain's security interests, however, if the German areas of Austria had been included in the German nation-state, which was still, after all, a mere blueprint, not a reality. From the British point of view, a power block would then exist in Central Europe strong enough to destroy the balance so essential to peace in Europe. Palmerston's preference was for a Northern Germany under Prussian leadership that was stronger than the fairly loose German Confederation and should therefore act as a counter-weight to both France and Russia. This did not mean, however, that Palmerston would not oppose any attempt by Prussia to expand in the north, for example in the direction of Denmark. Rather, it was in keeping with the policy he had pursued in the Italian question during and after the Revolution: a united northern Italy under Piedmont-Sardinia was, in his view, considerably better equipped to act as a counter-weight to both France and Austria. And indeed such a policy — for Prussia as well as for Piedmont-Sardinia — had historical roots. At the Congress of Vienna it was largely as a result of Castlereagh's initiative that Prussia, by her acquisition of the Rhineland, became the dominant power in the north German area, while Piedmont-Sardinia, through the incorporation of the old city republic of Genoa and its *terra ferma*, became the most powerful all-Italian power in the north of Appenine peninsula.[31] Both these states were to act as barriers between East and West in the interests of security. In the case of Prussia and the North German area, however, this was the most that Palmerston, in view of his security interests, could accept. For ulti-

31. Cf. C. Webster, *The Foreign Policy of Lord Castlereagh, 1812–1815*, vol. 1, London, 1931, pp. 313, 397.

mately the disruptions of the Revolution in Germany had served to make the complexity of German unification, with its various possible territorial combinations, all the more apparent. The inclusion of the southern German states or indeed the German territories of Austria was already enough, in British eyes, to make the size of the power block in Central Europe unacceptable. What is more, the inclusion of Austria's German territories would, in Palmerstons's view, strip her of her function as a 'pillar' in Eastern Central and South Eastern Europe.[32]

These were the main reasons why Palmerston favoured Prussia over Austria. A possible further motive was that any future political alliance between England and Prussia could potentially be strengthened by the fact that the two states were both Protestant.

Although Palmerston supported Prussia, this was by no means his optimal solution for the future of Germany. But the fiasco of the Revolution had made it quite clear that his ideals of the 'liberalisation and parliamentarisation of a united nation' were not yet possible.[33] After all, it was the moderate Liberals in Germany, the very ones who had been called upon to prevent revolution by means of reform, thereby realising Palmerston's political concept of preventative modernisation in Europe, who had failed at the decisive moment. They should have consolidated their newly-acquired political power by carefully weighing up their priorities and then given it the necessary legitimacy by means of a constitution. Instead they let themselves be carried away by the force of nationalism and lost their political reputation through their amateurish handling of the Schleswig-Holstein question. This mistake was irreversible. By the time a constitution was eventually drawn up, it was too late. And so it was merely a question of time before the established powers and elites recovered from the shock of the Revolution, gradually reconquered the political terrain and regained control of the political developments in Germany.

So the future of Germany and her main political problem of nation-building could not be foreseen. The events of the two years of revolution had rather shown that Great Britain had to watch the political development in Germany with the greatest attention.

32. Cf. Palmerston's House of Commons Speech on Hungary, 21 July 1849. *Hansard*, Third Series, CVII, pp. 808ff.
33. K. Hildebrand, 'Staatskunst oder Systemzwang? Die 'Deutsche Frage' als Problem der Weltpolitik', *HZ*, 228 (1979), pp. 624–44, p. 642.

HAGEN SCHULZE

Europe and the German Question in Historical Perspective

'German Unity is certain to come'. This is the title of a recent German book[1] in which former right-wing historians and journalists together with theoreticians of the 'new left' unfurled fairy-tale scenarios: in West Germany, the departure of all American, British and other foreign troops from the territory of the Federal Republic; in East Germany, a similar disengagement of the Soviet army, creating a peaceful demilitarised zone in the middle of Europe. Therein would exist two German states which, somehow overcoming the contradictions which arise from their opposing political systems, would fall into each other's brotherly arms and, through confederation and a federal constitution, find their way back to a unity of the Germans. The sensation was enormous: the book probably found more reviewers than buyers, and in the West it provided an occasion to seek a clue to transformations in the German soul. The result appeared disquieting: 'foreshadowing the danger of a new German nationalism which would bring together both the left and the right', wrote the Bonn correspondent of the *New York Times*.[2]

Are the Germans again departing for new national adventures? Is peace again threatened from the centre of Europe? Are the 'incertidues allemandes' beginning all over again? Anyone reading American,

1. W. Venohr (ed.), *Die deutsche Einheit kommt bestimmt*, Bergisch Gladbach, 1982.
2. J. Vinocour, 'Germany's Season of Discontent', *The New York Times Magazine*, 8 August 1982, p. 52.

British or French newspapers must have the impression that dangerous things are happening in Germany. The various warning voices taken together unfold the picture of a retreat of the Federal Republic to anti-Western, neutral positions. In the search for their lost identity, it is said, the Germans have fallen back on their old romantic attitude towards politics. Their anxiety for the future is mixed with an increasingly aggressive anti-Americanism, and the agitations of the 'Greens' and the Peace Movement remind many of the behaviour of another German movement fifty years earlier. In *Harper's Magazine*, Timothy Garton Ash even recalled a statement of Tucholsky's: 'It begins in green and ends bloody red'.[3] Is German history the eternal recurrence of the same?

This picture is indeed not without relation to reality. For example, anyone who observed the recent meeting of 3,000 representatives of European peace groups in Berlin could follow vehement debates between the guests from abroad and the German delegates. The unity of the German nation, it was said there, must concern every advocate of peace, for all of Germany would be the battlefield in the case of a nuclear conflict between East and West. For this reason, all of Germany should be divested of soldiers and weapons. When the 'occupiers' of both sides would leave the country, the result would be a neutral united Germany which would insure world peace. The non-German listeners, on the contrary, found the vision of a state with 80 million Germans in the middle of Europe to be predominantly horrifying; sharp controversies arose, and the disagreements remained.[4] Thus it seems as if the German Question were on the agenda again, although from another direction than the hitherto usual one. The idea of the German nation is commonly considered to be a right-wing phenomenon. But except for a handful of noisy neo-Nazis, who constitute a legal and pedagogical rather than a genuine political problem, there is no longer a uniform, politically effective right in the Federal Republic of Germany. Instead, the German question is predominantly discussed today where it originally arose at the beginning of the nineteenth century: on the left, from the Social Democrats to the Peace Movement and the Greens.

But one should not overrate this discussion. It is the normal reaction to the economic and political crisis in which the Western alliance stands, and it takes place in a largely intellectual sphere which is

3. T. G. Ash, 'Why the Germans don't love us', *Harper's Magazine*, May 1984, p. 23.
4. G. P. Hefty, 'Die deutsche Frage zwingst die Friedenskonferenz zu einer akribischen Debatte', *Frankfurter Allgemeine Zeitung*, 13 May 1984.

distant from politics. The population of the Federal Republic thinks quite differently: according to a 1984 poll, while 79 per cent believe that the reunification of Germany should be an important goal of German politics, only 16 per cent are prepared to pay for that reunification with a neutralisation of the Federal Republic. More than half of the population believes, on the contrary, that the reunification is a distant goal which must be left to time, and only half a percent hold the reunification to be the most important goal of German politics.[5] The authoritative politicians of the CDU, CSU, FDP and predominantly also of the SPD see no alternative to the Atlantic alliance and European integration, and the contacts between the two German states indeed solidify the division, because they lead to normalisation on the basis of the status quo.

There are, however, uncertainties. The Federal Republic's permanent tie to the West is not only a consequence of the Second World War and the confrontation between East and West, but also and most importantly a consequence of the teaching of history. Thus are the young revenged for the fact that none of them has received a decent historical education at school. Like all young movements which claim to be revolutionary, the Green and pacifist movements believe they will be able to spring from a present which they experience as miserable into an earthly paradise, without knowing how this present originated, and without knowing what the Germans in Europe were, what they are, and what they can be. The German Question is a question of European history.

Never in history was the political unity of the Germans taken for granted. It was always a problem, and indeed one for the whole of Europe. The great constant factor of German history, which survives every vicissitude and has decisively influenced every epoch, is Germany's central position in Europe; Germany's fate, one could say without much overstatement, is geography. Since the great upsurge of the Renaissance, with Reformation, Counter-Reformation, and the revolutions in communication and navigation, new physical and philosophic frontiers emerged, forming the world of nations which has determined Europe's destiny up to the present century. England, France, Spain, the Ottoman Empire, Russia, Sweden, the Netherlands

5. E. Noelle-Neumann, 'Im Wartesaal der Geschichte. Bleibt das Bewußtsein der deutschen Einheit lebendig?', in W. Weidenfeld (ed.), *Nachdenken über Deutschland. Materialien zur politischen Kultur der Deutschen Frage*, Cologne, 1985, pp. 133–46.

and Denmark ranged themselves, with more or less natural boundaries, on the periphery of Europe. In between lay European no man's
land, a profusion of 'Germanys' — 'les Allemagnes', as one says in
France — a multitude of larger or smaller territories between Maas
and Memel, Etsch and Belt, where German was generally spoken. For
the rest, however, each was dependent on the respective ruler and his
religion, and perceived the Kaiser and the Empire as most as a
colourful *fata Morgana*: stirring, but very distant and without substance.

The fact that a modern great power could not develop in this area as
in the rest of Europe had a number of causes: the absence of a natural
central point, the absence of natural boundaries; the country was
dispersed, open on all sides, and moreover, transportation was impeded by a landscape cut up by rivers and mountains. Certainly there
was an attempt at the beginning of the sixteenth century to form a
united German state out of the transnational, rather metaphysical
structure of the Holy Roman Empire. In the following period, however,
German unity became a victim of the Reformation and Counter-
Reformation. While the struggle between the two denominations was
decided one way or the other in every other European state, it remained undecided in Germany, petrified to a certain degree in the
territorial state principle of *cuius regio, eius religio*. The territorial division
was arched over by the religious one, with consequences for the
political culture of the Germans which have remained visible up to the
present.

This split remained the principle of the Holy Roman Empire, a
structure without its own statehood, organisation or power, all of which
were transferred to the territories and imperial cities. Their 'liberties'
(*Libertäten*), their sovereign rights were guaranteed after the Thirty
Years War by an international treaty, the Peace of Westphalia of 1648.
Since then, the constitution of the Empire — 'an irregular body of state
which resembles a monster', as Pufendorf says[6] — was considered to be
a component of European international law and the organisation,
order, and foundations of its internal politics the business of all the
European powers.

This constellation was no accident, but the logical result of the
European order. Only the amorphous condition of Central Europe held
the Continent in balance, and a glance at the map shows why: anyone
who possessed this region, whether it was one of the European Great

6. Severinus de Monzambano (= Samuel v. Pufendorf), *De statu imperii germanici*
(1666), ed. by H. Breßlau, Berlin, 1922, p. 94.

Powers or a power that developed in Central Europe itself, could be the master of the Continent. Hence every concentration of power in Germany was seen as a threat to the European equilibrium; the necessary consequence was the formation of hostile coalitions, whose success was all the more probable, as a Central European hegemonial power had to assert itself on several fronts at the same time, and had no defensible borders.

For this reason, the European neighbours considered the 'liberties' of the more than 300 small German states to be the guarantee of European freedom, the equilibrium of the states and their survival. Consequently, the European states guaranteed the survival and the independence of the German *Duodez*-principalities and the Imperial cities. Every encroachment of a great power unquestionably led to competition. Already in the course of earlier times, the attempt of the Habsburgs to transform the half-metaphysical Imperial conglomerate into a more or less modernised state power failed for this reason. In the following period, Austria–Habsburg oriented itself accordingly towards the European periphery, towards Eastern and South Eastern Europe as well as Italy, and in the same measure lost power in Central Europe: this was Austria's long migration out of German history, which found its provisional conclusion in 1866, and probably its final one in 1945.

The rise of Prussia in the course of the eighteenth century acutely disturbed the European balance. What developed here, through the Hohenzollern's desire for domination and thanks to their organisational talent, was a lasting, largely artificial territorial structure, which was torn into provinces that lay far from each other, cut into pieces by rivers, without safe boundaries. It was an unsolvable paradox dictated by the geographical facts: the central position of Prussia demanded a policy by which no neighbour felt threatened; but at the same time Prussia stood on the brink of extinction, as its borders were open and exposed to every pressure. There were two ways out of this dilemma: either Prussia, like Germany as a whole, must open itself to the political influences of its neighbours and allow them to at least partially control its politics. That was the path which Poland, the other large state in the European centre, followed; the consequences for the Polish state were the undermining of its sovereignty, internal anarchy and finally division between its neighbours. Or Prussia could organize itself and arm to the point that it was in a position to conduct and win every war against an adverse coalition on its far-flung borders. And victory was essential, since every conflict, for Prussia, was a question of existence or non-existence. This was the reason for the predominance of the military sector, the bureaucratic organisation of all areas of life, so that the last forces of this wholly destitute state could be organised. This was the source of every tendency towards strenuousness and earnestness, and the lack of urbanity and joy in life which made the Prussian and later the German nature so unpopular with the European neighbours:

That was the basic figuration of Prussian existence: a central position, uncertain borders, fear of hostile coalitions and war on several fronts, a position on the dividing line between East and West and an internal constitution which correspond to the external position. All of this recurred in changing constellations during the course of the centuries, and became all the more determining, as the German concentration of power became greater.

At the beginning of the nineteenth century a further element appeared in the Central European area which threatened the European system: the idea of a German nation-state, which was at first the concern of a few small intellectual circles but seeped down as a cultural value to the lower levels from the Wars of Liberation of 1813 to the Rhine Crisis of 1840, until the idea of a nation-state of all Germans, to echo Karl Marx, stirred the masses and became a material force. At first the European public viewed this benevolently, for — as everywhere in Europe — German nationalism was for the time being the other side of political liberalism, hence a part of the tendencies of the epoch. But as soon as the German nation-state appeared on the horizon as a possible reality, all international sympathy disappeared. In the Revolution of 1848, German nationalism threatened to rupture the Vienna Settlement of 1815; the British ambassador Sir Stratford Canning preached to the Prussian government that it must align its policies 'with the system of international law, the best guarantee of peace, which the enthusiasts of German unity seek so eagerly to overcome, and which the apostles of disorder strive to surrender to contempt and oblivion with such great success'.[7] Sir Stratford's agitators were the liberal champions of the German nation-state, the disorder was, for him, the unification of Germany. The peaceful activity of the Frankfurt Paulskirche delegates seemed, to the cabinets in London, Paris and Petersburg, to be sheer revolt against the holy principles of the balance of power in Europe. French envoys demanded guarantees of the continuation of the sovereign German independent states, British warships demonstrated in the North Sea, Russian troops marched up

---

7. Sir Stratford Canning to Lord Palmerston, 3 April 1848, in M. Stürmer, 'Die Geburt eines Dilemmas', *Merkur*, 35 (1981), p. 5.

to the east Prussian border, and the German Revolution of 1848 — the attempt to found a liberal Greater Germany on the basis of people's sovereignty and human rights — foundered not least on the threat of a danger of intervention by the three powers.

The next advance towards imperial unification, this time supported by Prussian weapons and an alliance of the German princes, succeeded in 1871. One can view the fact that the German national state received in this way a Prussian authoritarian rather than a liberal nation-state form as a tragedy of German history — but would Europe have tolerated another foundation of German unity? Moreover, the Bismarck coup only succeeded because Europe found itself in the depths of the crisis following the Crimean War; the European Concert was disturbed, England and Russia were pulled far apart from one another, France was pinned down by Prussian weapons: a unique historical constellation. But even now, the suspicion in the European capitals was not to be missed, put into words by the British opposition leader Benjamin Disraeli, who declared in the House of Commons on 9 February 1871 that the foundation of the German Empire was nothing less than 'the German revolution, a greater political event than the French revolution of last century. . . . There is not a diplomatic tradition,' continued Disraeli, 'which is not swept away. We have a new world, new influences at work, new and unknown powers and dangers, with which we must deal, and which at the present, like everything new, are still not understandable'.[8]

That the empirical unification signified a European revolution had as a consequence the fact that the new German Empire was enjoined to the utmost good conduct if it wanted to survive for long in the middle of Europe. Bismarck's assurance that the empire was satiated was insufficient for this. Above all, this required the capacity of the new Prussian-German state to subdue its restless internal forces, and to quell and control their pressure for expansion across the imperial borders. This was particularly valid for the fermenting German nationalism, for which the *kleindeutsch* empire was only a partial downpayment towards the realisation of the utopia of a nation-state of all Germans. For this reason, a German Empire under Prussian domination was, while not congenial to the other Great Powers, nevertheless more tolerable than a liberal nation-state behind which the European cabinets and courts suspected German Jacobinism. Also to be subdued

8. W.F. Monypenny, G.E. Buckle, *The Life of Benjamin Disraeli, Earl of Beaconsfield*, vol. 2, London, 1929, p. 473.

were the economic forces which pressed powerfully past the area of the former German Customs Union (Zollverein) and called for colonies and spheres of influence, and not least, the fourth estate, which was attaining self-consciousness and whose threat of a social revolution became increasingly loud — not for nothing was German social democracy considered to be the prime mover in the Socialist International.

That was the dialectic between internal and external politics which necessarily dominated Germany: a quick and thorough liberalisation and democratisation of the Empire, the emancipation of political and social forces stumbled, among other things, against the limits of the German capacity for existence within the balance of powers in Europe. The sentence of John Robert Seeley, according to which the measure of internal freedom within a state stands in inverse relation to the external pressure upon its borders, fits seldom so precisely as in the case of Germany's central position. Consequently it was no contradiction that Bismarck instigated an internal policy of social and political repression, while on the other hand carrying on a foreign policy of compensation and avoidance of war. In fact, the one would not have been possible without the other: Germany was just tolerated by its neighbours as long as the lid sat tight upon its bubbling interior. Accordingly the World War became, sooner or later, unavoidable, as Bismarck's successors abandoned his policy of strict self-limitations, and the power of the old Prussian upper class, which was very content with its position in Germany and didn't possess the least ambition beyond it, became increasingly undermined. The rise of organised interest groups, nationalist and imperialist mass organisations, the gradual process of parliamentarisation and the slow loss of power of the Prussian Ministry of State, the 'struggle for a place in the sun' and the building of a battleship fleet — all of this was connected and irresistibly destroyed the limits which the European system had set to the existence of the German nation-state. In these circumstances, the conflict was as foreseeable as was the German defeat, and probably also the dissolution of the German Empire.

Thus it was a miracle that this did not happen in 1919, after the First World War and the reason for this was the same one which allowed Prussia to survive in 1807 and allowed the German Empire to develop in 1871: a falling asunder of Western and Eastern Europe, and the Western European need for a strategic barrier against Russia. In London and in Washington there circulated the fearful idea that a bolshevist government could gain the upper hand in Germany, which would then co-operate with Soviet Russia to subjugate Europe. That was the sole argument with which a foreign minister of the Weimar Republic could make German policy. All Western policy of the German Empire stood henceforth under the spoken threat of an alliance between the two pariahs of the international system, Germany and the Soviet Union, while the Soviet Union was dealt with through the promise to remain neutral in the case of a new Western policy of intervention. The balancing act between East and West remained a clever trick, and there were observers who became uneasy watching it. Already in the 1920s, the mayor of Cologne, Konrad Adenauer, took exception to the 'fluctuations and swings', as he designated Stresemann's foreign policy,[9] and recommended instead the foundation of peace in Europe on the basis of a close and unilateral alliance between Germany and the Western powers. For the time being, the logic of the political situation as much as diplomatic tradition dictated against this, but the time would come for Adenauer's plans.

Next, however, Hitler appeared. There can be no doubt that the thoughts and actions of the Führer cannot be explained in the line of continuity discussed until now. Hitler did not think in the categories of the international balance of power or political hegemony — the themes of classical European diplomacy were alien and of no interest to him. He wanted something totally different: the world domination of a superior race, which haunted the mad minds of some ideologists, and which was to be established on top of the bones of other, allegedly inferior, races. That was the break away from all tradition, the destructive rule of pure ideology. But it is also true, that Hitler's rule was only possible because members of old German elites had misunderstood him and had helped him rise to power, because they thought that he was only interested in a revision of the outcome of the First World War. That was the most dreadful error in the history of German conservatism, a history rich in blunders. The consequence was not only the end of the German nation-state, but, in addition, the death of millions of people, the destruction of Europe, and the silence of the European Concert.

Only now could the era of Konrad Adenauer begin. The first Chancellor of the Federal Republic of Germany did not need, as he believed, to 'turn Germany's face towards the West' — there was simply no other direction left for the Federal Republic. The reason for this was obvious: the European Concert was silent. An iron curtain

9. Note by Konrad Adenauer on occasion of the Locarno conference, 1925, in P. Weymar, *Konrad Adenauer. Eine Biographie*, Munich, 1955, p. 28.

divided Europe, Germany, Berlin. In the place of one Germany in the middle there were now two Germanys, each on the endangered edge of global power systems and consequently favoured by each of the respective hegemonial powers, America and Soviet Russia. There can be no doubt that the Federal Republic's solid ties to the Western alliance did not in the first instance arise from the free decision of German parties or individual politicians, but from the constraint of the general geographical and political constellation. The choice was easy to make. There was no third option besides that of the Soviet Union or the United States, and as soon as this choice was made — and because of the particular position of the Western victorious powers in the German western zones, the decision was unavoidable — German politics obeyed henceforth the strict constraints of foreign policy. New research based upon American documentary material shows how small was Adenauer's influence on the formulation of the Western reply to the Soviet diplomatic campaign of 1952.[10] For the policies of the Federal Republic there has never existed a missed opportunity to establish German unity through a neutralisation of Germany as a whole. And nothing essential to this strict tie has changed; the new German *Ostpolitik* of 1970, which actually had its first impetus in the Adenauer era, only followed the change in American and French *Ostpolitik*. In the years of the most concentrated Soviet–German relationships there was never a doubt that the Federal Republic pursued and could only pursue its *Ostpolitik* under the protection of the Western alliance.

And this had a decisive effect upon West Germany's political culture. The stability of German democracy would hardly have been possible without the Federal Republic's close ties to the Western democracies. From the very beginning, the Allied support of Adenauer's government lent a considerable measure of prestige to the new German form of state. To exaggerate a bit: for the first time in German history to be a democrat meant to be successful. Who knows how the first German democracy, the Weimar Republic, would have developed had an Ebert, a Stresemann, indeed a Brüning been able to enjoy comparable goodwill from the Allies? Next to the economic success of the post-war years it was above all the political stability of Western Europe which has made possible the domestic political stability of German constitutional order.

10. H. Graml, 'Die Legende von der verpassten Gelegenheit. Zur sowjetischen Notenkampagne von 1952', *Vierteljahrschefte für Zeitgeschichte*, 29 (1981), pp. 307–41; P. März, 'Anmerkungen zur Legende von 1952', *Geschichte in Wissenschaft und Unterricht*, 34 (1983), pp. 643–58.

I will conclude by again taking up the question which was raised at the beginning: what can be said about the solution to the German Question from the perspective of historical experience? The historical lesson, it seems to me, is clear: those who hope for a neutral and demilitarised united Germany between the power blocks lose sight of three factors. One of these follows not from history, but from the present geographical situation: an American withdrawal from the Continent; the consequences for the political order of Europe, in view of the continuing Russian hegemonial power, do not need to be described here. But secondly, a state with 80 million Germans within its borders would be the second largest industrial power in the world, a state, which even with all controls and neutrality could again become the nightmare of Europe. The destabilisation of Europe would become incalculably greater; not peace and freedom, but either sovietisation or war would be the probable consequences. And thirdly, such a constellation would certainly have decisive consequences for the political culture of Germany, even if it remained, against expectations, stable for a period. Without solid institutional ties to the West, entirely dependent upon itself, this Germany would hardly be capable, in the long run, of a peaceful and free policy which remained steadily tied to the West. Thus the old 'incertitudes allemandes' would begin all over again with the serious promotion of neutralisation.

To learn from history means to learn against history. The problem of the German nation-state is inseparable from the problem of the entire European constellation of power; every resolution of the German Question would necessarily have decisive effects upon the entire European order, which must unavoidably, in turn, have repercussions upon the internal order of a reunited Germany. For this reason, not every conceivable reunification is desirable. To be ruled out is not only a solution according to a Communist prescription, but also the option of a neutral disengagement of the Federal Republic from its Western allies as the price for the creation of a German nation-state. The authors of the Federal Constitution recognised this more clearly than many of their sons and grandsons when, in addition to the task of 'securing national and state unity' they imposed upon the politicians the duty to mould this unity in such a way that the German people would be in a position 'to serve world peace as an equal member of a united Europe'. On the basis of the experience of European and German history, a resolution of the German Question — if it is to combine national unity with the secure continuation of free constitutional standards — is only conceivable within a Europe which is freely constituted as a whole, and politically federated in such a form as to exclude the development of disequilibriums of power, coalitions and military conflicts. European policy must become European domestic policy: only then can and may the German people carry out the constitutional commission to 'achieve in free self-determination the unity and freedom of Germany'.

For the inter-German policies of the Federal Republic, this means decisively and principally renouncing a weakened capacity for alliance as the price of a vague chance of reunification, a new German special path. Beyond all particular national interests, and beyond criticism, however justified, of allies in particular cases, the solid tie to the Western alliance remains a categorical imperative for the capacity for life and survival of the West German state and this part of the earth. As the example of other peoples sufficiently demonstrates, one can very well tolerate the status quo over a long period of time without losing sight of a great national goal.

To that end, a further historical experience, which is particularly valid for the Germans but also for other nations such as the Poles and the Italians, is helpful: the foundation of national identity can be maintained for centuries by cultural rather than political ties. Even during the times of the sharpest tensions and divisions, when Germany not only crumbled into hundreds of state structures but was also divided by a deep religious gulf, Germany possessed a common national language, a common culture, a common past. Out of this, in the course of the eighteenth century, a German national culture coalesced, which created a unity of the German spirit within its European involvements. The German national state could never have developed without this German cultural nation, and this spiritual bond, even when repeatedly endangered, has survived until today.

To preserve and further this unity in steady, invigorating competition with the cultural policies of the German Democratic Republic, and its historical and cultural claim to be the sole representative of a good Germany, without at the same time loosening the bonds with the Western alliance and its constitutional standards: the West German task in the future will be to live in this tension. Politically divided until the unforeseeable future, united in culture and history: thus the relationship between the two Germanys appears as the leaf in Goethe's poem on the Gingko-Biloba-tree:

> Ist es Ein lebendig Wesen,
> Das sich in sich selbst getrennt?

> Sind es zwei, die sich erlesen,
> Daß man sie als Eines kennt?
>
> Solche Frage zu erwidern
> Fänd ich wohl den rechten Sinn:
> Fühlst du nicht an meinen Liedern,
> Daß ich Eins und doppelt bin?

(Is it but one being single/Which as same itself divides?/Are there two which choose to mingle/So that one each other hides?/As the answer to such a question/I have found a sense that's true;/Is it not my songs' suggestion/That I'm one and also two?)

Select Bibliography

1. General

Alter, P., *Nationalismus*, Frankfurt on Main, 1985

Barraclough, G., 'German Unification. An Essay in Revision', in *Irish Conference of Historians. Historical Studies*, IV, 1963, pp. 62–81

Baumgart, W., *Vom Europäischen Konzert zum Völkerbund*, Darmstadt, 1974

Becker, J., A. Hillgruber (eds.), *Die Deutsche Frage im 19. und 20. Jahrhundert*, Munich, 1983

Berdahl, R. M., 'New Thoughts on German Nationalism', *American Historical Review*, 77, 1972, pp. 65–80

Bienefeld, M., M. Godfrey (eds.), *The Struggle for Development. National Strategies in an International Context*, Chichester, New York, Brisbane, Toronto and Singapore, 1982

Buse, D. K., J. C. Doerr, *German Nationalisms. A Bibliographical Approach*, New York and London, 1985

Calleo, D., *The German Problem Reconsidered. Germany and the World Order, 1870 to the Present*, Cambridge, 1978

Conze, W., *The Shaping of the German Nation. A Historical Analysis*, London, 1979

Dahrendorf, R., *Society and Democracy in Germany*, Garden City, 1969

Dann, O., 'Nationalismus und sozialer Wandel in Deutschland 1806–1850', in idem. (ed.), *Nationalismus und sozialer Wandel*, Hamburg, 1978, pp. 77–128

Dehio, L., *Gleichgewicht oder Hegemonie. Betrachtungen über ein Grundproblem der neueren Staatengeschichte*, Krefeld, 1948

Dorpalen, A., 'The Unification of Germany in East German Perspectve', *American Historical Review*, 73, 1968, pp. 1069–83

Eisenstadt, S. N., S. Rokkan (eds.), *Building States and Nations. Models and Data Resources*, 2 vols., Beverly Hills, 1973

Eley, G., *From Unification to Nazism. Reinterpreting the German Past*, Boston, 1986

Faber, K.-G., *Die nationalpolitische Publizistik Deutschlands von 1866 bis 1871*, 2 vols., Düsseldorf, 1963

Fehrenbach, E., 'Die Reichsgründung in der deutschen Geschichtsschreibung', in *Reichsgründung 1870/71. Tatsachen, Kontroversen, Interpretationen*, T. Schieder, E. Deuerlein (eds.), Stuttgart, 1970, pp. 259–290

Groote, W. v., *Die Entstehung des Nationalbewußtseins in Nordwestdeutschland 1790–1830*, Göttingen, 1955

Gruner, W. D., *Die deutsche Frage. Ein Problem der europäischen Geschichte seit 1800*, Munich, 1985

Hinrichs, C., W. Berges (eds.), *Die deutsche Frage als Problem der europäischen Geschichte*, Stuttgart, 1961

Hope, N. M., *The Alternative to German Unification. The Anti-Prussian Party Frankfurt, Nassau and the Two Hessen, 1859–1867*, Wiesbaden, 1973

Huber, E. R., *Deutsche Verfassungsgeschichte seit 1789*, vols. 1–4, Stuttgart, 1957–69

Katzenstein, P.J., *Disjoined Partners. Austria and Germany since 1815*, Berkeley, Los Angeles, 1976

Kedourie, E., *Nationalism*, London, 1966

Kohn, H., *The Mind of Germany: The Education of a Nation*, New York, 1960

——, *Prelude to Nation-States. The French and German Experience, 1789–1815*, Princeton, 1967

Lutz, H., *Osterreich-Ungarn und die Gründung des Deutschen Reiches. Europäische Entscheidungen 1867–1871*, Frankfurt on Main, Berlin, Vienna, 1979

Meinecke, F., *Cosmopolitism and the National State*, Princeton, 1970

Meyer, H. C., *Mitteleuropa in German Thought and Action, 1815–1945*, The Hague, 1955

Mitchell, B. R., *European Historical Statistics 1750–1970*, London and Basingstoke, 1978

Mosse, W. E., *The European Powers and the German Question 1848–71. With Special Reference to England and Russia*, Cambridge, 1958

Nipperdey, T., *Deutsche Geschichte 1800–1866. Bürgerwelt und starker Staat*, Munich, 1983

Pflanze, O., 'Nationalism in Europe', *Review of Politics*, 28, 1966, pp. 129–43

Pinson, K. S., *Pietism as a Factor in the Rise of German Nationalism*, New York, 1968

Plessner, H., *Die verspätete Nation. Über politische Verführbarkeit bürgerlichen Geistes*, Mainz, Berlin, Stuttgart and Cologne, 1959

Prignitz, C., *Vaterlandsliebe und Freiheit. Deutscher Patriotismus von 1750 bis 1850*, Wiesbaden, 1981

Sagarra, E., 'The National Movement', in *An Introduction to Nineteenth Century Germany*, Burnt Hill, 1980, Chap. 6

Schulze, H., 'Die Stein-Hardenbergschen Reformen und ihre Bedeutung für die deutsche Geschichte', in Fritz Thyssen Stiftung (ed.), *Preußen — Seine Wirkung auf die deutsche Geschichte*, Stuttgart, 1985

——, *Der Weg zum Nationalstaat. Die deutsche Nationalbewegung vom 18. Jahrhundert bis zur Reichsgründung*, Munich, 1985

Sheehan, J. J., 'What is German History? Reflections on the Role of the Nation in German History and Historiography', *Journal of Modern History*, 53, 1981, pp. 1–23

Showalter, D. E., *Railroads and Rifles. Soldiers, Technology and the Unification of Germany*, Hamden/Conn., 1975

Snyder, L. L., *German Nationalism: The Tragedy of a People. Extremism contra Liberalism in Modern German History*, New York, 1969

Taylor, A.J.P., *The Struggle for Mastery in Europe 1848–1918*, London, 1971

Tilly, C. (ed.), *The Formation of National States in Western Europe*, Princeton, 1975

Zechlin, E., *Die deutsche Einheitsbewegung*, Frankfurt on Main, Berlin, 1967

Zillessen, H., 'Volk — Nation — Vaterland — Die Bedeutungsgehalte und ihre Wandlungen', in H. Zillessen (ed.), *Volk — Nation — Vaterland: Der deutsche Protestantismus und der Nationalismus*, Gütersloh, 1970, pp. 13–47

2. Political and Social Movements

Baron, J., *Das deutsche Vereinswesen und der Staat im 19. Jahrhundert*, Diss. Göttingen, 1962

Becker, J., *Liberaler Staat und Kirche in der Ära von Reichsgründung und Kulturkampf*, Mainz, 1973

Birke, A. M., Introduction to *Church, State and Society in the 19th Century. An Anglo-German Comparison*, Prince Albert Studies, vol. 2, Munich, New York, London and Paris, 1984

——, *Bischof Ketteler und der deutsche Liberalismus*, Mainz, 1971

——, 'Bischof Ketteler und die Anfänge der Zentrumspartei', in F. Quarthal, W. Setzler (eds.), *Stadtverfassung — Verfassungsstaat — Pressepolitik*, Sigmaringen, 1980, pp. 339–48

Bussmann, W., 'Zur Geschichte des deutschen Liberalismus im 19. Jahrhundert', *Historische Zeitschrift*, 186, no. 3, 1958, pp. 527–57

Conze, W., D. Groh, *Die Arbeiterbewegung in der nationalen Bewegung. Die deutsche Sozialdemokratie vor, während und nach der Reichsgründung*, Stuttgart, 1966

Düding, D., *Organisierter gesellschaftlicher Nationalismus in Deutschland (1808–1847). Bedeutung und Funktion der Turner- und Sängervereine für die deutsche Nationalbewegung*, Munich, 1984

Eisfeld, G., *Die Entstehung der liberalen Parteien in Deutschland 1858–70*. Studie zu den Organisationen und Programmen der Liberalen und Demokraten, Hanover, 1969

Foerster, C., *Der Preß- und Vaterlandsverein von 1832/33. Sozialstruktur und Organisationsformen der bürgerlichen Bewegung in der Zeit des Hambacher Festes*, Trier, 1982

Gall, L., 'Liberalismus und Nationalstaat. Der deutsche Liberalismus und die Reichsgründung', in H. Berding, K. Düwell, L. Gall, W. J. Mommsen, H.-U. Wehler (eds.), *Vom Staat des Ancien Regime zum modernen Parteistaat. Festschrift für Theodor Schieder*, Munich and Vienna, 1978, pp. 287–300

——, *Der Liberalismus als regierende Partei. Das Großherzogtum Baden zwischen Restauration und Reichsgründung*, Wiesbaden, 1968

——, 'Liberalismus und Bürgerliche Gesellschaft: Zu Charakter und Entwicklung der liberalen Bewegung in Deutschland', *Historische Zeitschrift*, 220, no. 2, 1975, pp. 324–56

Gebhardt, H., *Revolution und liberale Bewegung. Die nationale Organisierung der konstitutionellen Partei in Deutschland 1848/49*, Bremen, 1974

Hale, D., 'The Press and Fatherland Society of 1832: Common Ancestor of

German Progressivism', *The Rocky Mountain Social Science Journal*, 9, 1972, pp. 69–78

Hertz, F., *The German Public Mind in the 19th Century: A Social History of German Political Sentiments, Aspirations and Ideas* (ed.) F. Eyck, Totowa, 1975

Hinton, T. R., *Liberalism, Nationalism and the German Intellectuals (1822–1847): An Analysis of the Academic and Scientific Conferences of the Period*, Cambridge, 1951

Kupisch, K., 'Die Wandlungen des Nationalismus im liberalen deutschen Bürgertum', in H. Zillessen (ed.), *Volk–Nation–Vaterland. Der deutsche Protestantismus und der Nationalismus*, Gütersloh, 1970, pp. 111–34

Langewiesche, D., *Liberalismus und Demokratie in Württemberg zwischen Revolution und Reichsgründung*, Düsseldorf, 1974

——, 'Die Anfänge der deutschen Parteien. Partei, Fraktion und Verein in der Revolution von 1848/49', *Geschichte und Gesellschaft*, 4, 1978, pp. 324–61

—— (ed.), *Die deutsche Revolution von 1848/49*, Darmstadt, 1983

Langner, A., 'Katholizismus und nationaler Gedanke', in H. Zillessen (ed.), *Volk–Nation–Vaterland. Der deutsche Protestantismus und der Nationalismus*, Gütersloh, 1970, pp. 239–69

Lill, R., 'Die deutschen Katholiken und Bismarcks Reichsgründung', in T. Schieder, E. Deuerlein (eds.), *Reichsgründung 1870/71. Tatsachen, Kontroversen, Interpretationen*, Stuttgart, 1970, pp. 345–65

——, *Die Beilegung der Kölner Wirren*, Düsseldorf, 1962

Lutz, R. R., 'The German Revolutionary Student Movement, 1819–1833', *Central European History*, 4, 1971, pp. 215–41

Maier, H., *Katholizismus, nationale Bewegung und Demokratie in Deutschland*, Hochland, 67, 1965, pp. 318–33

Mork, G. R., 'Bismarck and the "Capitulation" of German Liberalism', *Journal of Modern History*, 63, 1971, pp. 59–75

Müller, H., 'Der deutsche politische Katholizismus in der Entscheidung des Jahres 1866', *Pfälzische Kirchengeschichte und Volkskunde*, 33, 1966, pp. 46–75

Namier, L., *1848: The Revolution of the Intellectuals*, Garden City, 1964

O'Boyle, L., 'The German Nationalverein', *Journal of Central European Affairs*, 16, 1957, pp. 333–52

Pfülf, O., *Bischof Ketteler (1811–1877)*, vols. 1–3, Mainz, 1899

Real, W., *Der deutsche Reformverein. Großdeutsche Stimmen und Kräfte zwischen Villafranca und Königgrätz*, Lübeck and Hamburg, 1966

Repgen, K., *Märzbewegung und Maiwahlen des Revolutionsjahres 1848 im Rheinland*, Bonn, 1955

Rößler, C., *Das deutsche Reich und die kirchliche Frage*, Leipzig, 1876

Seeber, G., H. Wolter, 'Die Gründung des Deutschen Reiches und die Arbeiterbewegung', *Beiträge zur Geschichte der deutschen Arbeiterbewegung*, 13, 1971, pp. 3–22

Sell, F., *Die Tragödie des deutschen Liberalismus*, Stuttgart, 1953

Sheehan, J. J., *German Liberalism in the Nineteenth Century*, Chicago and London, 1978

Thomas, R. H., *Liberalism, Nationalism, and the German Intellectuals (1822–1847): An Analysis of the Academic and Scientific Conferences of the Period*, Cambridge, 1951

Valjavec, F., *Die Entstehung der politischen Strömungen in Deutschland 1770–1815*, Düsseldorf, 1978

Windell, G. C., *The Catholics and German Unity*, 1866–1871, Minneapolis, 1954
Winkler, H. A., *Preußischer Liberalismus und deutscher Nationalstaat*. *Studien zur Geschichte der Deutschen Fortschrittspartei 1861–1866*, Tübingen, 1964
Wollstein, G., *Das 'Großdeutschland' der Paulskirche: Nationale Ziele in der bürgerlichen Revolution 1848–49*, Düsseldorf, 1977
Woodhouse, C. M., *The Philhellenes*, London, 1969

3. Economic preconditions

Adler, A., *Die Entwicklungsgeschichte des deutschen Zollvereins*, Leipzig, 1879
Best, H., *Interessenpolitik und nationale Integration 1848/49*. *Handelspolitische Konflikte im frühindustriellen Deutschland*, Göttingen, 1980
Böhme, H., *Deutschlands Weg zur Großmacht. Studien zum Verhältnis von Wirtschaft und Staat während der Reichsgründungszeit 1848–1881*, Cologne and Berlin, 1966
Bondi, G., *Deutschlands Außenhandel 1815–1870*, Berlin, 1958
Brinkmann, C., 'The Place of Germany in the Economic History of the Nineteenth Century', *The Economic History Review*, 4, 1932–34, pp. 129–46
Dorn, A., *Pflege und Förderung des gewerblichen Fortschrittes durch die Regierung in Württemberg*, Vienna, 1868
Dowe, D., T. Offermann (eds.), *Deutsche Handwerker- und Arbeiterkongresse 1848–1852. Protokolle und Materialien*, Berlin and Bonn, 1983
Dumke, R. H., *The Political Economy of German Economic Unification: Tariffs, Trade and Politics of the Zollverein Era*, Ann Arbor/Mich. and London, 1977
———, 'Der Deutsche Zollverein als Modell ökonomischer Integration', in H. Berding (ed.), *Wirtschaftliche und politische Integration in Europa im 19. und 20. Jahrhundert*, Göttingen, 1984, pp. 71–101
Fischer, W., 'The German Zollverein. A Case Study in Customs Union', *Kyklos*, 13, 1960, pp. 65–89
———, *Der Staat und die Anfänge der Industrialisierung in Baden 1800–1850*, vol. I: *Die staatliche Gewerbepolitik*, Berlin, 1962
———, 'Government Activity and Industrialization in Germany (1815–1870)', in W.W. Rostow (ed.), *The Economics of Take-Off into Sustained Growth*, London, 1963, pp. 83–94
———, 'Der Deutsche Zollverein nach 150 Jahren — Modell einer erfolgreichen wirtschaftspolitischen Integration?', *List Forum*, 12, no. 6, Sept. 1984, pp. 349–60
———, 'Industrialisierung und soziale Frage in Preußen', in Fritz Thyssen Stiftung (ed.), *Preußen — Seine Wirkung auf die deutsche Geschichte*, Stuttgart, 1985, pp. 223–59
———, J. Krengel and J. Wietog, *Sozialgeschichtliches Arbeitsbuch*, vol. I: *Materialien zur Statistik des Deutschen Bundes 1815–1870*, Munich, 1982
Forberger, R., *Die Industrielle Revolution in Sachsen 1800–1861*, vol. 1/1: 'Die Revolution der Produktivkräfte in Sachsen 1800–1830', Berlin (East), 1982, pp. 508–19
Fremdling, R., 'Germany', in P. O'Brien (ed.), *Railways and the Economic Development of Western Europe, 1830–1914*, London, 1983, pp. 121–47

———, *Eisenbahnen und deutsches Wirtschaftswachstum 1840–1879. Ein Beitrag zur Entwicklungstheorie und zur Theorie der Infrastruktur*, 2nd edn., Dortmund, 1985

Gehrig, H., *Friedrich List und Deutschlands politisch-ökonomische Einheit*, Leipzig, 1956

Gerschenkron, A., *Economic Backwardness in Historical Perspective. A Book of Essays*, Cambridge/Mass., 1962

Hahn, H.-W., *Wirtschaftliche Integration im 19. Jahrhundert. Die hessischen Staaten und der Deutsche Zollverein*, Göttingen, 1982

Hamerow, T. S., *The Social Foundations of German Unification 1858–1871*, 2 vols., Princeton/N.J., 1969–72

———, *Restoration, Revolution, Reaction, Economics and Politics in Germany 1815–1871*, Princeton/N.J., 1958

Henderson, W. O., *The Zollverein*, London, 1939

———, *The Industrial Revolution on the Continent. Germany, France, Russia 1800–1914*, London, 1961

———, *Friedrich List*, London, 1983

Huertas, T. F., *Economic Growth and Economic Policy in a Multinational Setting. The Habsburg Monarchy, 1841–1865*, New York, 1977

Kahan, A., 'Nineteenth-Century European Experience with Policies of Economic Nationalism', in H.G. Johnson (ed.), *Economic Nationalism in Old and New States*, London, 1968, Chap. 2

Kiesewetter, H., 'Bevölkerung, Erwerbstätige und Landwirtschaft im Königreich Sachsen 1815–1871', in S. Pollard (ed.), *Region and Industrialization. Studies on the Role of the Region in the Economic History of the Last Two Centuries*, Göttingen, 1980, pp. 89–106

———, 'Regionale Industrialisierung in Deutschland zur Zeit der Reichsgründung. Ein vergleichend-quantitativer Versuch', *Vierteljahrschrift für Sozial- und Wirtschaftsgeschichte*, 73, 1986, pp. 38–60

———, R. Fremdling (eds.), *Staat, Region und Industrialisierung*, Ostfildern, 1985

Kindleberger, C. P., *Economic Response. Comparative Studies in Trade, Finance, and Growth*, Cambridge/Mass., 1978

Landes, D. S., *The Unbound Prometheus. Technological Change and Industrial Development in Western Europe from 1750 to the Present*, Cambridge, 1969

Megerle, K., *Württemberg im Industrialisierungsprozeß Deutschlands. Ein Beitrag zur regionalen Differenzierung der Industrialisierung*, Stuttgart, 1982

Pollard, S., *The Integration of the European Economy since 1815*, London, 1981

Price, A. H., *The Evolution of the Zollverein. A Study of the Ideas and Institutions Leading to German Economic Unification between 1815 and 1833*, Ann Arbor/Mich., 1949

Roussakis, E. N., *Friedrich List, the Zollverein, and the Uniting of Europe*, Brügge, 1968

Thimme, P., *Straßenbau und Straßenbaupolitik in Deutschland zur Zeit der Gründung des Zollvereins 1825–1835*, Stuttgart, 1931

Tipton, F. B., *Regional Variations in the Economic Development of Germany During the Nineteenth Century*, Middletown/Conn., 1976

———, 'The National Consensus in German Economic History', *Central European History*, 7, 1974, pp. 195–224

Vogel, B., *Allgemeine Gewerbefreiheit. Die Reformpolitik des preußischen Staatskanzlers Hardenberg (1810–1820)*, Göttingen, 1983

Zorn, W., 'Wirtschafts- und sozialgeschichtliche Zusammenhänge der deut-schen Reichsgründungszeit (1850–1879)', *Historische Zeitschrift*, 197, 1963, pp. 318–42
——, 'Wirtschaft und Gesellschaft in Deutschland in der Zeit der Reichs-gründung', in T. Schieder, E. Deuerlein (eds.), *Reichsgründung 1870/71. Tatsachen, Kontroversen, Interpretation*, Stuttgart, 1970, pp. 197–225
——, 'Die wirtschaftliche Integration Kleindeutschlands in den 1860er Jahren und die Reichsgründung', *Historische Zeitschrift*, 216, 1973, pp. 304–34

4. Germany and her neighbours

Birke, A.M., 'Die Revolution von 1848 und England', in K. Kluxen, A.M. Birke (eds.), *Viktorianisches England aus deutscher Perspektive*, Prince Albert Studies, vol. 1, Munich, New York, London and Paris, 1983, pp. 49–60
Bourne, K., *The Foreign Policy of Victorian England, 1830–1902*, Oxford, 1970
Bridge, F. R., R. Bullen, *The Great Powers and the European System 1815–1914*, London and New York, 1980
Carr, W., *Schleswig–Holstein, 1815–48: A Study in National Conflict*, Manchester, 1963
Droz, J., *L'Allemagne et la révolution française*, Paris, 1949
Eyck, F., *The Prince Consort. A Political Biography*, London, 1959
Fehrenbach, E., 'Preußen-Deutschland als Faktor der französischen Außen-politik in der Reichsgründungszeit', in E. Kolb (ed.), *Europa und die Reichsgründung. Preußen- Deutschland in der Sicht der großen europäischen Mächte 1860–1880*, Munich, 1980, pp. 109–37
Gillessen, G., *Lord Palmerston und die Einigung Deutschlands. Die englische Politik von der Paulskirche bis zu den Dresdener Konferenzen (1848–1851)*, Lübeck and Hamburg, 1961
Graus, F., 'Die Nationenbildung der Westslawen im Mittelalter', in H. Baumann, W. Schröder (eds.), *Nationes. Historische und philologische Untersuchungen zur Entstehung der europäischen Nationen im Mittelalter*, vol. III, Sigmaringen, 1980
Gruner, W., '"British Interest" und Friedenssicherung. Zur Interaktion von britischer Innen- und Außenpolitik', *Historische Zeitschrift*, 224, 1977, pp. 92–104
——, *Großbritannien, der Deutsche Bund und die Struktur des Europäischen Friedens im frühen 19. Jahrhundert*, Munich, 1979
Hagen, W., *Germans, Poles and Jews: The Nationality Conflict in the Prussian East, 1772–1914*, Chicago, 1980
Hildebrand, K., '"British interests" und "Pax Britannica". Grundfragen englischer Außenpolitik im 19. und 20. Jahrhundert', *Historische Zeitschrift*, 221, 1975, pp. 623–39
——, 'Die deutsche Reichsgründung im Urteil der britischen Politik', *Francia*, 5, 1977, pp. 399–424
——, 'Großbritannien und die deutsche Reichsgründung', in E. Kolb (ed.), *Europa und die Reichsgründung. Preußen-Deutschland in der Sicht der großen europäischen Mächte 1860–1880*, Munich, 1980, pp. 9–62

204 *Select Bibliography*

Holbraad, C., *The Concert of Europe: A Study in German and British International Theory, 1815–1914*, London, 1970

Howard, M., *The Franco-Prussian War. The German Invasion of France 1870–1871* Princeton/N.J., 1979

Jaworski, R., 'Zur Frage vormoderner Nationalismen in Ostmitteleuropa', *Geschichte und Gesellschaft*, 5, 1979, pp. 398–417

Kennan, G. F., *The Decline of Bismarck's European Order, Franco-Russian Relations 1875–1890*, Princeton/N.J., 1979

Kluxen, K., A. M. Birke (eds.), *Viktorianisches England aus deutscher Perspektive*, Prince Albert Studies, vol. 1, Munich, New York, London and Paris, 1983

Kolb, E., *Der schwierige Weg zum Frieden. Das Problem der Kriegsbeendigung 1870/71.* Schriften des Historischen Kollegs, Vorträge 11, Munich, 1985

Labuda, G., 'The Slavs in Nineteenth Century German Historiography', *Polish Western Affairs*, 2, 1961, pp. 177–234.

Lawaty, A., *Das Ende des Staates Preußen in polnischer Sicht*, Berlin, 1985

Lepowski, T., *Polska–narodziny nowoczesnego narodu 1764–1870*, Warsaw, 1967

Mander, J., *Our German Cousins. Anglo-American Relations in the 19th and 20th Centuries*, London, 1974

Markiewicz, W., 'Die Bildung der modernen polnischen Nation', in *Nationalgeschichte als Problem der deutschen und polnischen Geschichtsschreibung*, Brunswick, 1983, pp. 46–66

Mosse, W. E., *The European Powers and the German Question 1848–71 with special reference to England and Russia*, Cambridge, 1958

Müller, M. G., 'Deutsche und polnische Nation im Vormärz', in *Polen und die polnische Frage in der Hohenzollernmonarchie*, Berlin, 1982, pp. 69–95

——, *Die Teilungen Polens 1772, 1793, 1795*, Munich, 1984

Poidevin, R., J. Bariéty, *Les relations franco-allemandes 1815–1975*, Paris, 1975

Pottinger, E. A., *Napoleon III. and the German Crisis 1865–1866*, Cambridge, Mass., 1966

Rothfels, H., 'Die Nationalidee in westlicher und in östlicher Sicht', in H. Rothfels (ed.), *Osteuropa und der deutsche Osten*, Cologne, 1956, pp. 7–18

Sandiford, K., *Great Britain and the Schleswig-Holstein Question, 1848–1864. A Study in Diplomacy, Politics, and Public Opinion*, Toronto and Buffalo, 1975

Sked, A. (ed.), *Europe's Balance of Power*, London and Basingstoke, 1979

Stürmer, M., *Die Reichsgründung. Deutscher Nationalstaat und europäisches Gleichgewicht im Zeitalter Bismarcks*, Munich, 1984

Valentin, V., *Bismarcks Reichsgründung im Urteil englischer Diplomaten*, Amsterdam, 1937

Vogt, M., *Das vormärzliche Deutschland im Urteil englischer Schriften, Zeitschriften und Bücher (1830–1947)*, Phil. Diss., Göttingen, 1962

Wandycz, P. S., *The Lands of Partitioned Poland 1795–1918*, Seattle, 1974

Webster, C., *The Foreign Policy of Lord Castlereagh*, 2 vols., London, 1925–31

Wendt, B. J., *Das britische Deutschlandbild im Wandel des 19. und 20. Jahrhunderts*, Bochum, 1984

Zernack, K., 'Negative Polenpolitik als Grundlage deutsch-russischer Diplomatie in der Mächtepolitik des 18. Jahrhunderts', in *Deutschland und Rußland*. Festschrift für G. von Rauch, Stuttgart, 1974, pp. 144–59

——, *Osteuropa. Eine Einführung in seine Geschichte*, Munich, 1977

——, 'Das Jahrtausend der deutsch-polnischen Beziehungsgeschichte als

Problemfeld und Forschungsaufgabe', in *Grundfragen der Beziehungen zwischen Deutschen, Polaben und Polen*, Berlin, 1976, pp. 3–46

———, 'Das preußische Königtum und die polnische Republik im europäischen Mächtesystem des 18. Jahrhunderts (1701–1763)', *Jahrbuch für die Geschichte Mittel- und Ostdeutschlands*, 30, 1981, pp. 1–20

———, 'Die deutsche Nation zwischen Ost und West', in *Nationalgeschichte als Problem der deutschen und der polnischen Geschichtsschreibung*, Brunswick, 1983, pp. 67–80

About the Contributors

Adolf M. Birke: born 1939; Professor of Modern History, University of Bayreuth; 1980–1 Visiting Professor Trinity College, University of Toronto; since 1985 Director German Historical Institute London. Recent publications: *Bischof Ketteler und der deutsche Liberalismus*, Mainz, 1971; *Pluralismus und Gewerkschaftsautonomie in England*, Stuttgart, 1978; (Ed.) with Hermann Baumgarten, *Der deutsche Liberalismus*, Berlin, 1974; (Ed.), Prince Albert Studies, Munich and New York, 1983–

Harm-Hinrich Brandt: born 1935; Professor of Modern History, University of Würzburg. Recent publications: *Wirtschaft und Wirtschaftspolitik im Raum Hanau 1597–1962*, Frankfurt on Main, 1963; *Der österreichische Neoabsolutismus: Staatsfinanzen und Politik, 1848–1860*, 2 vols., Göttingen, 1978.

Dieter Düding: born 1940; *Privatdozent* of Modern History at the University of Cologne. Publications: *Der Nationalsoziale Verein 1896–1903. Der gescheiterte Versuch einer parteipolitischen Synthese von Nationalismus, Sozialismus und Liberalismus*, Munich and Vienna, 1972; *Organisierter gesellschaftlicher Nationalismus in Deutschland 1808–1847*, Munich, 1984.

Günther Heydemann: born 1950; 1977–85 Assistant Professor, Universities of Erlangen and Nuremberg; since 1985 German Historical Institute, London. Recent publications: *Geschichtswissenschaft im geteilten Deutschland*, Frankfurt on Main, 1980; *Carl Ludwig Sand. Ein Biographie*, Hof, 1985.

Hubert Kiesewetter: born 1939; *Privatdozent* for Economic History, Free University of Berlin. Recent publications: *Von Hegel zu Hitler. Eine Analyse der Hegelschen Machtstaatsideologie und der politischen Wirkungsgeschichte des Rechtshegelianismus*, Hamburg, 1974; *Industrialisierung und Landwirtschaft. Sachsens Stellung im regionalen Industrialisierungsprozeß Deutschlands im 19. Jahrhundert*, Cologne and Vienna, 1986.

Hagen Schulze: born 1943; Professor of Modern History and Methodology of Historiography, Free University of Berlin; 1985–6 Visiting Fellow St Antony's College, Oxford. Recent publications: *Otto Braun oder Preußens demokratische Sendung. Eine Biographie*, Frankfurt, Berlin and Vienna, 1977; *Weimar. Deutschland 1917–1933*, Berlin, 1982; *Der Weg zum Nationalstaat*, Munich, 1985; *Wir sind, was wir geworden sind*, Munich, 1987.

Alexander Schwan: born 1931; Professor of Political Theory and Philosophy, Free University of Berlin; Chairman of the Arnold Bergstraesser Institute for Socio-Political Research at Freiburg; 1980–1 Research Fellow, Woodrow Wilson Center, Washington. Recent publications: *Wahrheit — Pluralität — Freiheit*, Hamburg, 1976; *Geschichtstheologische Konstitution und Destruktion der Politik*, Berlin, etc., 1976; *Grundwerte der Demokratie*, Munich, 1978; *Theorie als Dienstmagd der Praxis*, Stuttgart, 1983.

Michael Stürmer: born 1938; Professor of Modern History, University of Erlangen–Nuremberg; 1976–7 Research Fellow Harvard University; *Professeur associé* Sorbonne 1982–3; columnist *Frankfurter Allgemeine Zeitung*. Recent publications: *Die Weimarer Republik — Belagerte Civitas*, Kronsberg, 1980; *Handwerk und höfische Kultur*, Munich, 1981; *Das ruhelose Reich. Deutschland 1866–1918*, Berlin, 1983; *Die Reichsgründung*, Munich, 1984

Klaus Zernack: born 1931; Professor of Modern History, Free University of Berlin; Chairman of the Historische Kommission zu Berlin. Recent publications: (Ed.), *Handbuch der Geschichte Rußlands*, Stuttgart, 1976–; *Osteuropa. Eine Einführung in seine Geschichte*, Munich, 1977; (Ed.), *Polen und die polnische Frage in der Geschichte der Hohenzollernmonarchie 1701–1871*, Berlin, 1982; (Ed.), *Schichtung und Entwicklung der Gesellschaft in Polen und Deutschland im 16. und 17. Jahrhundert*, Wiesbaden, 1983